Critical Review

Exceptionally well written, organized and presented, "Becoming an Architect: My Voyage of Discovery" is a highly recommended addition to personal, community, college, and university library Contemporary American Biography and American Architectural collections.
—James A. Cox, Midwest Book Review

Readers Praise Becoming an Architect

Enjoyable, fun and courageous! Although there are plenty of books about great architects, very few of them show how architects think and conceptualize…Despite the newer Design-Build delivery systems, it's still the vision of the owner and the and the architect that forms the seed of every project.
—Robert O. Little, Former President, Ittner Architects, St. Louis

Overall, I found the book very entertaining. I particularly liked the travels in Ireland, France and Turkey with…wonderful sketches of famous places…[and] some very funny anecdotes.
—David Margolis, Author of The Myth of Dr. Kugelman and *The Misadventures of Buddy Jones*

I loved the adventure of continuing to work while getting farther and farther from the nest. Milan! The Orient Express! Istanbul! Great characters—the South Africans, the Turkish vendor, Elias and Catherine ("Oh darn, I missed it by that much!"), Charlie, Stan, Bulent, Omar, the architecture in Milan and Istanbul, Turkish history and customs were all fascinating.
—C. Michael Lederer, Career Nuclear and Environmental Scientist, University of California, Berkeley

Enjoyed…[author's] youth in Chicago, fascinating world travels, attaining architecture degrees, and becoming a professional architect-planner eventually in St. Louis….enjoyable for a mass audience, even those who are not architects—some great laughs, too, as he describes his life's journey. He concludes with wisdom for any young person in a professional field about how to pursue career and family life. I think design-oriented students would especially enjoy his escapades; and those of us who are retired reflecting about our own journeys. Enjoyed reading for two days.

—Dr. Terry Farris, Associate Professor Emeritus
Dept. of City Planning and Real Estate Development
College of Architecture, Arts and Humanities
Clemson University

What a great read!
Highly recommended to all architects, students and all those who love to travel and experience the world!
What a great memory!
The author shares his life experience from school years, his many travels and his architectural career, as if it happened yesterday.

—Julius Juracsik, Architect, St. Louis

Manifest Destiny

"Grandpa followed the trail of Lewis and Clark, built rails to open up the West and helped fulfill America's Manifest Destiny. Learning what architecture was, what it should be and how I fit in would be mine."
—Peter H. Green, AIA, Architect and Author

Discovering Architecture

Once Peter had decided at an early age he wanted to design buildings, the desire turned into a quest: picking the right college, learning to compete in a larger arena and at last seeking an architectural degree. Along the way he met opponents and obstacles and dodged or overcame them. He traveled to study architecture in its original setting, absorbing its history and culture. En route he met many people and learned a lot about human nature. He sketched what he saw and told stories he recalled, honing his visual and verbal communication skills. It's all part of how he acquired his expertise, met a few great mentors and unlocked secrets of his survival in a complex, difficult and ever-changing profession.

Also by Peter H. Green:

BIOGRAPHICAL MEMOIR

Ben's War with the U. S. Marines
Radio: One Woman's Family
in War and Pieces (with Alice H. Green)

ARCHITECTURAL MYSTERY
Patrick MacKenna Series

Chicago's Designs
Crimes of Design
Fatal Designs

BECOMING AN ARCHITECT

My Voyage of Discovery

PETER H. GREEN

Greenskills Press

St. Louis

Becoming an Architect: My Voyage of Discovery
© 2021 by Peter H. Green

Cover design and drawings, text, original sketches and family photographs, except as otherwise attributed or credited to others, © 2021 by Peter H. Green

GREENSKILLS PRESS. Publisher, an imprint of GREENSKILLS ASSOCIATES, LLC

This is a work of creative nonfiction. Scenes from the past, events and historical figures may be compressed or treated fictionally to represent actual situations, based on historical research, letters and their writings, as noted in the text.
Address comments and inquiries to: GREENSKILLS PRESS P. O. Box 11292 St. Louis, MO 63105 or to:
writerpeter@authorpetergreen.com
Internet URL: www.authorpetergreen.com
Library of Congress PCN Control Number applied for.
Categories: 1. Architecture 2.Biography/Autobiography 3.Architectural Education
ISBN: 978-1-941402-17-7 (Trade Paperback)
ISBN: 978-1-941402-18-4 (Kindle e-book)
Printed in the United States of America

For Connie

My wife and life partner, whose love, dedication and good cheer have made it all worthwhile

TABLE OF CONTENTS

BECOMING AN
ARCHITECT

My Voyage of Discovery

F. J. Herlihy, Engineer on Horseback
Still riding in 1931

Indian Creek Bridge, Judith Basin, Montana, 1918

Part I: Manifest Destiny

SOMETIMES I WONDER if my role in life was predetermined. My maternal grandfather was a pioneer, builder and visionary: I found his example impossible to resist.

An engineer on horseback, Frank J. Herlihy designed and supervised construction of rail bridges for the Milwaukee Road in Montana, extending what had been the Northern Pacific Railroad all the way to Washington state. He rode a horse to inspect his construction projects.

In June 1913. he got news several days after the fact that his fourth child was born back in Lewistown, Montana. Although he was building a railroad to the west coast, no scheduled train was available on short notice to take him back home. He climbed on his steed and followed the rail tracks through the Montana Indian country of Custer's 1876 last stand, through the Judith mountains to the home he had established for his family, grown too large to follow him to construction camps along the route. The trip took him three days, but he arrived to comfort his pioneer wife Mary and meet his new daughter Alice, who would one day be my mother.

He was soon thereafter called to work in Montreal, superintending a large-scale sewer diversion system, a multi-million-dollar project, in the days when such massive jobs were rare. This assignment enabled him to save a stake large enough to start his own business and further develop his reputation for engineering innovation. On his return to Chicago in 1919, he opened Herlihy Brothers Construction Company, with his brothers Charlie, Ed, Bill, and Bob as his initial staff. A few years later, in the stock market crash in 1929, after losing all he invested in the stock of his client Samuel Insull's tottering electric power empire, he built it back again, bigger than ever, and produced numerous Chicago landmarks.

Although his achievements sparked my interest in building, I passed up the chance for a career in the family construction company, possibly to run it someday. Wanting control over what was designed and built, rather than the construction process itself, I chose to become an architect.

My facility in drawing came from both sides of the family. My dad Ben Green was fascinated with art and drawing and used these skills often in the advertising business. In staging a furrier's live commercials for black-and-white television, for example, he created visual effects with such simple devices as placing wide masking tape in converging, forced-perspective lines on the studio floor, so models wearing the fur coats were set in an abstract, Giorgio di Chirico landscape. As he neared retirement, he attended classes at the Art Institute of Chicago and produced some very distinguished oil paintings, which could easily be tagged "Grandpa Moses" primitives.

My maternal grandmother, Mary Howard Herlihy, coached by talented nuns in her convent school, occasionally brought out an old travel trunk and showed us her beautifully rendered pencil sketches of Irish ruins and buildings in their landscape settings. My mother used her inherited talents, in addition to decorating the many houses we lived in over the years, in pattern making and sewing dresses for herself in the latest modes at a fraction of the cost in stores. When my sister was in high school, Mom copied dresses she saw Debbie Reynolds wearing in films and made them for my sister to wear to her dances and proms. My sister inherited the family artistic skills, as well, and made a career of professional graphic art and then the fine arts— watercolor, oil and acrylic painting.

From my maternal grandfather Francis Jeremiah "F.J." Herlihy came an engineer's facility in design. He created a special rail car with a built-in crane, sketched construction assemblies, drew plans for locating his machines and materials on construction sites and made good construction interpretations of architects' designs on his many building projects.

So much for nature. The rest can be attributed to nurture.

I seemed to have many of the family genetic skills—visualization, writing ability and a desire to broadcast my visions to the world. But what could I do with them? The question remained, was my architectural career preordained destiny? Confined as we all were during the pandemic of 2020, faced with the possibility that this might be my last chance while I still had all my faculties, it was time to sort through my varied life adventures and answer these questions.

The MacGuffin of this docudrama—that mysterious fact which brings all the players together—is an architectural degree, a straightforward goal which eager professors try to award, and which many talented students strive for and earn—or not. Grandpa followed the trail of Lewis and Clark, built rails to open up the West and helped fulfill America's Manifest Destiny. Learning what architecture is, what it should be and how I fit in would be mine.

Therein lies my tale.

Pete and Ben in the Park, 1941

Ben Home on Leave, 1944

1

A Sense of Security

UNTIL I WAS THREE WE LIVED in a small apartment on Chicago's South Side. Then we moved for a couple of years to a rented, two-bedroom house on Kenwood Avenue in Hyde Park. Next, with Mom expecting a baby, we needed to move again to make more room. But in late 1943, with a war on, there was a housing shortage. Finally, they found a ten-room house on nearby Blackstone Avenue, larger than they needed, but the rent was affordable. The house was big, tall and old, with brown clapboard siding, full-height windows and a white oak in front, set into the curve of a metal picket fence. It also had a big backyard where I could play. In the shade of an ancient elm, Dad put a swing set with a wooden slide and kept it waxed so I could slide down fast. Inside a beveled-glass door from the vestibule, three flights of stairs wound around a tall front hall.

Grandpa Herlihy loved to show off: to the public, to his construction clients, and even to his family. When I was a child, he picked me up in his black limousine and took me to tour his job sites. He used to buy expensive Perfecto Garcia cigars from Havana and use them for chewing tobacco. Next to his easy chair in the study, he kept a mug for spitting it out, but when we got in his chauffeured car, he opened his right rear window and simply spit his mouthful in the general direction of outdoors. Invariably, this left a telltale trail of goo on the rear panel, which would spoil the brilliant shine Clarence, his cheerful driver, had polished earlier that morning.

When I rode in the back seat with him. he had me captive and worked on me, making sure I knew how to deal with my life. "Hey Pete," he'd say, "do you know how to comb your hair with a washcloth?" I was only seven years old at the time—this was a new one on me. "When you're late for school and have to get ready in a hurry," he added, "just get the cloth damp and wipe it across the top of your head to one side."

I tucked that one away with Grandpa's other bits of advice. First he took me north on Wacker Drive past the Civic Opera house, which had a multistory office building atop the great auditorium. "We built the foundations for that one," he said proudly. Next, in the center of the wide avenue, we entered a ramp leading beneath the street to an underworld illuminated in those days with eerie green lights. He explained that the lower level, which followed Wacker Drive as it turned right along the south bank of the Chicago River, formed an express route taking us past all the congested surface streets of downtown, a multi-level concept envisioned by Daniel Burnham in his Plan for Chicago. Then Clarence, his driver, entered another ramp that took us to an even lower level, where Grandpa pointed out all the loading docks and service entrances for the downtown office and commercial buildings.

Support columns for the above-ground streets were hexagonal and very thick. Grandpa left the vertical rough concrete "fins" on the columns, where the poured concrete had oozed into joints between the wooden forms, a modern touch to show how things were constructed. He also pioneered heating of the mix to permit pouring concrete in sub-freezing weather and was among the first in the U.S. to pump concrete through flexible tubes to speed construction.

Then we drove to one of his excavations, where a steam shovel was taking huge bites out of the ground and depositing the dirt in dump trucks lined up along the street to take it away. "This one is named after you." He pointed to the name "Peter" painted in white letters on the back of the red cab, under the firm's name, Herlihy Mid-Continent Construction Co. Each of my six cousins had a crane or steam shovel bearing their names. Family lore reports that one of my male cousins, while touring the site with Grandpa, found an interesting nut about the size of his head. Figuring it was part of his crane, which had been disassembled for oiling and maintenance, he picked it up as a souvenir and carried it away. The job had to be shut down for the rest of the morning until a replacement for the missing part could be located and the machine restored to use.

In March 1944, as the war escalated in the Pacific, the draft hung over the heads of even married men. To retain some control of his fate, Dad enlisted in the Marines. His physical exam completed, Dad left from the train station. It was a tearful farewell. That big old barn on Blackstone Avenue seemed all the more vacant with him gone.

Our house was drafty and chilly. Despite all attempts to warm the interior, the gas furnace pumped night and day to no avail. With little insulation, we were paying to heat all outdoors. It was all Mom could do to swaddle the baby in extra blankets and clothes.

At the end of 1944, a year after his enlistment in the Marine Corps, Dad received orders sending him and all his buddies to the Pacific for further training and what many suspected would be the final assault on Japan. By spring, he had completed a 43-day trip by troop carrier to a location ultimately revealed as Guam, in the Marianas.

For the summer of 1945, Mom's sister Helen and her husband Joseph had rented a cottage in Annisquam, northeast of Boston, and they invited us to join them. With no hope of Dad's early return, Mom conferred with him in her daily letters, and they both concluded this would be a relief for her and positive influence on the children, including my two younger cousins David and Alan. They hoped family solidarity and her psychological expertise might help return my baby sister and me to a feeling of normal life.

Mom's efforts to give her children plenty of love and a sense of security were difficult in wartime. As much as she tried to steer radio listening away from news broadcasts during the hours that we children were awake, war was on everyone's mind and difficult to conceal. I had apparently been acting up, wetting my bed and feeling terribly insecure without my father's reassuring presence, and Mom was running out of options for calming me down.

At the Fairbanks seaside beach cottage in Annisquam, Mom had nature's rugged beauty and the daily companionship of her sister Helen to sustain her. Helen's husband Joseph, a surgeon in Boston, had a medical gas ration card, which enabled him to commute to the cottage on weekends. His soothing presence in the household helped maintain our stable emotional state.

On sunny days I ran on the beach from dawn to sunset wearing only my swim trunks. The sun tanned my skin and bleached my dark brown hair to blond. I explored the sea's many new sights, mysteries and natural wonders. I watched the tides ebb and flow. On stormy days huge breakers crashed on the seawall and splashed spray into the air. Ebb tide each day revealed breathing holes in the wet sand at the water's edge for a new crop of clams..The strand, littered with the remains of undersea animals, shells and beautiful new stones, was a new, unexplored territory, hinting at the secrets hidden beneath the ocean.

But I loved the squalls best. As I stood facing the bay with the morning sun at my back, I could see slate blue clouds roll in from the west. The gale whipped up whitecaps, and a blue-gray western sky formed a backdrop for white gulls circling and cawing as they warned of the coming storm.

One early evening at about seven o'clock I heard a cry for help to the left beyond the big rocks. People came running to the water. Soon my mother and aunt ran to the beach and made me stay back. I couldn't see but waited by the rocks in silence until, after the longest time, men plodded slowly back up the beach in a line, their long shadows in front of them in the sunset, their heads bowed with sadness

I didn't need any further explanation. Since I didn't know how to swim I had been told not to go in the water alone, not to go in over my waist and especially not beyond the rocks. I knew it was bad to do this but until now I didn't know why. I was shocked that the boy's shouts had been his last; that his life had been so fragile that it could be snatched away from one minute to the next on a beautiful summer evening.

Dad did his part as well. On reading Mom's report about the incident, realizing that I didn't know how to swim, he wrote me detailed instructions in his letters. He based them on his Marine Corps swimming lessons: how to float, position one's fingers and swim efficiently in the water.

Dad's Virtual Swimming Lessons

One morning near the end of July, I eagerly picked up the newspaper from the steps and brought it up on the porch. I liked to make out the words in bold type and see how much I could understand of the stories. I stood on the screened porch of the Fairbanks Cottage, stunned in disbelief by the headline and the photograph of a damaged skyscraper, flames licking out of the 78th and 79th floor windows, the entire structure above that level shrouded in smoke.

A twin-engine B-25 Bomber, lost in a blinding fog, crashed into the Empire State Building today at a point 975 feet above the street level. Thirteen persons, including the three occupants of the plane, and ten persons within the building, were killed in the catastrophe and twenty-six were injured. Brilliant orange flames shot as high as the observatory on the eighty-sixth floor of the building, 1,050 feet above Fifth Avenue, as the gasoline tanks of the plane exploded.[1]

"How could that happen?" I asked my aunt, who had come out to drink her coffee and read the paper.

After she looked over the headline and the news story, Aunt Helen replied, "It seems that an experienced Army colonel got lost in a storm and thought he was over the river instead of the middle of New York."

"What happened to the pilot?" I asked.

"He and his crew were killed," Helen admitted reluctantly. A psychoanalyst, she was known for her tact and gentleness with patients and family alike, but she did not shrink from reality.

"Yeah, but did any people in the building get hurt?" I persisted.

"Yes, several office workers died," she replied firmly, "but many others escaped." Concerned that I was upset, she was quick to add, "But don't worry about it: this sort of accident doesn't happen very often."

Aunt Helen's reassurance didn't do much good. I couldn't understand how such a thing could happen. Men like Grandpa constructed huge buildings from the ground up. Airplanes were supposed to fly around them: it just couldn't be any other way. Many adults thought the same thing: how could an honored war hero make such a mistake, with such terrible consequences?

Until now I had faced wartime bravely, as when my father sent me a birthday letter just a year earlier:

> *Dear Peter:*
> *I hope you have a wonderful time on your birthday—it's your fifth and a very important one because you and Mommy have to take care of things without Daddy's help. It would be great if we could celebrate your birthday together, but I know you understand that Daddy is away for a*

very important reason and we must never forget that. If Daddy and millions of other daddies were not away from home to fight the bullies, we might never be able to have nice homes and live happily together. So, however much we miss one another, we should try to remember that things would be much worse if Daddy and other daddies were not willing to fight the bullies.

Have a wonderful birthday and Daddy will be thinking of you—and when I eat my ice cream here, I'll pretend it's your birthday ice cream. This is a real Marine pennant for your room.

Love, Dad.[2]

I remember standing in the glare of the living room window as Mom read me this letter, and how proud I was of my father. But the plane crashing into the Empire State Building got me worried about people dying, and whether Daddy would come home again to take care of our family. I knew Mommy was worried. too, about whether Daddy would have to use his gun to fight, and I worried that maybe he would die.

Among all the crannies in the over-sized Victorian house, I was most scared of the basement. Beyond the furnace a few bare light bulbs hung from the ceiling, casting pools of light on the cement floor. But past these warm, safe zones, visibility dropped off and I could just make out the rubble stone exterior walls, occasionally pierced by the glare of small high windows. When I was small I imagined that monsters and other spirits were hidden there, ready to pounce on me from the impenetrable Gothic gloom. At the foot of the stair on the right was the laundry room, where Mom spent so much of her time.

In the rear of the basement, next to the laundry room, was the water heater. Because of the large quantities of hot water we used, and the age of the mechanical equipment in the house, Mom was advised by her contractor father to get a new and larger capacity water heater. After the new one was installed, she put an ad in the neighborhood newspaper offering the old water heater for sale. I remember following Mom early one Saturday morning to the basement as she showed the used tank to a man who needed one.

I piped up, "Oh, that old thing? It doesn't work anymore!" Despite Mom's protestations to the contrary, this ended the discussion and killed the sale. The next day, I was again following Mom as she trooped back up the steep stairs. When I reached the winder treads where the stair began to reverse, I stared with fascination at the open side where there was no handrail. I peered into the mysterious and inviting darkness down below. Inexplicably, I gathered my nerve and leapt into the void.

What possessed me at that instant I have often wondered and only recently begun to understand.

How easily I could manipulate my mother's emotions! Discomfort with my power to destabilize the only person I had to guide me and the hidden hurt I bore from the absence of my father were apparently taking their toll in self-loathing and pain. The darkness promised peace, and relief from these heartaches. I was later shocked at how easily and painlessly the oblivion had come.

Fortunately for me, the only damage I suffered that day, after coming back to consciousness on the living room couch surrounded by concerned neighbors, were hurt pride and a lump on the back of my head. Grandpa sent out a carpenter Monday morning to add a handrail and enclose the open side at the bend in the basement stairs.

Dad arrived back in Chicago on October 28, 1945, owing to his skill and to serendipity, among the very first Marines to be released from duty after the peace was signed. It was none too soon.

The inevitable first clash between father and son developed over Dad's cooking. Mom enjoyed sleeping late on weekends, and on this particular Sunday morning so did my sister Linda. Always an early riser, Dad often prepared his own breakfast. On this occasion, a ham was left over from a family dinner; he sliced meat off the bone, browned it in the pan and cooked it into scrambled eggs. He put the food on plates, placed them before us on the kitchen table and began to eat.

"Uggh," I said.

"What's the matter? That's my special ham and eggs."

"It smells funny!"

"It smells good. Now eat your breakfast," Dad insisted, getting a little upset that his special offering was being rejected.

"No. I don't want it," I shouted angrily. I picked up my plate and dumped the eggs on the floor.

Ben had taken guff from officers, sergeants and his own reluctant fellow soldiers for too long; he wasn't going to take any from an ungrateful six-year-old, especially not a son of his. In fury he grabbed me, laid me across his knee and gave me several sound wallops on the behind. Terrified as well as hurt, I wailed in mortal agony.

Dad scraped the ham and eggs off the floor, put them back on the plate and commanded: "Now shut up and eat!"

Too frightened to disobey, I suppressed my howls and, whimpering, choked down the detested breakfast. By this time, the whole household was awake. Mom appeared in robe and slippers, trailed by my two-year-old sister, who was all eyes and ears. "What on earth are you doing to that child?" Mom demanded, to my utter relief.

"He threw his food on the floor. I taught him a lesson," he retorted.

I don't know what happened next, but I suspect that the harmonious homecoming was over. Mom and Dad probably had their first fight in a year and a half; reentry of the original man of the house had begun in earnest. I was never spanked again—Mom must have seen to that—and Dad regretted his impulsive reaction.

But some much-needed Marine Corps discipline asserted itself back home. Mom's tenure as both mother and father, which had stretched her to the limit of human endurance, was done, and Dad was finally able to reassert his role, in person. I never forgot this incident. It has always flashed through my mind whenever I was about to challenge someone over a disagreement: the memory that defying authority, especially Dad's, has consequences stuck with me.

As of that day, the readjustment process began.

The Green household headed back to normal. While I resented my loss of status as top dog, I felt a huge weight lift from me, as my sense of inadequacy to deal with things I didn't understand began to slip away. Now there was a boss, someone to ask, someone to rely on besides Mom. There was even someone to help me fight off evil spirits. While it would be years before I exorcised all the ghosts that haunted me during the war, I had at least made a beginning.

Ray School Class of 1952 50th Reunion, 2004

Top: Mort and Rowie; Top Left: Laurel, Mort and Susan; Top right: Alice and Ann; Center: Ray 100th Anniversary Student Painting; Lower left: Me, Puzzled; Lower Right: Martha; Bottom: Ray Auditorium

2

GRADE SCHOOL: CRUELTY AND KINDNESS

THE CHICAGO GRADE SCHOOL I ATTENDED in the 1950s, William H. Ray Elementary, offered kindergarten and all eight grades. Graduation constituted admission to high school. Common in those days was a practice called double promotion, in which a student was promoted, not to the next grade, but to the next half grade level above that. This happened to me twice: along with my whole class I skipped the first half of fourth grade and, with three other students, the second half of sixth grade. Since this meant I spent what is currently called middle school with a new crowd almost a year older than I, it later led to some problems with social adjustment.

The schoolyard, like Chicago and the wider world, could be a cruel place. Mom got creative with my outfits and loved to send me off in really neat kids' clothes, which I loved. When Davy Crockett and Daniel Boone ruled the afternoon TV channels, she bought me a coonskin cap with a real striped fur tail. Naturally, I was the only kid with a hat like that, and the older boys would yank off the tail, mercifully held on with a snap fastener, and play keep-away with it, tossing it back and forth to anyone but me. Ricky, a tall delinquent who became my personal bully, took the whole cap and ran away with it, until I was lucky enough to find the schoolyard monitor, who made him return it to me. One day I showed up in my new Hopalong Cassidy polo shirt, with my TV hero's name and a picture of him in his cowboy hat on the front. Ricky grabbed me by one shoulder and crumpled the front of the shirt in his fist until only a few letters showed. "Long…ass," he muttered in disgust, and stalked away. I never felt the same about that shirt or my proud appearance in it again.

This wasn't the last I heard from Ricky. One day as I reached in my locker I found the furry collar on my winter coat had been sliced with a sharp knife. The next morning Mom showed up at the school office with my coat, the principal called police and they found Ricky and his switchblade. I didn't find out what happened to him, but he never bothered me again.

Taking out our resentment for such abuse, in fifth grade, my classmates and I often persecuted a fat boy named Jay, who cowered when any of us approached him. Many of the other boys also picked on him. One day the word circulated among them, "We're going to *get* Jay after school." Led by some of the bigger boys, I joined the mob, who taunted him as he came out the school's doors. When confronted by the angry group, he ran. We chased him into the alley behind the school building. He cut between houses, crossed streets and tried to evade us. In desperation, he climbed the wooden rear porch of an apartment building, where, on the top floor, the boys caught up and cornered him. He whimpered. "What did I ever do to you?"

For the first time I saw him as human, just like me. I thought of Ricky, and how helpless he made me feel. My friend Mort was the first to read the situation and call off the dogs. He turned toward the others and said, "He's right. He's harmless, and we proved it. Now let's just leave him alone." Ashamed, the boys turned one by one and descended the stairs.

We had some great teachers in those grade school years. One who stands out was Mrs. Rose M. Aultz, my sixth-grade

English teacher, who was Scottish (think: *The Prime of Miss Jean Brodie*). She showed us how to diagram sentences and was a stickler for the English language and correct spelling. On our frequent tests we had to write our answers in ink, and a false start in writing a word, or an on-page correction was automatically marked wrong. She also administered the annual school spelling bee, in which I once took second place, after misspelling "amethyst."

I got encouragement from both sides of my family in verbal expression. Throughout my grade school years, Dad would sit down after dinner and read through a story or an essay I was trying to write. Looking at a confused sentence, he'd ask, "What were you trying to say here?" I would tell him, and he would reply, "Well, why don't you just write it that way?" He trained me to eliminate unnecessary words and clarify my writing.

Mom also wrote well. She had studied creative writing with Thornton Wilder at the University of Chicago. She loved the outdoors and verbalized her reactions to cloud shadows on the water, the scent of a fresh breeze, laundry dried on a clothesline and the smells of an ocean beach. I can't count the times she told me, "You write so well, Peter, you ought to do something with it."

We often had writers at our house. I recall telling one of them I might like to be a writer, and he responded by shaking his head. "Oh, you don't want to be a writer. What a terrible occupation!" I never knew what he meant, although low pay, lack of recognition and a long, uncertain climb toward success were no doubt the reasons. When it came time to prepare for a career, my parents never encouraged me to follow that line of work. They insisted I get proper training for a *real* job.

In eighth grade, the thirteen- and fourteen-year-old girls wanted to throw evening parties. But whom could they invite? Their classmates of course, consisting of shorter, younger-acting preadolescent boys. We were introduced to Spin the Bottle, Truth or Consequences and other parlor games. This meant the winner, or loser, as I saw it, was kissed by one of these nubile young teens. A year behind in social, not to mention physical, development—I wouldn't even turn thirteen until just before graduation—I was in that uncomfortable phase between boyhood, where I kicked cans, stepped in mud puddles and generally avoided girls, and the teen years, when I became aware of them. Nuzzled by some of the most attractive young women in the school, I was exposed to new feelings and had no clue what to do with them. Still innocent of lust, at least my curiosity was satisfied.

In these parlor games, I was often paired up with Susan Roth, who was as short as I. Apart from these encounters, what endeared me to her to was prompted by one incident. Still very fashion conscious, Mom continued to come up with creative ideas for my wardrobe. When I was in seventh grade, she bought me some blue jeans, marketed under the brand name, Snow Jeans, lined with flannel in bold, bright-colored plaid. With the cuffs rolled up, the lining showed. Although I was desperate to fit in with my classmates, I was likely the only kid in the school to own such pants and was mortified to show them off to my peers. Still, unwilling to disappoint my mother, who was so proud of her purchase, I bravely wore them to school.

The next day in math class Susan noticed: "Oh, your jeans have such fancy cuffs! That's so-o-o cool." At once I was in the very place I had tried to avoid—the center of attention. But it felt different. For a sweet, young girl, one I was already fond of, to notice, praise my outfit and and comment made me feel special. I recall that feeling to this day—her pure sweetness at that age, untainted by ulterior motives nor overshadowed by overruling passions, caused me to like her all the more.

Lagniappe, 1956. "The Heat's On"
My opening backdrop for the "Christopher Street" dance number

Dance Troupe with choreographer Penny Winston
Penny (center) raises the bar with her high kick

3

FROM SHOWING OFF TO SHOWMANSHIP

M Y FASCINATION WITH THE THEATER began as a child. My Aunt Sylvia, Dad's sister, took me on Saturday afternoons to children's performances at the Goodman Theater in downtown Chicago. When King Midas touched his beautiful daughter, and the stage lighting dimmed and flooded her crouching figure with amber light, the special effect was sheer magic. As the curtain closed for the act, I believed I had seen her transformed into a solid gold statue. The ability to transport audiences to faraway places and olden times and change the time of day and locale awakened me to the magic of my imagination. A "ham" at heart, I loved any excuse to appear before an audience and show off. In grade school I gave family magic shows and made special trips downtown to buy magic tricks. Dad encouraged me by taking the family to see Dante the magician and the famous illusionist Blackstone in person.

In high school I attended school plays and volunteered for the stage crew. There were two types of productions at New Trier, those run by faculty and the student show called *Lagniappe*, an annual musical production, so named, in New Orleans parlance, since it always promised "a little bit extra." In senior year I was appointed set designer for the show. The script involved Chicago and its gangsters and was called *The Heat's On*. Borrowing freely from Broadway shows, our talented musicians (perhaps influenced by the show itself), somehow "lifted" the rousing opening number from *Wonderful Town,* Leonard Bernstein's "Christopher Street," and adapted the Betty Comden and Adolph Green lyrics to a new plot on which to hang a student variety show. My friend Mike Lederer composed several original songs and wrote new lyrics for the borrowed ones. I designed the sets and supervised scene painting. Since this show was created entirely by students themselves, over 200 actors, singers, dancers and crew members, we all put heart and soul into it and thought we had created a new Broadway sensation.

As a high school senior thinking about careers, I decided to pursue my interest in set design and technical stage production. Encouraged by success in shows, I wanted to work in a professional stock company for the summer. The principal opportunity in our suburban Chicago area was at Music Theater, a musical comedy venue in Highland Park, Illinois, about ten minutes from my family's house. Dad advised me beginning with the spring thaw that I had better make contacts early for the season. Following up on a tiny ad in the paper announcing auditions, I called the New York number and was told to come to the Chicago try-outs.

My friend Ronnie, from our high-school drama club's lighting crew, accompanied me as we ventured downtown and entered an aging Michigan Avenue hotel, where the auditions were held. Reaching the top floor on an old elevator, we followed some signs up another stairway to a huge skylighted loft, a former ballroom, no doubt, with about forty metal folding chairs arranged around a creaking wooden stage. We found a singer belting out, "Oklahoma, where the wind comes sweeping down the plain," as a balding, reddish-haired rehearsal pianist with a cigarette dangling from his lower lip hammered out the bright chords on a battered upright. The candidates performed for a couple of men seated in the first row and another directly behind them. Aspiring singers and dancers in tights sat further back in the hall, tensely awaiting their turn.

"Thank you! We'll let you know," said the tallest of the men, who then stood up and walked over to us. He was suave, more casually dressed than we, and had a flourish—some might call it a swish—in his manner. "Hi! I'm David Tihmar, the director," he said. We introduced ourselves and stated our business. He told of his plans for an exciting season of summer musical theater and thanked us for coming. When I said I wanted to be a set designer and showed him designs from my high school portfolio, he said, "Ah yes, Peter, you've got to feed on the arts and let them become the grist for your mill!" He introduced us both to the stage manager, Bill Krot, a wiry, thin man of about 40, with crew-cut, black hair and dark, penetrating eyes. The director then excused himself turned around and called "Next!" as he returned to his auditions.

Krot told us the job of an apprentice offered no pay, a condition I was willing to accept in order to break in. I was hired on the spot. Ronnie said he had to think about it and, not surprisingly, was absent on the day we were asked to report to work.

The summer schedule promised six musicals that had enjoyed great popularity on Broadway. *Kismet* features the music of Borodin and is set in the opulence of an Arabian kingdom. It was richly rendered by a small yet talented and orchestra of a dozen musicians, a resident company of 30 singers and dancers and star talent brought in from New York. We went on to present five additional shows, each for a two-week run, including Frank Loesser's *Guys and Dolls*; Cole Porter's *Out of This World*, with Kaye Ballard, Bill Hayes and ballerina Mia Slavenska; Leonard Bernstein's *On the Town*; Rodgers and Hart's *Pal Joey*, starring Johnny Desmond—a popular singer and bandleader of the day who had recently been bitten by the acting bug—and, at season's end, the charming Rodgers and Hammerstein musical, *The King and I.* Our job was to construct scenery during the day for the next show, help with planning and design for the show after that and, every night, seven days a week, run the props and scenery down the five aisles to the arena stage for scene changes in the current show. While it was exhausting work, it was exciting to enjoy the camaraderie of the talented singers, dancers and musicians, to meet the big stars and to hear stories of life in the New York theater world. In breaks from scenery construction and painting, we got to know these people. Many of them, like Bill Hayes, were as kind and friendly to the lowliest apprentice in the scene shop as they were to the talented lead singers. He played Mercury in *Out of this World*, Cole Porter's musical romp through the Elysian fields of Greek and Roman mythology.

Highlights of my magical first season also included the night that we peered down the aisles to see Leonard Bernstein, in town to conduct at the nearby Ravinia Music Festival, and his wife, Felicia. They sat in the front row of canvas folding chairs on gravel terraces that made up the informal seating for our theater. He was laughing and enjoying his own show. *On the Town* depicts the comical adventures of three sailors turned loose in Manhattan on 24-hour liberty. The action takes them to the Museum of Natural History, Greenwich Village and the top of the Empire State Building and pairs each of them off with a genuine Broadway character. After the show, Maestro Bernstein graciously came backstage, congratulated the company and took the director aside for a heart-to-heart talk. The next day Bernstein himself appeared for a specially called rehearsal. He spent the entire afternoon assisting the director in refining cues, tightening transitions, re-staging scenes and, in general, improving the quality of the performance. The results were remarkable. The show ran twelve minutes shorter and sparkled with a new flair and enthusiasm, as only one of the show's creators could have imparted to the production. The event showed me that Leonard Bernstein, in addition to being one of the most notable composers of the twentieth century, was a first-class human being.

Penny Winston Stein recalls that she and I worked together, not only on Lagniappe, but also in the first season of Music

Theater, in On the Town, "when I fell in love with Bill Hayes and was complimented by Leonard Bernstein for my *pas de deux* in 'Lonely Town.' *In The King and I* (where I was Little Eva, who dies in the ballet of 'Small House of Uncle Thomas' and she has to climb a ladder on stage up to heaven)!" Her favorite memory of the Lagniappe production is that her name was more prominent in the program, "since I was not only a performer but was also the choreographer and was on the Lagniappe Board, while Ann-Margret Olsen was merely in the chorus, the only time in life when my billing would be better than hers."

The biggest challenge of all occurred every other Sunday evening on "strike night," when a show closed. We had to strike the set, remove the old scenery, re-hang the lighting, put the new scenery in place and have everything running like clockwork by 8 p.m. the next night for the new show's opening. While the actors had been rehearsing their lines, their songs and their dances every afternoon and had merely to adjust to their new physical setting, the changeover usually involved a 24-hour marathon—really 36 hours when you added the previous day's activities—for the technical crews.

None of this could start until 11:30 p.m., when the lights dimmed on the closing show and the audience had departed. We lowered scenery from the top of the tent, disconnected and stowed it. We hung a new show curtain on the wall of the stage house at the back of the main aisle, added new floodlights and spotlights, re-aimed them and changed their colored gelatin filters. Frequently, we repainted the stage floor in the show's theme colors. Without fail, we completed the bulk of the heavy work and hung most of the new scenery by sunrise. But we spent the day working frantically to attend to a thousand details: last-minute touch up and painting; rehearsing dozens of scene changes and practicing over 100 light cues. Often as the show began, paint was literally "drying under the lights."

Enchanted with the glamour, the excitement and the challenge involved in presenting 84 consecutive nightly performances, I didn't complain. By the third strike night, however, about mid season, my father was annoyed: "You've got to go over there and *insist* on a day off," he declared. "A day off is 24 consecutive hours without working," he explained, in case I didn't get it. Reluctantly I returned to the theater after breakfast on the morning after strike night and told Bill Krot I would not be returning until the show opened the next evening. He was not happy. He drove himself relentlessly and found it hard to understand anyone who didn't, but he grudgingly admitted that my father probably knew what was best for me. When I did return, Bill informed me he had cut me out of the scene changes. He said, "I'm not chastising you for taking time off, but since you were not here, you simply don't know the cues and will not be in a position to help us tonight." Fully rested by then and feeling left out, I watched the show, but on the next night of the production, he pressed me into service anyway, out of sheer necessity.

Bill Krot was my mentor and a real father figure—luckily, since I did not have any time that summer to spend with my own father—and taught me many life lessons, some if only by his example. He loaned me the book, *Slim*, by William Wister Haines, author of *Command Decision*, a play that debuted on Broadway in 1947. Slim—a top lineman with a risky and demanding job hanging power transmission lines—performs his arduous duties with precision, care and total dedication, because he loves his work.

Bill related how this job had become so important to him. "My first job was as an apprentice to a jeweler. The work was impossibly difficult: I was all thumbs with those tiny parts; one little slip of the hand and a whole day's work could end up in a mess on the floor. The hours were long, and the confinement was miserable. I used to curse the sun when it came up in the morning. I hated my job. Nowadays, in the winter, I work on Broadway shows when I can and do the auto shows for Chevy, Ford, and others—where the new models are presented to the sales force at a big annual sales meeting." These were elaborate productions with music, full scenery, lighting and costumes. In summer, he did stock. "Now, I love life, can't wait to get to work in the morning and can't bear to leave at night, because I'm *doin' what I want to do.*"

That fall, I began my freshman year at Yale. After the Christmas break I returned to school a few days early so I could spend time in New York, getting standing room tickets for Broadway shows and visiting friends I had made in the theater. At my Dad's recommendation that I get a paying job for the following summer, I looked up the producers and agents for Music Theater and made inquiries and about the coming season. I sent a follow-up letter to New York, complete with a resumé of my theatrical experience. By now it showed some strong theatrical credits: set design for Tennessee Williams' *Summer and Smoke* for our amateur summer players; set design for *Lagniappe*, the all-student high school production that showcased Ann-Margret Olsen on the way to her meteoric film career, and design and stagecraft for several other student productions. I eventually received a reply with an offer of the princely sum of thirty dollars a week, which I was proud to accept, since I could show Dad that, with the exception of previous summers spent cutting lawns for him and the neighbors, I had my first paying job.

The resident company now numbered only 17 singers, dancers and actors,, more than a dozen less than the previous summer, and the orchestra had shrunk to nine stalwart players and a new musical director, including a nervous, hep-cat drummer named Marvin, whose straight black hair was uncontrollable, especially after he began his frenetic attack on his skins, and Leo, a classical violinist who took great pride in playing the jazzy show tunes on a Stradivarius passed down to him through the generations of his family. A recent graduate of Parsons School of Design in New York was the new set designer.

The season promised six great shows—*The Pajama Game, Plain and Fancy, Can-Can, Wish You Were Here, Damn Yankees and South Pacific*—but the stars were dimming. The biggest names in the program for this season were Jimmie Komacs, who was remembered as one of the three ballplayers who sang "You've Gotta Have Heart" in Damn Yankees on Broadway. He coached the singers on that song in our production. Leonard Stone, who played Applegate (the Devil) in that show would top off the season as Luther Billis in South Pacific, a role he had played for two years in Australia and again in the United States. Despite this lack of star power, Gene Bayliss, a Broadway choreographer, was our new, energetic director; David, his lead dancer-assistant choreographer, and an outstanding dance troupe brought a new dynamism to the company.

In this theater-in-the-round, we had to run the scenery, furniture and props down the aisles onto the stage during the blackouts between scenes. To accomplish this, those of us on the scenery construction crew became stagehands. Every night at home after dinner, I changed into what Mom called my "ghost suit," all black. With precise timing, as soon as the stage went dark, the actors escaped down one or more of the five aisles, and we descended at a run, down the unoccupied aisles with chandeliers, set pieces, chests, chairs, roof beams, potted plants, statues, trees or whatever else was called for in the set design. Pity the poor patron who thought the blackout was a good time to pop up unnoticed and run to the toilet—the cause of a few near-catastrophes.

One of them occurred on the second night of the opening show, *The Pajama Game*, when we were just getting accustomed to our new scene changes. The scene to be set was the office of Mr. Hassler, President of Sleep-Tite Company. While our colleagues cleared the sewing machine tables from the previous factory floor scene, with Frank, klutz of the scene shop, in the lead, we dashed down an aisle with a desk, where we'd stacked an upended secretarial chair. True to form, Frank tripped and lurched forward. The desk tipped to the left toward the orchestra pit. I fell forward against the desk. The swivel chair bounced off the head of Marvin the drummer and hit Leo on the shoulder, grazing his violin. We untangled the mess in the dark, set the scene and scrambled to safety just as the stage manager, running the show from backstage and unable to wait a second longer, brought the lights up. As the actors began to recite their lines, I heard a low moan coming from the pit, in Leo's general direction. Only at intermission did we learn that Marvin's addled brain was not further damaged, but that the chair had chipped a nick in Leo's 400-year-old—and until that moment, perfectly preserved—Stradivarius. I escaped with only a cracked rib, which I nursed for the rest of the summer, but I considered myself lucky: it only hurt when I laughed.

There was more to do this summer than the last. Bill Krot had not returned; I never even met, much less received direction, from his replacement Production Stage Manager. Only Wally, the easygoing union Master Electrician, knew how to run the technical aspects of the production. The new set designer didn't know how to run a scene shop, nor did he have much interest in designing for our stage. He sat in the shop for what seemed like hours, mixing beautiful colors and moping. When it came time to design the barn-raising scene for *Plain & Fancy*, he threw up his hands and asked those of us in the scene shop what to do. A couple of days later I brought in some watercolor sketches of a sequence for assembling hinged frames that the actors could easily carry onto the stage and hook together. When all the pieces had been raised, they formed the skeleton of a Pennsylvania barn. By dimming the overhead lights and illuminating the angled floods, the red-tinted, gauze-like scrim covering on the frames would then appear solid just as the chorus sang "It comes a barn!" We adopted my plan.

By the time we launched the next show, Cole Porter's *Can-Can*, the set designer gave up the ghost. "This just isn't what I expected," whined the strapping, six-foot-tall artist. "I'm going back to New York."

Seizing my opportunity, I made a pitch to the director for the job. Stuck at mid-season without a designer, Gene Bayliss was all ears. "Why don't you work up some ideas for *Wish You Were Here*?" he suggested. In the next few days, in what little spare time I had, I prepared sketches. I devised a way of making clusters of pine needles from green plastic soda straws; suspending floating beams that suggested cabin roofs and designed a show curtain for the wall of the stage house that depicted a post card bearing the words: "Having a wonderful time—wish you were here!" After the overture, when the show curtain was raised, it would reveal a bright yellow bus in a perspective view. The cast would make made their grand entrance by swinging open the door of the bus and bounding into the main aisle to arrive at Kamp Karefree. The director was impressed, Bob and I requested raises, and I was hired, or so I thought. The next day I learned of Herb's decision to split the job between Bob Green (no relation), my fellow scene-builder, and me, and to offer only ten dollars a week to each of us. Good old Herb had eliminated the entire salary of the previous, higher-paid set designer, doubled our responsibilities and incurred an added cost of only twenty dollars a week.

Bob and I swallowed our pride and accepted our puny raises. With Bill Krot's words: "Now I love life…because I'm *doin' what I want to do*" echoing in my head, I settled in for the rest of the summer to do the job I was dying to do at any price.

It turned out Bob and I made a good team in creating the scenery. I prepared the designs and Bob, with his sunny, good-natured personality, showed people how to make them. David Crane, our stage manager, was doggedly determined to fulfill Gene's vision to convert the orchestra pit into a swimming pool, the signature feature of any production of *Wish You Were Here*, while relocating the musicians to the rear of one bank of seats. Jim Kiddle, our lanky, bespectacled assistant electrician, had moved up to Technical Director in the rash of mid-season desertions, He devised a way to line the orchestra pit with a heavy vinyl material that both contained most of the water and somehow kept the choristers who volunteered for aquatic duty from being electrocuted. He even draped the first three rows of seats behind the pit with long sheets of this black vinyl, a precautionary measure that savvy spectators quickly learned to deploy. At the opening of the second act, the chorus again burst down the main aisle, this time in swimming suits, and plunged into the pool, sending sheets of water in all directions, as squeals of shock and delight emitted from actors and audience alike.

Sweet revenge for our paltry raises came soon enough. Since there were few offerings in those days on the sleepy Chicago theater scene, Music Theater had the full attention of the town's daily newspapers. Roger Dettmer, one of two drama critics for the Chicago American, wrote:

'WISH YOU WERE HERE'—CRITIC DIDN'T

Six summers ago I saw "Wish You Were Here" in New York, on a humid Friday night—humid as only New York can be.

It was simple-minded fun, furiously paced and fetchingly cast. When the show docked here the following summer, it had been altered script-wise beyond recognition and not at all for the better. Still, this seemed an ideal show for the citronella circuit, and when Music Theater promised a pool (the orchestra pit), well, I fell in love with the idea.

I fall in love too easily…

Apart from the pool, (just big enough for a frolicsome full-grown seal or three aspiring chorines) and the charming decor by Robert and Peter Green, "Wish" was played with the speed of "Cyrano" on creative self-expression night at the Bayonne (N. J.) Opera House.

While Herb Rogers's bluff that he was putting on great theater had been called, Bob and I became an item for our set design talents. Dad and Mom were particularly proud of me. Not only were they tickled by Dettmer's acerbic wit. Because they both had been press agents, they also knew how hard it was to get free publicity, and they considered this a major coup for one so young. Dad made sure I wrote a letter to Mr. Dettmer thanking him for the recognition, and joking a little bit, inviting him to come again sometime, to see if he liked the next show any better. Now that my design reputation was solidly established, any actor who needed a special prop or service would ask me for help.

In August we launched our last show, *South Pacific*. During the dress rehearsal, a burly, fully costumed Leonard Stone, in his faded blue shirt with sleeves rolled, slouchy dungarees and weather-beaten sailor hat, found me in the scene shop.

"Hey, Green," he said in his gruffest Seabee voice, "You're an artist, aren't you? I need you to do the boat on my stomach. Come an hour before the cast call tonight so you can draw it."

I was so pleased to help him create his character, I could barely resist saluting and saying. "Aye-aye, sir!" It was the talk of our family dinner table as I bolted down my meal so I could show up earlier than usual. When I sat down in the scene shop to do this elaborate make-up job for Billis—Stone, that is—he handed me one of those indelible pencils with one sharpened end red and the other blue and told me to create a two-masted schooner precisely in the center of his belly. Using both colors I drew a graceful sailing ship, straining in the wind, headed from left to right, with several square sails billowing out toward the bow. The two masts sloped gracefully from front to rear, accentuating the impression of speed. Checking the mirror, he scorned my first attempt: "Naw, dammit, that's not it!" he cursed like a sailor, as he scrubbed off my efforts with a wet cloth. "Here's how to do it!" With emphatic strokes he grabbed a scrap of brown wrapping paper and drew the same ship, but foursquare, its masts perfectly vertical and sails trapezoidal and flat, with lines much thicker and bolder than I had dared inscribe on his famous abdomen. Finally, he was satisfied, and I was invited to come back every night to reestablish the accepted design.

Billis's Nightly Tattoo

That night I got a front row seat for the action. Owing to our penny-pinching producer's tight budget, we male apprentices and all the male singers and dancers assumed positions at the edge of the round stage floor as the onstage military audience. When the lights came up, in his grass skirt and halter top made of half coconut shells, blonde wig and smeared lipstick, he was a sight. As the chorus sang, he edged his way toward center stage:

> *A hundred and one*
> *Pounds of fun*
> *That's my little Honey Bun.*
> *Get a load of Honey Bun tonight!*

The trombone blared at the conclusion of the third line, the verse ended and the orchestra repeated the tune. Marvin, our punch-drunk drummer, launched into his drum solo, his black hair flying: BOOM-boom-ba-doom-doom, BOOM-boom-ba-doom-doom. Billis sprang into action. His hips gyrated, the grass skirt swayed, and the blond mop flopped. He was in his element, in total control. He relaxed, lifted one cup of his halter top, took out a pack of cigarettes and matches, lit one and replaced the pack. As his audience of sailors and soldiers, we clapped, hooted and cheered. Gripping his smoke tightly with his lips and puffing, he raised both arms and started a serious bump and grind. The ship caught the wind. The waterline undulated; the hull bobbed on the swells of his gut; sails alternately billowed and collapsed in the gale, and foam splashed from Billis's stomach as the schooner knifed through the waves. When I saw how Lenny performed the number, at last I knew why he didn't need to have any motion expressed in the line work of my drawing. In thinking that the total effect rested on my artistry, I had forgotten to allow for his!

This work with Leonard Stone gave me my first inkling of a truth commonly obscured by myth of the solitary genius: many artistic works are collaborative. While individual creativity is often the origin of an idea, great works of theater, architecture and music are never realized without the participation of many backers, entrepreneurs, artists, artisans, engineers, technicians and others in support of the effort. My two summers at Music Theater disabused me of the notion that art is the work of a lone artist and taught me how much people have to work together. They must collaborate to produce the show, communicate a vision, inspire others to contribute the best of their own talents and finally share it with the audience, the ultimate participant and interpreter in the artistic experience.

Throughout my musical theater summers, as always, Dad was there again for me. When I was five he had admired my drawings from his post halfway around the world and drew pictures of his surroundings for me. When I was 13, he encouraged me to take art classes at the Chicago Art Institute on Saturday, and both he and Mom praised my progress and encouraged me to continue. He was always interested in drawing, painting, architectural design, construction and everything that my grandfather knew how to build; he nurtured those interests in me. As I set out to use my talents to earn a living, he was there at every point along the way, guiding me as I took my first tentative steps. I reflected how he had taught me to avoid exploitation, to hold my ground in a financial negotiation and to compromise when it was in my own best interest. Moreover, not without some early misgivings, he had encouraged me to follow my heart and seek a career I could follow with passion.

And what a sense I had gained of the power of teamwork to accomplish any complex endeavor! I had begun my summer stock career believing art was the province of the solitary creative genius. But I soon found that it took hundreds of people, beginning with the show's original creators on Broadway and extending to our small but talented company. And it was not complete, after all, without our audience—which in my rough calculation approached 100,000 per season— as we launched daring and wide-ranging voyages of imagination from a few dilapidated farm buildings, a water-filled orchestra pit big enough for a full-grown, frolicsome seal and a makeshift, stuffy, and leaky tent.

My urge to show off had earned me a little bit of extra money—making a splash, attracting the public's attention, impressing an audience. I knew it was a dead-end occupation. Only a handful of theatrical set designers in America earned a living wage. Still, in choosing a career, maybe there was a larger demand in the wider business world to use my knack for showmanship.

Ben Green, Ad Executive
Preparing his children for college

4

AN OUTSIDER STORMS THE BARRICADES

DAD WAS EXTREMELY PROUD I was admitted to Yale. Since his own father, an unsuccessful real estate promoter, either didn't steer him at all or gave him mostly bum steers, he never finished college. He determined to do a better job on me. Mom coached me, too, based on the teachings of her mentors: her fearsome father and Thornton Wilder, who taught her creative writing at the University of Chicago. I began my first semester at the South Side high school Mom had attended during more placid times. I sneaked around the savage halls of Hyde Park High as inconspicuously as possible, trying to avoid the hoodlums who shook us down for "change."

The plan to send my sister and me to college was carefully laid and years in the making. After my first month of running the gauntlet in city high school, my parents decided their next move up was overdue. With my sister coming along four years after me, they were ready for the open spaces and the celebrated school systems of the suburbs. After spending a delightful summer in Glencoe, renting a house across the street from his former business colleague Bob Cunningham and commuting daily by train to his job downtown, Dad was sold. Mom was charmed by the prospect of village life in the north suburbs, and she hoped for a spacious house with a modern kitchen and a big yard where she could plant a garden. We spent many golden fall weekends that year with our real estate agent, searching for the perfect home. As a budding photographer, I was absorbed in capturing images of the gold, orange and crimson leaves, contrasted with the cloudless, cobalt skies of autumn.

We finally found an ideal house—a tri-level on a double lot in the village of Glencoe, within the district of New Trier Township High School. Linda, age nine, clinched the deal when she said, "This house likes us." Their choice was validated soon thereafter through an article in a national publication drawing attention to this institution as the second highest ranking high school in the nation, under the title, "A Right to Be Proud."

By junior year I was getting plenty of pressure to think about the choice of a college. I was busy enough keeping up with my coursework in English, chemistry, advanced algebra and Latin, but found time for set design in the school's dramatic productions, including musicals—both school-sponsored, shows, such as Lerner and Loew's *Brigadoon*, and the student-produced musical, *Lagniappe*. I was having fun in high school and wasn't devoting much thought to my future. Still, guidance counselors at school planned College Night, so we could meet alumni from all the famous universities and small, liberal arts colleges and hear them tout their alma maters. In addition to the preference tests and personality analyses to which we were all subjected as part of our schooling, we then began college guidance testing and in late sophomore year, a practice round of Scholastic Aptitude Tests (SATs). These activities uncovered many possible directions for my career and further education.

Nonetheless, Mom and Dad—among the ranks of those frightened parents who didn't want to slip up in child-rearing—decided it was time for even more guidance and hired a career consultant named Florence "Rusty" Miller to set me straight. I recall some discussion at the time that this was a big investment on my parents' part, and they elicited from me a pledge to take it seriously and give it my best shot. After meeting Rusty, a middle aged, very bright and intellectual woman with glasses and a mop of curly red hair, I spent an arduous Saturday taking yet another battery of tests in her downtown office. A couple of weeks later Mom took me back there for our summary and evaluation session.

The conclusions were definitive: I had high aptitudes in math, writing and abstract social relations — less so in personal interactions, due apparently to an innate shyness. Possible fields of were engineering, architecture, social work, and even a counseling role as a pastor. The last one was a weird outlier—religion was the last thing either of my parents (or I, for that matter) were interested in or encouraged me to pursue.

We were referred to her by business or social contacts in the suburbs. My case was not Rusty's first rodeo. She asked plenty of questions about family occupations and learned I had an interest in construction, owing to my grandfather's business. Furthermore, she knew many of my high school peers were headed for Eastern colleges. They were well positioned for acceptance, due to the high success rate of New Trier graduates at the finest universities. Well-oiled with this background information, Rusty proposed the colleges I might be eligible for and which ones offered fields of study for which I had aptitude, as well as extracurricular activities meeting my interests. They included Harvard, Yale, Princeton and Cornell.

So far, the only university campuses I had ever seen were the University of Chicago in our old Hyde Park neighborhood, which both my parents had attended; Harvard, where my aunt and uncle, whom we visited periodically, both taught, and Eastern Illinois State Teacher's College (now Eastern Illinois University) in Charleston in the southeastern part of the state, where the finals of the State Latin contest were held. My visit there was successful: I placed second in the State of Illinois, Freshman Division. As a junior in high school, I also got wind of a college trip sponsored by the Cornell Club of Chicago. Dad called the club's president and got invitations for me and a friend on an all-expenses-paid trip for a weekend on the Cornell campus.

To my parents' delight, I was accepted everywhere I applied, Harvard, Yale and Cornell. Although he didn't stay in college long—a year at Illinois in Champaign-Urbana and a year at the University of Chicago, Dad knew what it took to fit in on campus and wanted me, at the very least, to be properly attired. When I was ready to go off to Yale, he made a formal date with me to go downtown and took the day off from work. His stated purpose was to buy me some school clothes. Reflecting on his own experience, he wanted to make sure I'd fit in with my "betters." He knew I could overcome any Midwestern social crudity that might be apparent to Easterners by dressing like them. We were not only shopping; we were acquiring my "college man's wardrobe" and the mental attitudes necessary to dress for success.

He had learned the men's clothing business shortly after he dropped out of college in his sophomore year, when his father died. He went on to work in a department store that offered quality men's wear. He learned the dos and don'ts of sales: Don't pressure your customer, select well for him, let *him* decide how good he looks and never show him an ill-fitting garment. He had an eye for color harmony—subtle was best: "See the little thread of yellow worked through the Harris Tweed weave? This is a beautiful jacket," he said, and he bought it for me. Dad liked subtle shoulder pads and an easy fit. When it was right, you felt different—at ease, confident, pleased with your image in the mirror and ready to take on the world.

We combed the downtown department stores: Marshall Field, Brooks Brothers, and several smaller men's stores. But their selections in my size (36 short) were limited, and we could not find anything satisfactory. When I got bored with shopping and was rude to a salesman, Dad brought me up sharply. He reminded me from his own experience how hard the man worked and explained that he would get paid only if we bought something. By example, he was scrupulously polite to each individual who waited on us, making sure to thank him even if we could find nothing to buy.

When we arrived at Maurice L. Rothschild, we struck gold. Our salesman was a master, and the selection was immense. Like kids in a candy store, we could hardly decide which of the many handsome available garments I should try on. We settled on a basic navy wool suit with a faint pinstripe, a Harris Tweed gray wool jacket with a vertical stripe and a dark brown suit that complemented my hair color. Dad said it fit me like a dream—I agreed. The next step was to find the right accessories. Dad showed me how to select a shirt that contrasted nicely and picked up tones found in the suit fabric. He carried a sport jacket over to the tie counter and showed me how to decide what went well together. As a result of our educational shopping trip, I went off to college with a fine new wardrobe and the confidence that I could hold my own in any group because of the way I dressed.

At times, though, he went a bit overboard in his efforts to perfect me.

He was never hesitant to criticize my table manners for example: "Don't bob your head up and down when you eat soup—it's not polite." He taught me how to tie my necktie in a Windsor knot, dimple it just so, adjust the length of both ends and make sure it was pulled tight, with no white showing above the knot. He insisted my nails always be clean and trimmed— difficult for me, a nail-biter as a teen—since, he pointed out, unkempt hands jarred a business interviewer's first impression. Perfect diction and pronunciation were expected, and he closely he monitored the expressions I picked up from friends. He was quick to call attention to anyone we encountered in public who was "one of those 'dese, dem and dose guys.'"

He insisted I join mainstream society. He loved my Jewish friends, but as he had done in his own case, he purged my language of any ethnic expressions which might have identified me with a disadvantaged social group. When I picked up their speech habits, he scorned them, commenting: "Don't say. *'oi vey.'* It means 'Oh, God,' and it's coarse language." Actually, it's a Yiddish expression meaning "woe is me," but Dad still wanted to make sure I didn't use it. Mom did her part to refine me as well, teaching me the fine points of manners, introductions and courteous behavior with women.

For the most part, my parents' coaching smoothed my way. I made fewer *faux pas* in polite society. On the other hand, it took some of my natural reactions to other people away, made me self-conscious and left me more inhibited, certainly more than he, in relating comfortably to other people. Ready or not, I hopped on a plane and set off for a college campus I'd read about but had never seen, assuming, like others of my age, that I was prepared to take on the world.

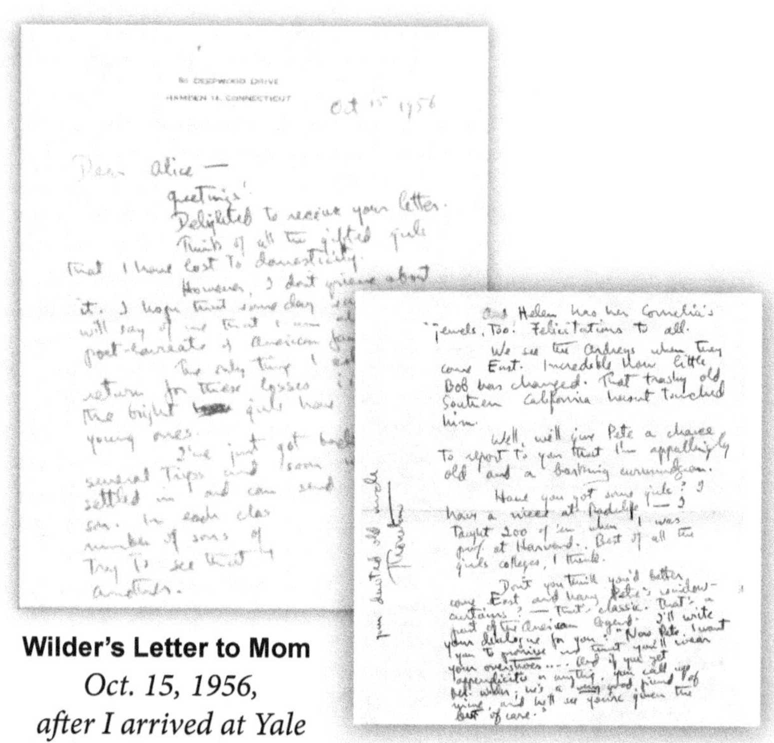

Wilder's Letter to Mom
Oct. 15, 1956,
after I arrived at Yale

Thornton Wilder at the University of Chicago, 1931
About when when he taught Mom creative writing

5

WELCOMED BY THORNTON WILDER AT YALE

I N SEPTEMBER 1956, I arrived in a cab from the New Haven Railroad station, suitcase in hand, a trunk to follow by Railway Express, for my first view of a different campus. Relying on my trusty consultants, I had picked the college with not so much as a sightseeing visit. I met my assigned roommates, whom I knew only by name. That very evening, we were serenaded from the courtyard below by one of Yale's celebrated singing groups, the Spizzwinks(?), with:

> *Wake, wake, freshmen wake,*
> *Wake while our song smites the sky.*
> *And now, ere we leave you,*
> *We heartily give you*
> *A welcome to Delta Theta Psi!*

My roommates Paul, Tom and I agreed: we liked the setup. The only thing we dreaded was the reason we were here: the classes and the hard work, which we knew lay just ahead. The preppies considered the three of us "public school weenies"— Paul local and Tom and I Midwestern—and we all could be construed by Yale officialdom as Jewish, although I was undeclared. Nevertheless, they assigned some genuine preppies to a room across the hall, one of them the son of a *bona fide* Washington D. C. socialite, who rubbed elbows with presidents, congressmen and diplomats at her frequent Capital entertainments. At least we got to see how the other half lived and—to our distress—hear how they carried on into the middle of the night.

During the first week of classes, I attended the President's Tea and met A. Whitney Griswold. Stumped over what to talk about with a university president, I babbled on about the fact that my mother knew Thornton Wilder, who lived nearby. Griswold said, in fact, he had sent Mr. Wilder home at a very late hour the previous evening. He learned that the writer had just returned from Mexico. I wrote Mom that this was her chance to catch him while he was in the country. She sent him a letter letting him know that I was in the vicinity. Three weeks later, she received a response to her letter:

> *50 Deepwood Drive*
> *Hamden 14, Connecticut*
> *Oct 15, 1956*
> *Dear Alice —*
> *Greetings!*
>
> *Delighted to receive your letter.*
> *Think of all the gifted girls that I have lost to domesticity.*
>
> *However, I don't grieve about it. I hope that someday someone will say that I am also the poet laureate of American family life.*
>
> *The only thing I ask in return for these losses is that the bright girls have bright young ones.*

*I've just got back from several trips and soon will become
settled in and can send for your son. In each class we have
a number of sons of friends, and we try to see that they meet me—*

And Helen has her Cornelia's jewels, too! Felicitations to all.

*We see the Ardreys when they come east. Incredible how
little Bob has changed. That trashy old Southern
California hasn't touched him.*

*Well, we'll give Pete a chance to report to you that I'm
appallingly old and a barking curmudgeon.*

*Have you got some girls? I have a niece at Radcliffe—I
taught 200 of 'em when I was prof. at Harvard. Best of
all girls colleges, I think. Don't you think you'd better
come east and hang Pete's window curtains?—That's
classic. That's a part of the American legend. I'll write
your dialogue for you: "Now Pete, I want you to
promise us that you will wear your overshoes... And if
you get appendicitis or anything, you call up Mr. Wilder;
he's a very good friend of mine, and he'll see you're given
the best of care."*

Your devoted old uncle,

Thornton

I had indeed sent Mom the measurements for our window
curtains—and she did send us a lovely set of red café curtains to
warm up our living room.

I was thrilled that the self-nominated "poet laureate of
American family life" was willing to receive me and delighted
Mom's former professor was so friendly to her. Mom sent the
original letter to me, and my roommates were very impressed.
From his comments it was clear I could call and visit him when
I got the opportunity. Perhaps the onrush of college life, my
basic shyness and the lack of access to a car prevented me (a
poor excuse: I knew how to summon taxicabs), but I never

arranged to go see him—one of the regrets I have over those chances of a lifetime I've missed.

My letters of that busy fall illustrate this onrush. My classmates clued me in to the many things I had to do to keep up: buy a block of season football tickets, for fourteen dollars; sign a contract with the student laundry; take a bus trip to Manhattanville College to meet the freshman girls and get dates for football weekends—I was being pulled in many directions.

Oh, and the classwork. I was enrolled in the two-year Directed Studies (D.S) program, an immersion course in the liberal arts, which both Mom and Dad felt I needed. Its core courses freshman year were Philosophy I (ways of knowing), Literature and History of Art, and my two electives were French and calculus. Each of the D.S. courses included a weekly seminar composed of ten to a dozen students and an instructor. The lit course required weekly papers—in fact, every course required frequent writing of papers. I commented that each week was like a rough week at New Trier High.

What wasn't like high school was the grading system. Yale stuck with numerical grades, rather than converting them to letter grades, the practice at our high school. I worked hard, yet amid the increased competition, grades above 85 were much harder to earn. I scrambled to maintain an average of 80 to 81, or the equivalent of a B, while in high school I was used to achieving grades in a range of 90 to 100, which typically converted to an A.

My calculus course was taught by the head of the math department, who preferred to regale us with memories of making gin in the bathtub during his college years and never got across, to me anyway, the point or the operating concepts of calculus. French pronunciation was easier for me than most, so I enjoyed the conversational approach in class, failed to drill on vocabulary or grammar and did poorly on both oral and written exams. As our professors and section leaders reminded us, we were now among the top ten percent of the classes from Eastern prep schools and top high schools across the country. I wondered whether they were better prepared than I, although I attended one of the best public high schools in the country, or just smarter to begin with, which would be a real blow to my pride. Moreover, while I worked hard to maintain my grades, it really burned me that some prep-schoolers had learned how to coast along without seeming to try too hard, join fraternities and still maintain a 70 to 75 average, that is, the equivalent at other colleges of a "Gentleman's C." What did these Easterners know that I didn't?

I stayed afloat the first year with good grades in the Directed Studies program but barely passed my neglected French and calculus courses. In my spare time, I took advantage of my route through New York to see a few Broadway shows, to call on the team packaging our shows for the forthcoming Music Theater season back home and to line up a backstage job in the summer stock company. Yale's residential policy required dormitory living on the Old Campus for freshmen and residential college assignments for upperclassmen, except for a few privileged seniors and married students.

Consequently, fraternities were more like social clubs, a luxury both of my parents scorned and were unwilling to subsidize. Frankly, I had no time, interest or need for fraternity life. But it was yet another factor that distinguished me and many of my friends as outsiders by the comfortable "legacy" members of our student body.

6

SEEKING ROOTS IN EUROPE

I N THE SUMMER BETWEEN our junior and senior years in college, like many of our classmates, my friend Mike Lederer and I were itching to travel. I dipped into my savings from summer work, and we planned a trip to Europe. American demand for travel was so great in the Fifties that a Dutch steamship company offered a bargain fare for students, and anyone else who didn't mind the ruckus and the absence of finer amenities, on older vessels in their fleet. Those of us on our first ocean voyage found the freedom, the bargain bar prices and round-the-clock social scene irresistible, and we signed on for the week-long party. I took a boat and Mike, already a seasoned traveler, would fly and join me in London.

On June 13, 1959, aboard the S.S. Waterman, a student ship of the Holland-America Line, I wrote home, apologizing for the delay and explaining that "you can't mail letters from the ship and also because I haven't had anything to say." The old tub limped along slowly. Due to a problem with one of the screw propellers, the crew announced, the scheduled seven-day voyage would take ten days. I was more interested in being on my way than speed. Besides, it gave me more time to meet the girls. At first I felt very detached, and the trip seemed unreal, but things got wilder and wilder. The realization that I might never see my shipboard acquaintances again took a point of reference away but freed me from my customary social inhibitions.

The company had also promoted the cruise by offering classes with teachers and professors on board who taught European social graces and languages and explained differences between our culture and Europe's. I even picked up a few German phrases in a shipboard class. I didn't do any reading but spent a lot of time talking with people from different regions and countries. I decided that I really love America and Americans, a healthy attitude, I concluded, in approaching my adventure.

"Drinks are cheap," I wrote, "only 12 cents for a Heineken's beer and 25 cents for scotch and soda. Despite this happy fact, and I suppose because of it, I seem to have spent about 20 dollars at the bar. One feels free to buy other people drinks at these prices and my personal consumption is slow but sure." It was also a good way to try all different kinds of drinks. For the family's benefit I marked our course and position on the inside of the envelope, special gift stationery with a colorful map of the world printed on the interior.

Some of my cabin mates were polite and interesting, but two of them, Mark and Aaron, turned out to be jerks — loud and combative, New York's lowest form of life. The plumbing on the in-room lavatory was stacked: common supply and drain piping served both ours and the adjacent cabin. To ensure consistent supply, the water was under high pressure, with spring shut off valves. When one pressed on the faucet, it spouted forcefully and, on release, sprang closed with a loud "thump," which could be heard through the thin steel bulkhead separating cabins. Regardless of the time of day or night, we heard the adjacent cabin's lavatory usage and they heard ours through the thin walls. Annoyed whenever our neighbors used their faucets, Mark and Aaron retaliated with double the number of thumps they heard through the wall.

One night at midnight I was awakened by an argument:

"Aw, shut up. You're wrong!" Thump

"You can't transfer to the A-Train from that stop." Thump, thump.

Cries of "Quiet!" and "I'm trying to sleep," arose from other bunks.

"Like hell you can't. I do it every day!" Thump, thump, THUMP. "Just the other day I met a beautiful babe sitting at the station."

"Oh sure, you were probably wearing a dress!" THUMP.

"Go to hell!" Thump, thump, thump — THUMP.

Protests of "Shut up," and "Go back to sleep" added to the growing din.

A loud knock cut through the uproar. I answered the door.

"Vould you pleass keep qviet in here?" a Dutch steward in his nautical uniform addressed me with cold formality. "Ve are gettink complaints from de udder bessin-chers."

"Hey, I'm just trying to sleep." I shrugged and nodded toward the warring pair, who were still arguing loudly, and threw up my hands.

The steward entered, took names and warned the whole group that the offenders would be severely punished if we failed to keep the peace.

I hoped they would be set adrift on a raft.

At a discreet hour the next morning, I knocked on the door of the adjacent cabin. An elderly lady in a smart-looking black suit and low heels answered. She reminded me of my sweet grandmother. She introduced herself as Mrs. Jaczi (Yah'-zi).

I apologized profusely for my rude and rowdy roommates. She agreed it cut into her sleep. She invited me in and introduced me to her lady companion. They both appeared to be about 60. She explained they were headed to Vienna to visit her relatives for the first time in many years.

That afternoon, I saw Mrs. Jaczi again in the main salon and sat next to her on a padded banquette. When I mentioned I was studying architecture, her eyes lit up. Back in the 1920s at the university, she told me, she had studied architecture and made friends with a handsome student named Adolf Loos. He was outspoken in his attitudes about architecture and cut a very distinctive figure among his fellow students. I recognized the name. In architectural history class, we had learned about the school of the Vienna Secession—a revolt against Beaux-Arts classicism. The work of Loos stood out, with his simple geometric forms for houses and his most famous pronouncement, "Ornament is crime!" This quiet, elderly woman, it seemed, had breathed the rarefied air of the leading intellectuals in Europe during the Bauhaus years. I apologized again for my cabin mates. That evening, I returned early to our stateroom and tried to explain to my fellows that I had met our next-door neighbors and found them to be gentle, intelligent souls, who knew some very famous people in Europe. Apparently, my pleas fell on deaf ears. A half-hour later Mark and Aaron were at it again. Resentful of the steward's official intrusion of the previous night, they took out their feelings on the pressurized faucet valve. Soon the thumping reached a fever pitch.

"Why, you ass!" I had reached my limit. Like David attacking Goliath, I lunged at Aaron, grabbed his shirt and delivered a punch to his face. He swung back, I dodged, and his fist landed on my shoulder. Two of the taller boys pulled us apart and gripped us firmly. I resisted, with a fierce passion to bean Aaron, but I couldn't move. Silence descended at last. My cabin mates threatened physical consequences if this behavior recurred—the only language these lowlife jerks seemed to understand. An uneasy truce prevailed for the rest of the voyage.

I stayed in contact with Mrs. Jaczi after I returned to Yale. She responded with a long letter describing Adolf Loos, his personality and her friendship with him. I realized the letter I held in my hands was a valuable historical document and offered it to a historian at the Yale library who had helped me with a research paper. To my horror, he contacted the poor woman and pursued her for further information and documents she might have, related to the Bauhaus school of architecture. I was mortified by the fact that her kindness to me had resulted in yet another irritation by an annoying outsider. But the kind lady wrote me again and expressed how thrilled and flattered she was that her humble memories would become part of a collection in the university's library. I assume that her letter about Adolf Loos, and perhaps more, resides in the Yale library's historical collection to this day.

We arrived in Southampton, I picked up the car at the dealership and drove to London. In my next letter on June 18, postmarked London, I wrote, "After infinite complications. I finally got enough insurance so I could drive. I got a cover note which lasts until Monday And I have an insurance broker in London who is pretty sure he can get a policy for me before the cover note runs out. The problem is that I'm a year too young, and all companies that used to cover young American tourists have stopped, because they are such a bad risk. Anyway, I had to make a special trip to London before I could even start for Torquay. I would have stayed in London, except that Maureen and the family had already been expecting me for two days, and I was dying to get to the country. I finally arrived in Torquay at midnight Tuesday Since then I've been relaxing. It's beautiful here, just like Annisquam in some respects—in its elderly tourists and its complete lack of a Miami Beach air. The town is built on seven hills, or *tors*. but I forgot—you've been here, Mom. I love it. It would be a wonderful place to come and paint."

Maureen was an Irish cousin of my mother who had settled in England and married a hotel worker named Ernie Brown. They had a young teen daughter, Mary. I met's Maureen brother Paddy and his Greek wife Dina. Paddy then took me on a tour of the area and an old town named Stokenteenhedge. We went to an ancient pub there and had a draft beer. Paddy has a very good feeling for architecture, and he showed me some wonderful stuccoed-stone houses with thatched roofs, which have been there for centuries. I asked whether they leak, and he said, remarkably, they are quite reliable, provided you replace the thatch every few years.

"In London I stayed at a bed and breakfast while waiting for Mike to arrive on the following Sunday at London airport. I visited the Tate gallery. I didn't see much that was exciting, but British painting never was my favorite. Strangely enough, aside from a few by Gainsborough and Copley, the only paintings I found really good were by Sargent, Whistler and Turner. They also had a room full of impressionists, so that made the visit worthwhile—they had always been my real love. I also discovered one Rodin marble statue, *Le Baiser*, with figures that melt into the white stone from which they are carved, proving that there are comfortable ways to sit when you kiss, a fact that I always found hard to believe."

On Thursday, June 25, I reported "This is the first chance I've had all week to write. "Boy, have I got adventures to tell you!

"Mike arrived reasonably on time at the airport and we were off. I had a hotel room arranged and he agreed to stay in London for four days, so I got a chance to see the sights. Sunday night we took a walk before dinner in Hyde Park. We went to the speaker's corner and heard the big time equivalent of Chicago's bug house square. We got into a couple of arguments and proved some points to the speakers. Mike offered to light two girls' cigarettes and we got talking with them. We took them to dinner and found them delightful, both Irish, who were living in Harlesden district of London and working in the city. They took us back to meet one girl's' mother, who was a warm, relaxed and homely woman. She didn't apologize much for being in her bathrobe when we arrived—it didn't seem to bother her—and she served us tea. The next night we took the girls out again and returned there for more tea. I'm really sold on the Irish, and I can't wait to meet our cousins. Monday morning, we attended to business and got it all done. We went to AA (the British version of AAA), which we joined when we bought the car. They arranged our passage from Fishguard to Cork (sans car) and from Dover to Calais (with car, the next Wednesday), then routed us all through Europe and gave us stacks of valuable maps. I also got an international driver's license. I have every document that a traveler can have, I think.

"Monday night with the girls we saw a play called "All in the Family," a very well-produced drama about a family terrorized and subjugated by the old man, and still feel his domination when he dies. But his influence (symbolized by a phonograph record of his voice which he wanted played after his death) is finally broken by the strong son, who has always been the black sheep of the family. It was quite a good play. After the performance they played "God Save the Queen," a nice touch.

"Tuesday we went to the National Gallery, which Mike enjoyed as much as I; the Tower of London (and saw the crown jewels), and St. Paul's, by architect Sir Christopher Wren."

Wednesday we set out at one o'clock for a leisurely trip to Fishguard. We spent the night at the youth hostel at Mitcheldean, a picturesque English town where there was not even a restaurant. We had to go to a neighboring town for dinner, and to our delight we discovered a fashionable country dining spot, a Speech House, of the "Trust Houses" chain of hotels, alleged to have been a hunting lodge of Charles II. It was most welcome after a long day's drive.

We had to be sneaky about English hostels, since they didn't allow motorists, so, we parked around the block. While getting out of the car, when we saw a "youth" headed for the same lodging, we had to decide if he looked "hostile."

We delighted in the food: breakfasts were meaty and delicious. "Puddings were wonderful because they put custard on them," I wrote. "They eat a lot of meat, but it isn't as good as ours, needless to say. They make good tea and spoil it all with milk."

Leaving the car at Fishguard, we set sail across the Irish Sea. Patty Beale my mother's Irish cousin, met us at the pier with two of her daughters, young teens Mary and Pam. Her husband Mick was making his annual visit to relatives in London on a schedule arranged with his employer in advance, which could not be changed. She looked just like photos we have of my grandmother Mary Herlihy when she was middle aged. She talked just like her and had that same glint in her eye and some of self-reliant, "to blazes with what they" say spirit. It was just like talking to Granny again.

Mike relaxed and made a great hit with everybody. He was very domestic and joked and played with Patty's toddler Sinead, as well as having lots of fun with the family. At night we had hilarious fun at the pubs. We stopped the first night in a place called Mike's later in the evening really just for a laugh, because when her sister Maureen visited them from Torquay, and they took her there, Mike got drunk and hosed down the customers in order to get them out at midnight.

"We had a good time at Mike's that night," I wrote, "and besides, he has a 16-year-old daughter who is really cute I really took a liking to her. It occurred to me why: Granny did the same thing—she served in her father's pub until her relatives sent for her. I told her to come, look me up and promised to show her around when she got there.

"As a result of the good time we had at Mike's Pub Friday, we went back on Saturday. This time I brought my uke and serenaded the publican's daughter, Eiblish (Eye-leash'). Well, anyway, that night Mike's wife invited us back for a going away celebration for us Sunday night."

My friend Mike recalls, "We (you, I and members of the Beale family) entered through the back door leading to the kitchen, which I recall being on a floor above the pub itself. Mike's (the pub owner's) wife greeted us at the door, looked at our ID's, which surprised us, since they hadn't checked them when we went into the pub legally on previous days. She seated us around a large table, took our orders, and went downstairs to the pub to pour the beers at the taps behind the bar. Of course, this was strictly illegal, for pubs are supposed to be closed on Sunday nights."

As a further precaution, Mike's wife posted her fourteen-year-old daughter on the lookout at the landing and her eight-year old to watch from a window at the bottom of the stair below. As I serenaded Eiblish with folk songs on my ukulele, the older folks were laughing and making bets on whether she would fall in love with the foreign stranger.

Just then, the two daughters burst into the room, while Eiblish glanced out from the kitchen. "The Guards!" announced the youngest. "They're almost up to the door."

Two officers came in and walked around the kitchen, very serious, writing down everyone's names and addresses.

Patty Beale was very nervous, whispering that her husband would be very angry to return from England and have to get her out of jail.

"We were just havin' friends and our American relations in for little drink and a visit," the pub keeper said.

"Sure, and you were," said the one in charge.

"The officer collected your ID and mine," Mike recalls, "and then asked his wife to name us. After our third night there, Mike Condon's wife knew us so well, she did it from memory."

The policeman left, defeated.

We kidded on the way to the boat that we had not only eaten and drunk the Beales out of house and home, we had also gotten them kicked out of house and home and almost put in jail. Mike Condon's Pub probably wouldn't get into trouble, but they were all much more worried than we would've been over it.

"Poor Patty!" I said. "Mick will find how much mischief his wife has gotten into while he was away."

I felt, since they reminded me of my Irish grandmother, I had known them all my life. As parting gifts, they gave Mike and me each small bottle of Paddy—the classic Irish whiskey—and an Irish linen table napkin with instructions for making Irish coffee on it.

On Monday, June 29, as the M.V. Innisfallen pulled away from the Irish shore, I could still see the hills of Ireland on our left as I wrote a letter home. I had found my roots, and it was a very satisfying to feel at home in a place I had thought of as a foreign land.

We returned to London and Mike guided me to Dover, We drove the car aboard the ferry, made the crossing to Calais and rolled it off. We headed straight for Paris.

In the Latin quarter of the fifth arondissement, we landed on the third floor of a little hotel in the crooked rue de la Harpe. Street life held our attention until late at night. The clatter of trash cans awoke us at 6 a.m. Donning the drip-dry shirts we had washed overnight, we found a café for croissants and coffee and set out.

Mike's previous visit had coached him on getting around, and we visited the Louvre, the Jeu de Paume (tennis court) art museum, at that time home to the Impressionist collection, and the stylish women's shops along the rue de Rivoli, where we bought gifts. At Nina Ricci I found an elegant bottle of L'Air du Temps with two doves circling around its stopper and had it sent home to Mom. At Montmartre I traded sketches with a street artist. Back at school, when my drawing professor Neil Welliver saw what I got in trade, he grinned. "I hope you didn't give him anything good!"

Mike and I en route
Summer, 1959

Notre Dame du Haut, Ronchamp, France,

7

THE CONTINENTALS

IN THE POST WORLD WAR II ERA Europeans welcomed Americans, in gratitude toward the Allies for helping restore their freedom, recall their greatness in the past and imagine a new future.

Sylvia Beach, who founded the original English-language bookstore in Paris, Shakespeare and Company in 1919 at 12 rue de l'Odéon, created a gathering place for the great expat writers of the time—Joyce, Hemingway, Stein, Fitzgerald, Eliot and Pound. Hemingway called Paris a movable feast, which stayed with you ever after. We arrived 30 years later to partake of what these and other creative spirits such as Cezanne and Miro had discovered.

For us, 1959 was a very good year, and not only for its legendary wine harvest. Mike and I took our Mutt and Jeff act on the road. I relied a lot on Mike—tall, ebullient and affable, with his self-effacing charm—he appeared to me much more confident. He does not admit to having such poise in new situations at that age. In fact we were about equally unsure of ourselves. In discussions about this book, he reminded me that, despite my inbred shyness, I was also able to confront strangers, ask questions and make new friends. I thought of myself, nonetheless, as the quiet, contemplative one, Mutt sans mustache, spouting observations, coining jokes and adding comments on humorous aspects of our encounters.

We forged ahead—with only the vaguest of plans, with an optimism based merely on the absence of obstruction on an endless open road. Lured by Europe's cultural treasures, we acted as if they were placed at points of interest along the way for our sole information, entertainment and delight.

We continued our French lessons as we drove. I recalled that at the youth hostel, an old château where we had stayed the previous night, our host's little boy spoke better French than I did. Playing on the front steps, he said «*Voiçi mon ballon!* » (Look at my ball) in a perfect French accent. At the cafés in Paris, Mike had taught me that ordering a *"limonade"* would get me a fizzy bottled soda. Ordering a *citron pressé* would reward me with a much better drink. I insisted on my "limonade" and soon realized my error. The waiter brought me a bottle of lemon Pschitt, which tasted about like it sounded, but Mike got a plate with a knife, a fresh lemon and a bowl of sugar, so he could make himself a real lemonade.

We joked about language a lot that day. Although I had the advantage of three years of college French, Mike had taken a student tour of Europe in 1956 as a senior in high school. It was a great combination. He knew about service issues: restaurants, hotels and local customs, and he spoke German. I have always had a good ear for language, and I was somewhat fluent in a natural-sounding French. It also made for great fun. When a Citroën crossed into the opposite lane to sail past us at 110 miles an hour, Mike said, «*Ça va être un Citroën pressé.*» When I saw a cow in a field, he'd say, «*Voila une vache francaise.*»

«*Ç'est comme une vache normale,* (it's like a regular cow), I responded, «*mais plus amoureuse* (but more amorous).»

I was to be the art and architecture guide for the tour, while Mike would find us the best musical and entertainment events. We were headed to the valley of the Loire, but a necessary stop on the way was the Cathedral in Chartres, which, according to Henry Adams, 19th century architect Viollet-le-Duc called, "The greatest and surely the most beautiful monument of this kind that we possess in France."

As we approached from the north, the cathedral loomed over the low buildings of the town, dominating the landscape, with its two steeples of unequal height, completed about 400 years apart. When we arrived in the wooded town square, we faced the west front's three statuary-lined Gothic portals, beneath a round rose window and flanked by the towers rising out of sight above us. A crowd of tourists gathered on the *parvis*, or ceremonial front terrace, even on a weekday morning in 1959.

The rose window was added in the 13th century when the church was expanded after a fire in 1194. The west front containing three sculptured portals was moved and painstakingly rebuilt stone by stone 40 feet further forward, to expand the capacity of the interior. This had the effect of removing the sculptural setback between the two towers and altering the bold massing of the original design, with a contrast between the older south tower, dating from 1150, and the northern tower, which was not completed until three centuries later during the early Renaissance. The character of the two towers could not be more different: Divided into several clearly demarcated stories, it rises taller and is more ornate; the earlier tower rises simply, from a square base to its octagonal peak, the finest expression of the high Gothic style. Abbé Bulteau, a contemporary of the project's construction, desscribes the architecture of old tower:

> This clocher, whose base is broad (*pleine*), massive, and free from ornament, transforms itself as it springs, into a sharp spire with eight faces, without its being possible to say where the massive construction ends and the light constructor begins.

We entered through an open side portal, whose embrasures are lined with attenuated figural sculpture of which Henry Adams said: "These statues are the Eginetan marbles of French art; from them all modern French sculpture dates, or ought to date."[3]

In his in-depth analysis of the Middle Ages and its architecture, *Mont-Saint-Michel and Chartres,* Adams contrasts the two churches, each representing a different era. Romanesque-styled Mont-Saint-Michel is sited on its peninsular rock to challenge all comers and the perils of the sea, The complex represented the masculine Church Militant of the 11th century. This church inspired a political triumph: the Norman conquest of England in 1066. While St. Michael's church was dominated by soldiers of Christ, Chartres was the Virgin Mary's church, with feminine grace in the finest example of the high Gothic style. By 1200, Norman influence had declined, and the Virgin Mary's church rose to its peak of authority and power throughout Europe. Politically, Adams concludes, "In all Europe, at that time, there was no power to enforce justice or to maintain order, and no symbol of such a power except Christ and His Mother and the Imperial Crown"—that of the "Queen of Heaven."[4]

For perfection in this style, art historians and architects favor the south tower, completed first and dated about 1150. Viollet-le-Duc commented in the 19th century: "Of Norman origin, the design is direct, unembellished and derives beauty from its simple, structurally expressive lines; it also solves a tricky design problem with grace and beauty. …The transition, so hard to adjust, between the square base and the octagon of the *flèche,* is managed and carried out with an address which has not been surpassed in similar monuments."[5]

Then, in the Loire valley, we stayed in one chateau and visited another in Blois. Our visit to Tours concluded that evening in a sound and light show at Chenonceaux. Once the home of Marie de Medici, it straddles a river. At the one castle where I pictured one could live in comfort, we enjoyed the *son et lumière* historical presentation after dark.

We then headed southeast to Ronchamp to see Notre Dame du Haut, a free-form church on a hilltop designed by Charles-Èdouard Jeanneret-Gris, a Swiss-French architect who called himself Le Corbusier. As we rounded the curve in the mountainous country of southeastern France on a dull day, a sunbeam burst through the clouds and fell on a gleam of white on a hilltop: the church, as the architect wanted us to discover it. Following the signs to our destination, we periodically lost sight of the church and began to climb. As we neared the summit, around the bend we came upon the building itself. Atop two upswept curving walls of white stucco, a roof billowed up to its apex, piercing the sky with a simple cross. On the interior, we left the blinding light of the approach and plunged into a dark, compressed space, which exploded inside to the higher roof above and focused upon a simple raised pulpit. The dark space was lit by several tiny square openings punched in the right wall and a vertical slit at the intersection of two converging enclosure walls. A few black-clad French ladies knelt in prayer, scattered among the pews, setting the stage for the great solemnity and piety the sculpted interior evoked. Among the few buildings the influential architectural theorist actually constructed, it was worth going out of our way to visit.

Our stop in Switzerland was a bust, since mountain destinations like the Jungfrau were shrouded in rain and mist, and the funiculars giving access to them, accordingly, were closed. At a youth hostel in Montreux, however, we breakfasted with a hundred youths on fresh-baked French bread and the best semi-sweet hot chocolate I've ever tasted. Mike couldn't resist showing me the French Riviera, however, and we spent a couple of lovely days in Cannes, while he went scuba diving, and I practiced my sketching on the beach. Mike drove us on a harrowing ride along the *Grande Corniche,* an important site, yet for me a planning lesson on the possibilities for road design in rugged coastal landscapes. We pushed on to Italy by way of Genoa on a slow route along the crowded waterfront highway.

It was after dinner when we arrived in Florence. We found Albergo Turismo, a small hotel on a side street, and claimed the reservation Mike had arranged by writing from Chicago. The innkeeper spoke Italian and little English, but she did a good job of leading us to our rooms and pointing, her English limited to: "Pleass, Mister" and "This way, Mister." We spent three days combing the Ponte Vecchio, every palazzo that would admit visitors and the Uffizi Gallery. There loomed Michelangelo's statue of David, powerful, and from certain angles menacing, and his many Prisoners, emerging from, but still trapped in their original blocks of stone. We were well started on the art leg of our tour, and I had to thank Mike for his patience and open attitude while we awaited the choice musical events to come.

We didn't have to wait much longer. We drove on to Rome. Mike made sure we attended an outdoor concert in a park setting. We started with a concert featuring Beethoven's Ninth, "Choral" symphony, conducted by William Steinberg. Mike was very impressed with the way the maestro interpreted Beethoven, with a steady, determined beat: "Very Germanic, as intended," he said.

But the concert ran off the rails from there. The night was hot, and the Italian ladies in the chorus made a distracting spectacle, incessantly waving their fans. Mike recalls the scene:

> The Italian singers were not only waving fans throughout the first three movements, they were also carrying huge purses. But the worst was yet to come. The soloists sang in thick, guttural German, but the chorus sang in Italian! Following the orchestral introduction to the final movement, "Ode to Joy," *O freunde...* (Oh, friend), the Baritone sang his tale in the recitative, followed by: *Freude!* But the chorus echoed him with a sing-song *Gioia.*"

We also attended a performance of Tosca at the Baths of Caracalla. Opera was grand indeed in this amphitheater surrounded by the ruined arches of this public bath house dating back to Roman times. The fact that this space alone accommodated a crowd I estimated to number 10,000 spectators attested to the architectural skills of the Romans, to have envisioned and constructed such a vast interior space. The unenclosed remains of the central part of the bath complex (the *caldarium*) hosted summer performances of the Rome Opera company from 1937 to 1993. In 2001 the opera resumed use of the venue, but now on a temporary movable stage outside of the main structure, which relieved stress on the antique ruin.

At intermission I bought a container of iced coffee—it was spiked with strong brandy—and I sailed through the second act, immersed in grand opera and a lovely fog. Mike had whetted my appetite for concerts. And Salzburg was less than a week away.

The Pantheon, Rome

Wasting no time, we trekked to the Roman forum, took note of the sleek central railroad station and visited the Pantheon. I concluded that the Romans had been a race of designers for the last 2000 years and continued uninterrupted up to modern times. We had a delicious rabbit stew for dinner that night and the next day went on to visit St. Peter's Square, with Bernini's arcade, the extended nave and the original cruciform portion of the building featuring Michelangelo's dome.

Quarters during our Roman stay were a youth hostel in an old house—in Italy that can mean 400 to 500 years. People here were traveling from all over Europe: Harry and Elfie, a couple from Germany; Willem, a heavyset Dutch boy who spoke slowly and, despite some school English training, seemed to understand very little, and a couple of witty French students we met sitting on the patio wall finishing off a bottle of wine. We had fun joking around with them. One boy held up the empty, «*Soldat morte* (Dead soldier). » A girl sitting next to him tipped up the bottle: «*Je lui donnerai le coup de grace* (I'll give him the final stroke).»

The boys' dormitory, a large bedroom with two windows, was packed with double bunks, fully occupied with eighteen of us. On our first night, the day's heat, built up during the afternoon, caused the inside temperature to be much higher than outside. The only relief was an occasional breath of fresh air though unscreened, open windows. When darkness fell, the guests collapsed in their beds.

It wasn't long before I learned a new vocabulary. The operative word was *zanzara*, and no one had to translate. We tried to lie still and soundless, but incoming dive bombers approached from all directions. I had mosquito bites all over my arms and legs after the first half hour of tossing in this private hell. I learned how to say mosquito in four languages and swear words in five. Although it was already 95 degrees in the room; the only escape from the merciless menace was to hide completely under the thin blanket. Finally, an Italian youth turned on the light, closed the shutters, cutting off all outside air, and organized us into a brigade to kill every one of the little devils. With no fresh air at all, it was a hot compromise at best, but at least it reduced our misery to a level where we could sleep.

After visiting the obligatory historical sites, baking in the hot streets of Rome and suffering nights in our mosquito-ridden hostel, Mike came up with the perfect destination outside the city. We had met a beautiful Israeli girl named Chava, whom we squired around Rome. We took her along for an afternoon at Tivoli.

Villa d'Este, the country residence of popes in Tivoli, a few miles east of the city, is a UNESCO World Heritage site, owned and maintained by the Italian government since 1920. A classic example of Renaissance architecture, landscape and water feature design, it was further enhanced by baroque artists and architects during the 17th century. It was laid out by Pirro Ligorio (1500-1583) on behalf of Cardinal Ippolito II d'Este of Ferrara (1509-1572), who, after being named governor of Tivoli in 1550, wanted a palace and gardens suitable to his new, elevated status.

While Mike toured the estate with the lovely Chava, I was free to plant myself in front of magnificent fountains, alongside a valley of pools sourced by water that flowed from the hills, descended into this valley and was then released to water gardens even further below. One description of the sites is reported online:

> The most striking effect is produced by the big cascade flowing out of a krater perched in the middle of the exedra. Jets of water were activated whenever unsuspecting people walked under the arcades. The Fontana del Bicchierone (Fountain of the Great Glass) built according to a design by Bernini (1660-61) was added to the decoration of the central longitudinal axis in the 17th century. This fountain is in the shape of a serrated chalice, from which a high jet of water falls into a conch shell. The garden with the fountains is a masterpiece of hydraulic engineering, both for the general layout of the plan and the complex system of water distribution, as well as for the many

water features, with the introduction of the first hydraulic automatons ever built.[6]

Just as I began drawing the main fountain, a busload of schoolchildren burst upon the scene. With squeals of delight , they ran for the exedra, a semicircular arcade surrounding the main fountain and pool, tripping the sensor to start the water jets. When the chaperons regained control, the school group moved on and I resumed sketching the most refreshing scene of the trip.

In the evening we took Chava to a kosher restaurant so she wouldn't have to worry about dietary restrictions. All the Brooklyn, Miami and Chicago Jews in the restaurant came over to ask us where we were from in the states. The contrast between them and this young woman was striking: in their typical tourist garb—shorts, tennis shoes, cameras and huge purses, they compared less favorably with this stylish, petite Israeli girl with impish brown eyes and a grin on a hair trigger. We were afraid she would go back home thinking these tourists were what all Americans are like. As to tourists, of course, she would have been mostly correct.

Back at our hostel that night, Willem walked around, stewing over one predicament or the other. "What's the matter, Willem?" I asked him. "Ach, I have not much money left, and I must get back home." I consulted with Mike, and we told Willem we could probably manage to take him as far as Venice, but our delays along the way would probably not suit his schedule. Still, he accepted our offer and we planned to leave in the morning.

We had not been out of Rome for two hours when Willem started moaning in the back seat. "What is it?" I asked him. "I haff left my passport at the youth hostel in Rome "

Mike responded cheerfully, "There's no going back now, but at least you can call when we get to Bologna and arrange to have it sent to Venice, where we'll be staying a couple of days." He did this and made his arrangements to pick up his passport when we got there.

I wrote home on July 19th:

> After we left Rome we…spent the night in
> Bologna. I like the town very much, with its
> Renaissance arcades over the sidewalks. Even the
> modern buildings there are built on this idea of
> arcades. As a result, the whole town hangs
> together. There are quite a few art galleries and
> churches there. One could easily spend a week
> there and not get bored.

Our little band set out for Venice. As Mike put it, "My recollection was that Willem continued to be a pest over a number of days, perhaps over three legs of our drive…a hopeless sad sack who was driving us crazy."

We were halfway there when Willem reached for his backpack and realized he had left it in Bologna. More moans came from the back seat. "Ach, I must turn back and get it."

Slow at most mental tasks, at least Willem had a quick grasp of the obvious.

At the train terminal in Venice, we parted with our Dutch friend and wished him the best of luck. We feared he would need it.

"We spent just the right amount of time there," I wrote, "one-and-a-half days, two nights. I loved St. Mark's, with its mosaics and intersecting arches and domes, typical of the Byzantine style of architecture. I was also impressed by the doge's Palace in St. Mark's Square, which has beautiful murals and grand scale paintings by Titian, Tintoretto and Paolo Veronese. It had never occurred to me, in lectures and art books, that that the Venetian school of painting came from Venice. I saw many works of these three painters and gained a high respect for them. My July 19 letter continued:

> I wasn't completely enchanted by the canals and
> gondolas, but then I didn't really expect to be. I

think it's a neat trick to have boats instead of cars, but that was my only reaction. We thought that this would remove the noise but were rudely awakened at 6:30 AM, not by traffic, but bells. They are everywhere and they ring long and loud.

We're in Salzburg now. We drove up by the Grossglockner Pass, a very good mountain road. From here on we'll be on autobahns in Germany, so we're through with the bad roads.

In Austria the difference is refreshing. The Salzburg crowd, although just a bunch of tourists, was an international group, including many native Austrians. You never know what language you're going to hear next on the street. We scrounged for tickets and have heard one orchestra concert—it was very good according to Mike, the expert. I enjoyed it, too: *Eine kleine Nachtmusik* (A Little Night Music), and a Mozart Symphony.

We also obtained tickets for *Faust* at the Felsenreitschule, an old riding academy carved out of a sheer cliff. The stage was built in front of the former horse stalls, framed by columns, which support arches stacked up in several tiers. The stalls, carved out of the solid stone of the cliff, also surrounded the main interior space. When the riding hall was converted to a theater, the audience filled the arched arcades surrounding the great hall and the stage occupied the large center floor. The more recent arrangement for opera was the reverse, with the side and rear horse stalls and the central floor converted to audience seating, and the tiered arches at the front of the room used as acting areas and a backdrop for the stage.

The built-in scenery was used to good effect in the

performance we saw of Gounod's opera. Faust's descent into hell started at the top of the arches, and he progressed through each tier down to ground level. The chorus, now dressed as devils, had black capes and red helmets, each framed by one of the arched openings at the stage end of the hall. When they spread their arms wide to sing the chorus, the insides of their capes showed brilliant red, changing the backdrop to hellish fire. The historical architecture formed an authentic setting for this imaginative and visually rich production.

For the last leg of our grand tour, we drove on the autobahns to Munich, a very modern industrial city and major shipping port, where I met Karin and her little sister from a small town near Stuttgart. While my German was non-existent, she was fluent in French and managed to communicate her thoughts and feelings directly to me without difficulty. She had a short, pixie haircut, a sweet disposition and determination, at eighteen, to widen her experience, with me as a starting point. She and her sister left, headed for summer camp at the Hague. I arranged to visit them there the next day, took the car and arrived there in time for a twilight visit.

I don't know what she told her younger sister in German, but from her serious tone I gathered it was that we had important, grownup things to discuss, and the younger girl retired meekly to her dormitory. Free at last, our two minds with a single thought, we found a secluded bower for concluding these important matters amid the luxuriant informal gardens of the camp, sheltered from outside view. Time stood still, and the stars were out when we kissed a sweet farewell. I floated home seemingly above the road to our hotel in Munich, humming in harmony with the spheres, savoring the sweet secrets we had shared.

We then drove to Grossenbröde and spent the night. The next day we took a ferry to Gedser and on to Copenhagen, to see the famous Tivoli Gardens amusement park, drink beer and enjoy modern jazz for a few days with the blonde Danish girls.

It was time to go home, I on an Air France flight from Paris,

Mike on a return flight from London. Thanks to my dad's arrangements, the car would travel by boat to New York, with a box on the back seat containing various items we could not carry in our suitcases, including a dozen cans of large Portuguese sardines for Mike's father.

My folks met me in New York, and we finished our vacation with a visit to friends and relatives on the East Coast. I had a full sketchbook, and both Mike and I had enough memories of our full summer to last a lifetime.

**Notre Dame de Chartres - South tower (1150)
New Tower beyond (1507-1515)**

Chartres Cathedral: Two Concepts- West front

Left: Architect's intent–1150   *Right: Actual result -1515*
Vertical lines, recessed entrance   *Facade rebuilt for larger nave*

Framed by the exedra, La Fontana del Bicchierone
Fountain of the Great Glass. Villa D'Este, Tivoli

Preparing for Exams
Al Puryear Photo

Danish Beach Maiden: Cannes
Neil Welliver, my drawing teacher, loved this one: loose line work, good three-dimensional form—although somehow I failed to notice her face.

Exhibit: Glass Sets the Mood for Indoor Light
First Year sketch problem: Yale School of Architecture

8

THE INITIATE

I N 1956, THE YEAR I ARRIVED as a freshman on the undergraduate campus, Yale's venerated graduate architecture program stood at a critical crossroads. After a scheduled visit, the National Architectural Accreditation Board (NAAB) concluded the program had lost its way and refused to renew its national accreditation. Of course, I knew nothing of this. Although I had selected Yale because it offered an architectural career path, which interested me greatly, graduate school was a long way off. First I had to deal with a rigorous undergraduate program.

A picture my roommate snapped of me preparing for exams at the end of sophomore year shows me reading intently, with one leg slung over a huge, overstuffed chair, the other chair arm piled high with books, the surrounding floor littered with stacks of notes and other papers. I have a recent crew cut, shined wing-tip shoes and a white dress shirt, prepared to quit working at a moment's notice, throw on a jacket and tie and head out to our Silliman College dining hall for dinner. Oh, how we resented that some influential alumnus had pressured the administration secretly during the summer to reinstate an antiquated nineteenth-century rule requiring students to wear coats and ties at all meals!

The following year when I had to declare my undergraduate major, a new option existed. By choosing an architecture major early, I could save a year of their four-year professional degree program, an essential milestone on the path to becoming an architect. Moreover, a year after that, when I entered the program as a senior, I learned the architectural program had a new chairman, a rising star in the architecture field, Paul Rudolph, who had promised a new and forward-looking curriculum.

But I had not yet experienced my first encounter with the jury system, where each student faces a jury of architects and faculty to explain his design. In the fall semester, we had two sketch problems in a row: the first was a vacation house, for a peninsular site on the Maine coast, for which I designed hexagonal rooms stacked on different levels. The second was design of an exhibit for an imaginary client, the Glass Manufacturers of America. We had just heard a lecture from Richard Kelly, a prominent lighting designer and visiting lecturer, who had explained three types of interior light: focal glow, play of brilliants and ambient luminescence That same week, he stopped by our class and positively glowed with insights on architectural lighting. I chose an advertising slogan for the theme of the exhibit, "Glass Sets the Mood of Indoor Light." I sketched a space with undulating widths and variable heights composed of curved glass walls and overhand swelling clouds at varying heights. I took it to the print shop and had negative photostats made of my sketches. It was designed so various spaces would have different types of light we'd learned about from Richard Kelly: glittering, glowing and luminescent; curved stairways, a wide exhibit space and narrow passages. T. Gorm Hansen, chief critic for our class, said: "This design has guts. I think it's magnificent!"

Mr. Rudolph, who made it his business to attend most juries, asked, "Won't the ins and outs of the walls become monotonous?" I pointed out that the ceiling heights and levels varied, thus altering the volume of space in all dimensions, and different levels and moods of lighting occurred as you moved through the space. Mr. Rudolph appeared satisfied with my answer. Mr. Hanson defended my design: "We just don't appreciate the richness of your concept."

I felt I was on my way.

The bias of the school was a different story.

In addition to my own heritage, Yale's architecture program also had a legacy. Ever since its founding in 1916, the program was devoted to the Beaux-Arts ideal of combining all the fine and applied arts in one interdisciplinary center. Here the intermingling of the student body would exert cross-cultural influences and enrich students' understanding and vision. Egerton Swartwout, architect for the Romanesque art gallery building (1928), joined Street Hall's painting and sculpture studios with a bridge over High Street to classrooms and offices for the art history department. In the 1950s the newer art collections and the architecture school were expanded into Louis I. Kahn's new Art and Design Building. Architecture was located on the top floor of the new building. Graphic Design occupied a basement space below the art gallery. When Yale's architecture and painting school broadened to incorporate the modern influences of Europe's Walter Gropius, this was the closest the school had come to realizing its multidisciplinary ideal.

When I arrived, the school also retained other original features of Beaux-Arts education: a strong emphasis on graphic representation and exhaustive, laborious visual presentation, and the jury system, in which all student work was reviewed by a panel of professors and professional experts. Adapting traditional teaching methods from the past to the present, Rudolph liked many features of the old system, but he wanted to broaden it to include original designs by the talented student body. Nonetheless certain aspects of the European architecture of the 1930s, as developed with in the newer Bauhaus school, had such wide influence on U.S. architecture schools that it was tolerated at Yale, as at design schools throughout the country.

In fact, the new design influence was hard to ignore—it was rising all around them in the major cities. Beginning in the 1930s, German architect Walter Gropius conceived a less costly, flat-roofed and boxy design for worker housing and founded a design studio to develop it, called the Bauhaus. The new look was adopted by American architects, claiming freedom from previous historical revival traditions. Instead, they managed only to copy these "avant-garde" Europeans. They applied this new aesthetic, not even particularly well-suited to its worker housing origins, to luxury housing, to office buildings, to factories and to any other use which could be crammed into a rectangular, concrete, steel and glass box.

But how did the style spread so quickly and universally? Obviously, it wasn't the "in" thing. But how did it catch on so fast? Was it hastened by social pressure? Now, we're on to something: everyone wanted to belong to the colony of the avant garde that started in the 1930s in Europe.

In 1932, architectural historian Henry Russell Hitchcock and architect Phillip Johnson, director of New York's Museum of Modern Art, wrote an essay for the catalog of an exhibition of photos and drawings by Gropius and his followers to America, called, "The International Style." This exhibit title and essay were destined to become the founding document for a movement. In tracing the effect of America's adoption of the Bauhaus ideas and this style in the 1950s, Tom Wolfe comments:

> At Yale, students gradually began to notice that everything they designed, everything the faculty members designed, everything the visiting critics (who gave critiques of the students designs) designed…looked the same. Everyone designed the same…box…of glass and steel and concrete, with tiny beige bricks substituted occasionally. This became known as the Yale Box…the truth was that by now architectural students all over

America were inside that very box, the same box the compound architects had closed in upon themselves in Europe twenty years before.[7]

When I recently reread Tom Wolfe's book, *From Bauhaus to Our House*, I had a flash of insight. There I found a clarifying vision of the people I had met, the obstacles I had encountered and the ordeals I had endured, beginning with my architectural courses at Yale. The clarity of Wolfe's conclusion, from the objective view of an articulate outside observer, was as refreshing as a plunge in a mountain stream and as valuable as a year of psychoanalysis. It helped me reorder my priorities, shed the vain aspirations for "Modern Architecture" I had been taught and regain a stable sense of self. It occurred to me then, I did have an architectural story to write.

My art education began at age thirteen, when I attended Saturday morning classes at the Art Institute of Chicago. I continued these studies and attended summer sessions well into high school and had ample opportunity to "feed on the arts," as the theater director had advised me. Entering past the iconic bronze lions of the museum, I became familiar with each collection: Impressionists (my early favorite), the Renaissance painters, African art, Roman sculpture and pottery. In the two-block-long Frank W. Gunsaulus Hall, bridging over the Illinois Central tracks, I passed Asian, decorative arts and a host of other galleries on the way to class. In addition to the school, the Kenneth Sawyer Goodman Theater—also one of my childhood haunts, thanks to my father's sister Sylvia, who took me to children's performances there—is accessible from Columbus Drive in Grant Park.

My architectural training began in earnest at Yale, with my favorite architecture professor Vincent Scully. His reputation among students grew to legendary proportions. Fit but slight of build, with his downward sloping Irish eyes and inquiring gaze, he revealed his insatiable curiosity. Everyone had a Scully story. In his days as a younger professor, he attended student parties.

He appeared at his lecture one day with his arm in a cast. Students back then reported on good authority that he had fallen from a dormitory window.

In his popular history of architecture lectures, he began with the Greeks, illustrating his lecture on the 30-by-40-foot screen spanning from stage floor to ceiling of the cavernous lecture hall, Room 101 Art Gallery. He employed a 20-foot pointer stored in the corner of the stage to refer to the details of his arresting slides of the ancient temples at Corinth, Paestum, Crete and the other Mediterranean island city-states. He contrasted the Minoan civilization of Crete, with their rounded, natural forms, against the jagged, masculine shapes of the invading Achaeans from the north. He showed how, during the peak period in their civilization, the Greeks had built the Parthenon on the Acropolis. They juxtaposed Achaean, man-made forms within the setting of Mother Earth, as symbolized by the two-horned peak of the distant Mt. Hymettus and the sea, in perfect balance between man and nature.

In his spellbinding conclusion Scully displayed a dramatic slide, a corner of the iconic temple bathed in Aegean sunlight, and another of the temple, golden in the dying rays of sunset. As I vividly if only partially recall, he intoned in his rich Irish tenor: "And so, burned in our memory is the image of the column in the light, perfectly proportioned, the symbol of man and his striving, set within the natural world."

The all-male, overflow audience greeted his conclusion with thunderous applause.

Once when I was present in his modern architecture class, he described the work and character of Louis Sullivan. He showed the architect's portrait—a stocky, bearded man dressed in a wool suit with a matching vest covering his rotund abdomen—and said he modeled himself after the 19th-century titans of industry, whom he described. Striding across the wide speaker's platform for emphasis, he declared, "They consumed huge roasts, devoured great bowls of mashed potatoes and ate schooners of peas…" He got so carried away, he stopped cold and said, "Gentlemen, I seem to have forgotten my point…" and was greeted with howls of laughter. Another time, he was describing the details of high-rise buildings and reached in the corner for his pointer. The class comics had hidden the real one and substituted the long, crooked branch of a tree. When he had it in his hand he stopped to examine it quizzically. He shrugged and employed it, to the vociferous delight of his listeners, for the rest of his lecture.

During college, my art training paused. But junior year, as a prerequisite to the architecture major, students were required to take a course called Basic Design, an intensive graphic art and sculpture program. We met for three hours twice a week with professional artists, painter Neil Welliver (1929-2005) and sculptor Robert Engman (1927-2018), who had both come to Yale to study under Joseph Albers. In addition to his continued abstract and figurative painting career and teaching at Yale, Welliver taught at Cooper Union, and at University of Pennsylvania Graduate School of Fine Art, from 1966 until his retirement as department chairman in 1989.

Bob Engman was an accomplished sculptor and professor of fine arts whose outdoor sculptures in Philadelphia and beyond reached civic scale. During the period he taught our class he was making sculptures with the winged look of a manta ray. He led us to experiment in many materials— tempera paint, wood blocks, cardboard, toothpicks and glue, applicator sticks and modeling clay. The objective was to discover the forms that grew out of each material's properties. Toothpicks made great tetrahedrons, which could in turn create domes, vertical towers and crystalline structures. Thin cardboard could be scored and folded into geometric shapes. When folded, curving score lines resulted in bulging or concave boxes. Six-inch applicator sticks could be glued side-by-side in twisted planes, connected to other twisted planes, which enclosed spaces or formed stand-alone sculptural objects. Clay had endless possibilities, including warped planes which, when connected to other warped planes, formed curved, flower-like objects, some of them Möbius strips with a single surface. One of my friends, classmate Austin Towle, who qualified as genius material, could fill a table with objects in paper, glue sticks or clay during an afternoon class, each form unique and varied in a different way.

Engman played the autoharp, and our graduate assistant Will played bass on a gut bucket, a plucked instrument consisting of an inverted washtub with a clothesline attached and strung to the top of a broomstick. While we worked, they serenaded us with their favorite folk songs, those of folk-protest singer Pete Seeger (1919-2014), who wrote "Where Have all the Flowers Gone?" "If I Had a Hammer," and "Turn, Turn, Turn," and his half-brother Mike Seeger (1933-2009) and his New Lost City Ramblers. Bob's and Will's favorite tunes included the Carter family's "Wildwood Flower." When not playing music, Bob would put their records on a small portable phonograph. If architecture and sculpture can be considered "frozen music," the rhythms and harmonies of these songs were certainly reflected in the forms we created in that class.

In addition to these class exercises, Welliver required us to keep a sketchbook. He recommended rough newsprint paper, sold cheaply in thick tablets of varying sizes. "I don't care what you use to draw with," he said, "a pencil, pen, or a nail, for that matter—anything that will make a mark. Just make at least one sketch per day. When I was at Philadelphia Academy of Fine Arts, we were required to sketch many more than that. We drew all the time, even while we brushed our teeth, I don't care what you draw, either—the chair in your room, people, trees outside your window, even the dog. Just draw. Your main objective will be to depict three-dimensional objects and spaces with simple lines on the flat page."

Neil reviewed our sketchbooks every week. He found my early attempts stiff, my line work too feathery and the resulting forms rigid and lifeless. "You need to loosen up," he insisted. This became his mantra with all of us. I didn't know what he meant until about the third week. He flipped through my pages and stopped.

"What's this?" One night I had returned to my room after a few drinks and started drawing the couch. I sketched its main outlines and gave up.

"Oh, that," I replied, "I was half drunk when I sketched it."

"If it lets you draw like that, you need to get drunk and stay that way!"

So that was what he meant.

"Relax, follow the pen and let your lines do the work," he said.

In a flash, I understood. From then on I began to depict deep spaces and solid objects with economy of line. In the years to come, I learned how draw buildings with lines alone, in a technique Frank Lloyd Wright, Helmut Jacoby, Paul Rudolph and others took to great lengths and perfected. When visiting my Boston relatives. I saw Welliver's show at the Boston Public Library and then, a block away across Copley Square, I sat on the sidewalk to sketch H. H. Richardson's Trinity Church using this technique.

Welliver became an advocate of my work. When I returned from Europe to begin senior year in my architectural studio courses, he spent many hours dry mounting each one of my line sketches and exhibited them in Weir Hall. I received a 25-dollar "Award for Excellence and the Best Presentation, Summer Sketchbook Project." The best presentation part was surely due to Neil Welliver's time spent at the dry-mounting press. I used the proceeds to buy an adjustable drafting lamp.

Senior year started on a high note. All my courses, except for an elective on the nineteenth century novel, were in architectural subjects. Statics and Strength of Materials was taught by Herman D. J. Spiegel, a personable professor who genuinely liked his students and made these dense concepts— moments, stress moduli, statics, strength of materials and graphic truss analysis—clear and understandable. He led us through the equations for beam and column design and the design of an entire structure for a four-story steel building. Although as architects we would not design such structures ourselves, we needed to understand the process so we could hire and coordinate the work of our structural engineering consultants.

A special seminar in the fall semester of 1959 on architecture of the nineteenth and twentieth centuries entailed a weekly visit from Smith College Professor Henry Russell Hitchcock. While the course material was dry, he enlivened it with his own personal recollections in making and writing about architectural history. The portly professor had a Hemingway beard and a jolly temperament. "When I saw Mrs. Wright at the opening of the Guggen-ha-ha-ha," he said, half-chuckling and half-coughing as he recalled it, "she told me, 'You know, if Frank had lived' (he had died earlier that year), 'he would not have come here today. The changes others made to his building were unacceptable.'" He was referring to compromises made by Baroness Hildegarde Rebay von Ehrenweisen (commonly known as Hilla Rebay), who mediated a testy relationship between the practical donor, Solomon Guggenheim, and Wright, the high-strung architect. An abstract painter who educated the millionaire copper magnate on modern non-objective painting—she called him "Guggi"— , she had built the collection to be displayed there, thus becoming the de facto client for the project. Wright hated painters in general, especially artists of abstractions, and he had never agreed with Rebay on how her collection should be hung. She wanted the paintings, including her work, to be permanently fastened to the exterior walls; he insisted they be mounted in front of the walls and removable, part of continuously changing exhibitions. She also negotiated an architectural exterior finish and other practical changes and maintained sufficient peace between architect and client to reach solutions, not always acceptable to Wright, so the project could proceed.[8]

Afternoons in that senior year, my initiation into architecture school, were devoted to the centerpiece of the program, the first-year design studio A highlight of that semester was a class field trip to New Canaan, arranged by one of our instructors, architect Ed Winter, to visit several different modern houses, with a final stop at Phillip Johnson's glass house. Johnson personally welcomed our class to the site and gave us a tour of the main house and the windowless separate building where he had built his bedroom, both structures set atop a long hill, which dropped abruptly to a lagoon below. The main house looked exactly as it appeared in the architectural magazines, pristine, with the Mies van der Rohe furniture perfectly aligned in the clutter-free interior, amid a view of trees in all directions through the glass walls. I recall one classmate asking multiple questions about a huge water jet the architect had recently installed in the pond below, which shot at least 50 feet in the air to provide a water feature for the viewers above at their eye level. Johnson was mightily pleased at the student's fawning enthusiasm for his latest project.

This tour was in preparation for a vacation house design project. on an oceanside property. My solution was to design a hexagonal volume with a central fireplace and chimney and balconies, many windows on the water and sleeping balconies above the main living space, open and outward-looking in summer and cave-like in colder weather. The project received reasonable acceptance by the jury.

A major design problem assigned to the first-year class was a riding hall adjacent to a polo field, with horse stables, exercise areas, practice track and audience seating, for all-weather polo competitions. Our class visited polo games, learned the rules and gathered information on the care, feeding, and stabling of horses. I consulted my cousin Susy, who kept horses and a few other farm animals on their property in Comstock, Michigan, and received a letter on the subject, which I tacked up on the bulletin board to share with my classmates. If Susy had ever shown up at our school, she would have been received as a celebrated expert.

As my design progressed, I developed a wide-span wood structure, with three-hinged arches spaced along a gable roof. At each end, the arches converged at the hip in an octagonal design.

Another of my classmates designed a Mies van der Rohe style box in steel and glass, with infill of small bricks. Other students developed their own individual designs. T. Gorm Hansen, instructor for the first-year design studio, encouraged my direction. An older gentleman, modest in his manner, he maintained, "We Danes are not originators, merely refiners." He proved his skill in this area by encouraging me to develop this concept and showing me how. For the riding hall, I had designed a series of slits along the length of the gable to admit light in the roof, which got smaller and closer together as the roof reached its peak. He admired the long horizontals I sketched and even showed me how to modify my three-hinged arches to be proportioned correctly for structural support of the roof joists and window slits.

I later discovered Wright's Herbert Johnson house, "Wingspread," also had a stepped gable roof, four rows of skylight strips and octagonal ends. Yet I had arrived at this solution on my own. It's possible I had seen it and felt it was so right as a solution for letting light into a gable roof, it should always be done that way. My design grew out of Mr. Hansen's suggested reshaping of the three-hinged arches supporting the roof: it was natural and easy to step them up them a bit at four points along their climb to the peak, thus allowing the slits to appear for much needed natural light on the interior. But when I designed it, they grew organically from the structure. I had no conscious idea anyone had ever designed such a roof before.

Nonetheless, Edwin de Cossy, an associate of Rudolph's who had accompanied him to New Haven from Florida, came by my desk one day and remarked: "You think you're Frank Lloyd Wright? You're just copying his style."

I stared at him, too appalled to reply, thinking, "And what would be wrong with that—learning from one of the great masters of the twentieth century?" Certainly, my classmate David across the aisle was copying Mies van der Rohe's Crown Hall on the Illinois Institute of Technology's campus—a boxy, Miesian steel structure with exposed steel girders above the flat roof to achieve the required wide span; he wasn't receiving such scathing criticism.

Soon afterward, I caught the instructor's drift. Something I was doing was jarring to the very ethos of the Yale Architecture School. Years later, when I re-read Wolfe's book, I realized how protective these disciples of the Bauhaus faith were of their own kind:

> Composers, artists or architects in a compound began to have the instincts of a medieval clergy, much of whose activity was devoted exclusively to separating itself from the mob. For mob, substitute bourgeoisie—and you have the spirit of avant-gardism in the twentieth century. Once inside a compound, an artist can become part of a clerisy, to use an old term for an intelligentsia with clerical presumptions.[9]

What artist had not learned technique by copying the great masters first and then developing his own unique style? At Yale it was okay to copy Gropius, Mies and Le Corbusier, or Corbu, as American architects familiarly called him.

What was not okay was to imitate Frank Lloyd Wright.

Gropius and his postulants inside the compound, whom Wolfe called hierophants, or priestly advocates in the old sense of the word, considered Wright a nineteenth century architect. In fact, when they tagged him with that label in the 1930s, Wright was far from finished. In 1935 he designed Fallingwater, the Edgar Kauffman house, majestically poised over a western Pennsylvania waterfall. At age 68 he began the second half of his career. Between that time and his death at age 91 in 1959—the year before I was accused of copying his work—Wolfe reports he had "designed 180 buildings, including the Johnson's Wax headquarters in Racine, Wisconsin, Herbert F. Johnson's mansion, "Wingspread," Taliesin West, the Florida Southern campus, the Usonian homes, the Price Company Tower, and the

Guggenheim Museum. Nevertheless, I was excoriated, while copyists of the Bauhaus were praised. Wolfe's commentary explains why:

> For a hierophant of the compound, confidence
> came easy! What did it matter if you said you are
> imitating Mies or Gropius or Corbu or any of the
> rest? It was like accusing a Christian of imitating
> Jesus Christ." [11]

It appeared I was not acceptable as an adherent of the faith, nor for the membership in the compound—and I never would be.

A Riding Hall for New Haven

Frank Lloyd Wright, Wingspread, Herbert Johnson House, Racine, Wisc.

Part II: My Voyage of Discovery

Just as Grandpa followed the trail blazed by Lewis and Clark and helped to seal America's Manifest Destiny with a railroad, it was my turn to strike out in a new direction to find mine. My voyage of discovery took me to Europe and as far east as Anatolian Turkey.

September 1960 marked a turning point in my education. Coming from a family of business promoters on the one hand and builders on the other, I had an innate sense of my natural abilities and what I wanted to do, and with the help of my testers and prognosticators, of what I ought to become. I looked back at a family of striving achievers and a solid liberal arts education. Ahead I saw challenges to be met. I could apply my talents to the urgent needs of a rapidly rising generation facing social discontent, unsolved urban challenges and economic growth. With the energy of youth and seemingly unlimited time stretching out before me, I knew I must prepare for the future.

Unwittingly, I had found myself at the mecca for formation of new architects. I arrived at a moment in Yale University's history where she was poised for expansion, and yet her architectural school had stumbled badly. Gropius's day at Harvard had come and gone, Penn lacked a strong leader, and other schools training architects were turning out a corps of technicians with only the basic drawing skills necessary to work immediately in offices. Amid all this change, Yale's president, expansionist A. Whitney Griswold, had hand-picked a new leader.

While graduates of other schools had sought admission to Yale graduate architecture, by virtue of my early selection of an architectural major I had been admitted and well launched into the first-year program by the beginning of senior year. Graduates of other schools had joined me in that first-year class. Paul M. Rudolph, the school's new chairman, was fast developing a strong standing among clients and fellow architects and an educational reputation for collegiality among visiting experts. He was also known for toughness, demanding courses and determination to create graduates who sought to become the leading form givers among the world's great architects. After graduating with my undergraduate degree, I looked forward in the fall of 1960 to the second-year program of graduate school.

I was trying to enter an entirely new field of endeavor, unfamiliar to me or my mentors. In order to utilize my visionary, technical, descriptive and promotional skills—all inherited from various branches of my family—was I attempting too much? Was I tackling more obstacles than necessary? Why hadn't I looked more seriously, despite its known drawbacks, into following a career in the family construction company?

My reasoning at that time was based on the architectural profession's prevailing attitude toward construction. An architect's traditional role was to act as a check on the tendency of some contractors to seek unsuitable, money-saving shortcuts, which compromised building quality. At the time I entered the field, the profession was dead set against collaborative arrangements between architects and contractors: They considered them unethical, unprofessional and even dishonest, ignoring the architect's traditional duty to regulate contracting and enforce building standards. Would I spend too many years breaking into architectural firms? In the family construction firm, I might have begun building earlier and, in maturity, arrived in the era when professional architects could indeed work in concert with building contractors in a new field, known today as Design-Build contracting? That was hard to foresee. Moreover, as a supplicant, I was beholden to established architects to gain entry into the profession.

Rudolph took contradiction personally and had fought too hard against his own obstacles to be bested by others. He and his sycophants dared all comers to challenge him. Only those with a supreme self-confidence, like battered prizefighters, could survive his knockout blows, lick their wounds and stagger to their feet to fight another day. Other students, more circumspect in their analysis, might survive if they chose not to challenge but meekly to follow the great leader. They found another path to survival and completed the course. I took a third route: I moved elsewhere. I asked myself, "What does all this nonsense have to do with learning what architecture is and how to do it?"

For me, a neophyte in search of tools and techniques to earn a living, it was a different struggle. I already had the confidence of several years' Art Institute training in manipulation and representation of visual form. With a Yale education and a Bachelor of Arts in Architecture degree under my belt, I had a clear sense of how to create and illustrate the buildings I saw in my imagination. What I lacked was knowledge and experience to suit them for human use. I wanted to learn what makes buildings adequate, in terms of the classic requirements— Commodity (function), Firmness (structural strength) and Delight (visual beauty).

Now I needed more instruction in building and design techniques, wider exposure to urban planning and design and more open discussion about the broadening scope of architecture. I would eventually find it in the free, fresh air of my own Midwest. Whether I had made the right decision, it would take years to tell. But more and different approaches could not hurt. I had gotten the best Yale could give. Her insular graduate program had no answers for a changing world—as the school's development, or lack of it, as national and local events in 1965 would show. I now had to move into a wider circle, beyond the purview of the lone creator and solitary genius to the collaborative world of the larger community of those many who build and inhabit the urban environment.

9

TRAIN WRECK

I N FALL, 1960, I ARRIVED IN NEW HAVEN a week early so I could get to know my new housemate Roberto, an Art School student who had posted his need to share his housing costs, and to get settled in our rental quarters.

Our apartment was on the upper floors of an old house on Chapel Street, about two blocks west of the Yale Art Gallery and Design building, where my classes in the School of Architecture were held. When I arrived at our rental property, my new housemate was there. Roberto had charged several gallons of paint, for the sum of over fifty dollars. He said he was a little short—would I mind paying for it? Since it represented more than a week's wages from my twelve-week theater season, I told him I thought it would be fair to split the cost. Of course, I'd be glad to share the work of applying the paint. He then informed me he had already claimed the second-floor bedroom, but I was welcome to take over the entire attic space above. Even this early in architecture school, I observed the space was not insulated, only separated from New Haven's harsh winter by rough roofing boards and a few old layers of asphalt shingles. Moreover, the floor of the attic consisted of sub-flooring, without a finished floor. Roberto pointed out he had thought of this: He bought some wood filler and a spatula tool for applying it at the paint store, charging it, naturally, along with the paint.

When I challenged him on his prior claim of the second-floor bedroom, he assured me, "You'll be happier on the upper floor, separated from me and my boyfriends. We're likely to stay up late and be a bit noisy."

"Boyfriends?" I asked. Since our rental arrangements had been completed by mail and phone, I'd had no chance to notice his gay demeanor and manner of speaking. Even in those early days, I tried to keep an open mind about sexual preferences of others. In fact, I'd heard even our new head of school was gay. So was Michelangelo, I thought. Maybe it didn't matter, and I should get used to the idea. In 1960, however, tolerating such goings-on in one's rental quarters would not be considered an asset to one's reputation or dating life. His financial conduct was already disturbing, and this surprise made me even less happy.

Roberto noted my displeasure: "You said you would have to buy some furniture. The girl who used to live up there said she'd be happy to sell the bed and the dresser, so she didn't have to haul them away. I bought them, all for only twenty-five dollars." The bed was a double, in fair condition, with a mattress cover and new box spring, set directly on the floor. With a deep sigh, I handed him the cash. The dresser was old, but the drawers worked.

That night next to the bed I discovered a diary kept by its former owner, with no name to identify her. I opened it, wondering if I had stumbled upon some precious secrets of her soul. It didn't take long to get my answer. Two or three days a week, along with her pedestrian entries on attending class, and her evaluation of them—boring—she confided:

"April 3. Went to bed early last night, sad. Ted joined me, and we talked. I was up until 3 a.m. with Ted."

And so it went with the mysterious woman. No name, no photo, no clue as to what she was like. And no raw passion to confess—just pages recording dates and times she was "up late with Ted." I should have asked Roberto to return it to her, but what was the point?

The next afternoon, I began unpacking my suitcase and duffel bag, making use of a crude closet and the old dresser. I set to work with the wood filler on the worst cracks and missing chinks of the floor. Roberto came by, and I said I had to quit this for now and leave: "They're having a welcome party for Mr. Rudolph, so he can meet the new students."

"Ooh, I've got to come. Paul Rudolph is my idol. I'm so glad he came to the school. I've got to meet him."

"I don't think so, Roberto. This is just for the Architecture School, and you're not invited."

"The Art Department is right next door," he said, with a hurt look on his face, "and this is the School of Art and Architecture."

On this point I was uncertain. Maybe art students were invited, after all.

"Oh, I guess you can tag along, if you like," I said, against my better judgment.

We showed up promptly at four at one of the professors' homes. I quickly ditched my housemate in the crowd, greeted old classmates and met new ones. There apparently were some art students there, and I met several attractive girls in the incoming class. A petite blonde caught my eye. Her words tumbled out in low, musical tones like water playing over rocks in a mountain stream. Her blue eyes regarded me coolly and crinkled when she laughed, her name—Julie. We hit it off. I promised to give her a personal tour of the school the next day, and she gave me her phone number. Then I got talking with a classmate, Austin Towle, who had arrived early.

"Have you talked with Mr. Rudolph, yet?" Austin said.

"Just got here."

He led me through the crowd, and we waited until the guest of honor was free.

Rudolph, slightly taller than me, wore a tweed sport jacket, his gray-white hair in a crew-cut, an alert expression, his bright blue eyes set in a perpetually pink face. He greeted me cordially, recognizing me from juries in first year. I hoped he recalled liking my some of my design output.

Just then, Roberto found me and walked up. "Oh, and this is Roberto," I said, "my house-mate. He's in the Art School."

Before Rudolph could even speak," Roberto gushed, "Ooh Mr. Rudolph. I've been dying to meet you. I admire your work. I love you, I love you, I LOVE YOU!"

Rudolph stared at Roberto and back at me. "This guy must be off his rocker!"

Roberto may have been crazy, but he wasn't stupid. If Mr. Rudolph was unaware of his reputation for preferring males, what else didn't he know? I was mortified, but our new leader seemed clueless. I was certain, however, that this was the absolute worst thing that could or ever would happen to me, and I had caused it. Rudolph turned to other guests, I excused myself and abruptly left the room. I left the party and walked home to lie on my new bed and weep.

My luck at Yale had changed. That day, after my rude reunion with our respected, highly touted new leader, I wouldn't have given you a nickel for my prospects of success in the architecture program. The only benefits to be salvaged from the fiasco were my reunion with last year's favorite classmates and meeting Julie. When she smiled, she radiated inner joy. We had one evening together when we so delighted each other just by the fact that we felt beautiful and yet were shaped so comically, that afterwards as I walked home, I repeatedly burst out laughing.

The next day we toured the fourth, top floor of Louis Kahn's 1953 Art Gallery and Design Center. We passed through glass entry doors into the lobby, entered a concrete cylinder containing straight runs of stairs attached to the curved, bare gray walls at the landings and skylit from above. We mounted the dizzying isosceles triangular spiral, past second- and third-floor art galleries to the top. Through a door in the curving concrete wall, we entered a much larger space. A plane of triangular concrete coffers formed a wide-span structural ceiling hovering almost uninterrupted over the four quadrants of the room, each occupied by one year's class of the architecture school. My second-year class would be in the southwest quarter, enclosed by the blank exterior concrete block and brick south wall facing Chapel Street. The west wall of floor-to-ceiling glass faced the excavation for the new Art and Architecture Building across York Street.

The top floor was much beloved by students. Its understated design provided unrestricted space for drawings and models to evolve on drafting boards and tables within. The ceiling, a honeycomb of poured concrete coffers alternating with open spaces, accommodated track lights, air conditioning vents, sprinkler heads and other necessary fixtures, concealed in the dark voids. This hovering ceiling felt cozy and comforting, especially at night. Floodlit trees across the courtyard were visible through the glass wall on the north side facing Weir Hall, a variable backdrop that changed with the seasons.

The space was also pleasant in the daytime. A few people were working at their drafting boards. The presence of all four classes in one loosely defined open space on one level, from beginners to master's candidates, encouraged free interchange among younger and more experienced students. It was easy to make friends and offer or obtain help—a frequent occurrence among the classes.

Julie and I went to lunch and talked about our likes, dislikes and favorite things. Two hours flew by. I loved the way her voice, matter of fact, first sophisticated and low, a river along smooth banks, rose naturally when she laughed. I told her I used to date a girl named Julie, and she confessed the only man she had ever loved was named Peter. Her smile illuminated the dingy cafe with sunlight. I was smitten, and her expressions suggested the attraction was mutual.

"I love you," I wanted to say. She was perfect and I wanted and needed her.

But I was torn between opening up to her and charging

ahead on my own. It would give her some claim on me, on my precious time. I was about to start an important semester, and somehow she was in my way. Her opinions could not be ignored, but they could cloud my thinking and weaken my resolve.

The subject of my housemate came up. She had met him at the party as well. I told her how he had embarrassed me in front of the new head of the school.

"Let me see this apartment," she said.

I led her up the street to the house and took her to my quarters in the attic. She pointed to the bed. "This is the only thing worth keeping in this dump," she said. "You should get out of here."

"We arranged this rental over the whole summer. Where else could I live?"

"I don't know, but I'll help you look for a new place."

We set out along Chapel Street and soon found a For Rent sign in the lobby window of an apartment building even closer to the school. It was one of those buildings with a long center hallway and apartments on each of three floors. We entered the lobby with a bank of mailboxes, each with its own bell to an apartment, allowing residents to buzz guests in. I pressed the one labeled "Manager." A buzzer let us through the vestibule door and the woman showed us a second-floor apartment with a Pullman kitchen and an alcove for a Murphy bed, but no bed. A large double window was centered on the main living space, with a dismal view of a hotel's side brick wall and windows.

"You should take it," Julie said, "but you'll need to make sure to move in that nice bed."

Her interest in that bed was okay with me. I was dazzled by this lovely person who had walked into my life.

"You should put a little table and two chairs by the windows. You need a reading chair in that corner."

"You are what I need," I wanted to say.

She put a hand on my arm and turned toward me. She was standing very close, looking in my eyes. I wanted to pull her toward me and kiss her. But my feet were riveted to the floor, my arms paralyzed, my voice mute.

"Sure, good idea," I managed to utter in a thin, attenuated squeak.

I writhed with my need for her. I fidgeted. She waited. Then she looked at her watch "Oh, I promised to meet Ann at the art library."

With the assurance we'd meet again soon, she went to meet her friend. I paid the landlady for my month's advance rent and received the keys.

The next day as I headed toward down Chapel Street to the school, I ran into Roberto.

"What happened? Your bed is gone, and the spatula and the wood filler are still on the floor, right where you left them."

I explained to him why I couldn't live there. I reminded him I'd paid for the furniture. I figured the fifty dollars' worth of paint he had charged without my consent was his problem.

From the drafting room phone, I called the number Julie had given me to tell her I had moved in, and she congratulated me.

On Saturday morning when I called she wasn't home. With no phone installed in my apartment yet, communication was cut off. Three days later on a Tuesday, I met Julie on her way to class. She said, "I was really lonesome Saturday afternoon, and I rang your bell, but there was no answer."

"Oh, darn. I was there all afternoon, waiting for the phone man."

"Oh, it's okay," she said, "we'll talk another time."

But the light in her eyes had dimmed—our moment had passed. Later, I checked the apartment intercom—the doorbell for my unit was broken, and I notified the manager to get it fixed.

When I saw her a week later she was with a tall, blond god from the undergraduate school. I learned his name was Peter— so she had slid back into her former relationship! She had slipped through my fingers and out of reach. All possibility for romance was gone.

I returned to my new apartment. I was at least grateful she had helped me accomplish one thing. I was living in heated space, with enough privacy to conduct my own life, unaffected by Roberto's. But the week's events did not bode well for my new venture into the unknown world of graduate **school**. I sat in our anticipated love nest that evening, reflecting on how I had gotten into this situation. With nothing to do I peered through the Venetian blind across the light well at uncurtained hotel windows fifteen feet away.

In plain view a couple were going at it hot and heavy on the bed, further accenting my loneliness. When the man rolled over and walked out of the frame, the woman sat nude and motionless on the end of the bed for a long time. A lamp cast a strong chiaroscuro glow on her Rubens figure. I stood on the low windowsill to get a better look, gripping the edge of the window frame for balance, and peered through the partially opened blind. I lost my grip on the top window frame, kicked the blind and landed on the carpet, as the whole assembly descended on my head. I don't know if the hotel occupants noticed, but I didn't care. I laughed myself silly to keep from crying.

I felt I had been cast in a bad movie, where the hero misses his train, is attacked on the platform and by the third scene ends up shot, lying on the tracks. When would something good happen?

10

A LESSON IN FAILURE, MINE AND OTHERS'

AFTER MY EMBARRASSING ENCOUNTER with Paul Rudolph, I settled down to classes and the studio course. Our first design problem in the second year started with a class trip to Hammonasset Beach, a short drive from New Haven on the shore of Long Island Sound. On this November day under a cloudy sky, the wide beach appeared windswept and desolate. Our assignment was to design a pavilion for the active days of summer, to shelter, shade and provide concessions and dressing rooms for beach goers. We had been working with visiting critic Frei Otto, an architect-engineer specializing in lightweight structures. "Remember," he consistently advised, "the job with these structures is not so much to hold them up as to tie them down." My solution was to place a lightweight truss structure winged like a butterfly at the end of a long pier extending out into the water.

Our design work on most projects began with conceptual drawings sketched out on transparent buff-colored paper. Then, after much discussion with our design critics in class and comments by classmates, we evolved floor plans, elevations (direct, front-on views of each exterior wall)—all drawn to scale— and perspective sketches. Based on our observations at the building site, we would place the buildings on our site plans, adjusting them to the contours of the land, orientation toward the sun and exposure to promote cross ventilation in summer and protect them from harsh winter winds. We finished our sketched designs on flimsy buff tissue and then transferred them to presentation boards in India ink as detailed presentation drawings. This was a laborious process, extending deep into most nights, especially as we approached deadlines.

To keep us going in the long hours required to finish our work, we listened to music, some on portable phonographs, some on the radio. The soothing classical sounds of Music Till Dawn on WQXR, the New York Times radio station, spurred us on. Just as we thought we could not possibly draw another line, a cup of vending-machine coffee, a sweet roll and the stirring notes of Handel's Water Music or Purcell's Trumpet Tune, floating among classes through the open space of the fourth floor, would wake us up and drive us for another two hours. Music had the power to alter our moods, recalling old times and happy events.

One afternoon, the familiar strains of the William Tell Overture greeted my ears. Wound up with enthusiasm for my design and the lack of a physical outlet for my energy, without a thought I galloped from my desk into the first-year quadrant, bellowing, "Hi-yo Silver, away!" Much to the amusement of all Lone Ranger listeners and the eye-rolls of a few stuffy easterners, my impromptu performance met with chuckles, guffaws and good-natured approval.

Encouraged by the temper of the times, and classes with Welliver and Engman in the Art School, a few of the third-year students played music. George Buchanan had a nice guitar stowed beside his drafting desk. When morale in the room sagged, he brought out his instrument and played a few folk songs, accompanied by a classmate plucking out the bass line on his gut bucket and the swish of snare drums furnished by a draftsman tapping his drafting brush on flimsy drawing tissue. One of my favorites, which he delivered in a creditable baritone, was The Golden Vanity:

There was a ship that sailed upon the Lowland sea,
And the name of the ship was the Golden Vanity,
And we feared she would be taken by the Spanish enemy,
As we sailed upon the Lowland, Lowland. Lowland,
We sailed upon the Lowland sea.

The wrong music could also have the opposite of a soothing effect. Tensions ran high the night before the beach pavilion assignment was due. Someone in third year turned on some loud dissonant rock music, annoying me and my classmates as we struggled to finish our drawings. I made a fuss about it, mocking the unpleasant, squawking sounds with my own voice. George intervened, looking like a big papa bear, to calm our warring parties down and restore peace in the drafting room. But apparently the damage was done. The loud music lovers turned down their radio but glared menacingly in my direction.

I had presented my concept on half a dozen 20" x 30" illustration boards. The next morning, I carried some of them over to the exhibit area on the ground floor of Weir Hall, setting them at the base of the wall where I would pin them up for display. I had a bit more work to finish on the site and floor plans, so I went back to work for couple of hours and returned with the remaining three boards. My first three boards had disappeared. Panicked, I asked another student who was setting up his display if he had seen anybody take my boards. He mentioned he had seen a janitor come by cleaning up anything sitting on the floor. It seemed unlikely, but I had no other explanation for the mystery: Apparently, I had made an enemy in the third-year class.

I liked to think of myself as a merciless analyst of my own soul. In our late-night talks, Mom's belief in her sister's psychoanalytic skill often led to the topic of me—my early trauma, what must be upsetting me now and the hidden influences on my feelings. This little bit of self-knowledge convinced me that no one knew my weaknesses and flaws better than I did. I thought it impossible that others ever talked about me among themselves—in just as free, critical and mildly condescending way as I did about them. As I saw it, I had flaws, but I was the only one privileged to see them. Everyone must necessarily see me as the perfect person I tried to present to the world. That went without saying.

But the damage I caused resulted in making a presentation without half of my rendered final drawings—as bad at Yale as appearing in my underwear.

Charles Brewer was chief critic for second-year design. During the jury, my only choice was to pin up the rough sketches of my design along with the finished boards that escaped the fiasco. Frei Otto appeared to like the structural concept well enough, but Paul Rudolph was mystified at my lack of complete presentation work. I tried to explain the mysterious disappearance of my presentation boards, but to no avail. He pointed out that the pier, which was not part of the design program, would require a lot of maintenance. Once the other jurors tasted the blood of Rudolph's disapproval, they piled on. "It looks as if that building is trying to fly away, but its tail is too heavy," Brewer said. "Besides," said another instructor, "that pier is cutting the beach in half."

On the defensive, thinking as clearly as possible under the circumstances, I said this was an attempt to express a human act in a landscape where people did not usually make much difference. This, no doubt, was the result of Vincent Scully's lectures, a fact Rudolph might have recognized and resented. The art historian's growing fame tended to eclipse and rival Rudolph's national reputation. He thought Scully should stick to his history and not impose ideas upon architecture: students, who should focus on making visual forms. Judging my design on its own terms, they said, I hadn't accomplished this. Brewer confirmed this later, saying my ideas were too literary. In a school where form-making was everything and ideas about building use, meaning and historical association were less important, I was beginning to understand, I didn't fit in.

M. J. Long, one of several female students admitted to the first-year program during the sabbatical of Carroll Meeks (the art history professor who served as admissions chairman for the program) was in the first-year class when I was in second year. In their definitive history of Yale Architecture School, *Pedagogy and Place*, Robert A. M. Stern and Jimmy Stamp summarized her feeling about education at the school:

> For Long, Yale's great failure was that its approach to history was overly formal: "There was a kind of distrust of theory. Yale wasn't anti-intellectual but it was anti-idea," so that form making was emphasized, but forms were not seen as combined with fixed or social meanings. "Yale just wasn't interested in ideas at all." [11]

Impressed with the British approach, Long moved to England after graduation and practiced with Colin St. John Wilson, whom she met at Yale and eventually married.

Under Rudolph's lead, disregarding history, urban context and sometimes even bending functionality, we were expected to become form makers, in order to create spatial experiences with varying effects on the senses, levels of activity and emotions. These ranged from excitement to mystery—each valuable attributes of architecture, but far from its total meaning.

Among the best courses in the second-year program were those required in construction and structural engineering. We had a course in methods and materials of construction with Henry Pfisterer, who discussed his work on structural design of the Empire State Building. "Construction progressed," he said, "at the rate of one story per day." Tall with an athletic build, he had chipped a couple of his front teeth, no doubt climbing on the structural framework of what was then the tallest building in the world. The result was difficulty enunciating his r's, which came out as l's, and a slight whistle with the letter "s". Because his construction stories were so fascinating and authentic, we allowed for his hissing sibilants and missing r's and listened attentively as he brought construction history and techniques to life, along with information on "stlesses and stlains in leinforced conclete." He familiarized us with structural and mechanical systems we could employ in our work or might encounter in rehabilitating older buildings, including masonry bearing walls, patented masonry vaults, reinforced concrete frames and the many mechanical systems for heating and air conditioning buildings.

A highlight of that year was a course in statically indeterminate structures, taught by Clarence P. Dunham, who literally wrote the book on the topic. Such a structure, for example, has columns and beams continuously formed with rigid joints. Their combined resistance to loads is greater than bolted assemblies, but their strength is more complicated to calculate. Mr. Dunham, short and stocky, with a shock of graying hair and thick glasses, explained. He grinned as he drew little circular arrows on the board, diagramming internal forces in a beam joined to a column. "This little feller wants to turn left, but the joint resists him with an opposite force." His descriptions delighted the young women in our class, who thought he was cute and called him Clarence behind his back: "Oh, I just love Clarence and his little fellers." Moreover, he made this difficult subject approachable, and we learned a lot in his class, a bright spot in that semester's studies.

During this tense fall session, I reported in a letter home that ten students had failed to cope with the beach pavilion project in one way or another. Under the Pass-Fail grading system, out of thirty-one students, seven received a grade of Fail. Three others declined to present their work. This was a dodge I had not yet caught on to—at least by not submitting work, these students had nothing to grade, and judgment had to be postponed. I was not the type of person to avoid a challenge, but I soon learned, in this case, discretion would have been the better part of valor. I noticed later in the semester that these non-submitters had conferences with the chief critic at their drafting boards to discuss a few drawings completed after the jury. They had received a passing grade, totally sidestepping a jury's merciless scrutiny and the rigid, arbitrary Pass-Fail system. I was beginning to wonder, who had failed: Was it I, or the school?

My misgivings about the place had increased. The rules at that time stipulated that, although a student could progress to the next level in the program if one of his projects received a grade of "Fail," he was expected to redo the project and present it again for review. In the second semester of that year, I calmed down, and during a few days of my spring vacation, which I spent in New Haven, I wrote to the family that "one night I drew a horizontal line and suddenly knew what I was doing." I realized what kind of building belonged on that beach, and all the passion of that sere November poured into a rational, clear exposition of an idea. "Ever since our site planning problem, I've been discovering that I have a great ability to interpret land and integrate it with the architecture I place on it." I told my parents, "My beach pavilion is finished and beautiful—an easy 'Pass.'"

Second Design for the Beach Pavilion

I had dodged the bullet. Nonetheless Norman Foster, a British architect who sought his master's degree during the following year, when I was absent in the Army, commented on the terrifying habit Rudolph had of coming on to the struggling student at the last minute or, if he had not seen many drawings and studies of a student's design before final presentation, at the actual jury session:

> In retrospect, Norman Foster believes the students ultimately benefited from Rudolph's policy of terrifying eleventh-hour crits: "The one thing it really made you realize is that the more immersed you were in the issues of design; the more you knew about it, you did have the ability, at this very last moment, to question everything you'd done and to reshape the project — either modify it or go back to square one… I think that ability to really concentrate your energy, to make you question and to challenge is architectural but, in a way it's beyond architecture." Under Rudolph, rhetoric and reasoning were no substitute for completed drawings and models. If it couldn't be pinned up, it didn't matter.[12]

The stress I was feeling, I later learned, was not all of my own creation. By second year, which I began in my first postgraduate academic year, 1960-61, Paul Rudolph was hitting his stride. Born in Elkton, Kentucky in 1918, son of an itinerant preacher, he was gaining national prominence for his work and was popular with students. A shy person, he wore his heart on his sleeve and was approachable, at first. No one seemed to be his close friend, but he warmed quickly to the subject of architecture and was always eager to share his beliefs about it with his students.

One condition of Paul Rudolph's accepting the chairmanship of Yale's architecture school was that he also be employed as architect for some of the University's new buildings in an era of unprecedented university growth. The president, A. Whitney Griswold, had plenty of commissions and stayed closely tied to the planning and architectural process for expanding the campus. Eero Saarinen, a graduate of Yale architecture school, was also on an advisory and planning committee to help steer the institution's overall physical growth.

The first of these assignments for architect Rudolph was the forestry school on the north side of the university near the engineering departments. I visited the building, with its branching Y-shaped concrete columns reaching upward to support the roof, and felt it was appropriate to its forestry occupants.

The School of Art and Architecture's mission to combine all the visual arts in one building had by now exceeded the practical limits for its existing complex along Chapel Street. But the possibility of combining sculpture, painting, graphic design and architecture in one new building near the existing art gallery remained, and the university acquired land along Chapel on the opposite side of York Street to accommodate the expansion. Rudolph pressed for the job of design architect and was selected. He had made himself indispensable to the university, and any students' complaints might reasonably be dismissed as normal discontent rooted in their own failure to keep up with the curriculum's demands.

Students defended Rudolph for his helpful, personable side. One day as a second-year student, I happened to walk by the first-year class quadrant of the architectural floor. He was sitting on a drafting stool, expressing his candid opinions about the working world for architects.

While I don't remember the exact words, the tone of his comments was sincere and open, the gist of it something like this: "Now, let me just tell you," he said, "as you look for summer employment, many of you will get offers to work in the large firms. The types of jobs you'll find in those settings, however, will be very limiting. You may be assigned to working drawings on just one portion of the building, or to very large projects with many sheets of floor plans. When your exposure is so limited, it's hard to get a feel for the overall picture of architecture." Even in design, he cautioned, the jobs were likely to be menial, such as preparing presentation drawings for the principal architect's designs. He recommended working with smaller firms, where every person in the office played a key role and helped work through every phase of the job, from initial concept to inspection of construction. He made his conclusion clear, "Now, I don't want to hear in the fall that a whole lot of you have gone to work for the large firms."

He also confided great architectural tips. At one jury I attended, he defended one critic's comment on an inelegant rear façade: "You're entitled to one bad elevation—that's where you put your exhaust fans, loading docks, electric and gas meters and other necessities that will never look good." On another occasion, addressing the class, he shared his technique: "When you're working late into the night trying to render trees, you try for hours to make your trees work. You scribble loosely, trying to get the leaves right. Then, at two in the morning, your efforts begin to work, and you can't draw a false line. Every twitch of your pen creates a branch or a clump of leaves. Pretty soon, it looks like a real tree." I'd frequently experienced this and knew he spoke the truth.

While my own experience on the beach pavilion proved Foster's point and convinced me that I did have the resources within and the accumulated knowledge to do a better job on the second try, I hadn't come to Yale to become a "great architect." Rather, I wanted to learn how to design buildings and earn a living doing it. The second semester's principal design problem was an elementary school for a hillside site. I combined a row of hexagonal classroom modules with hexagonal-pyramid roofs and repeated that form on a larger scale for the major spaces, such as gym, cafeteria and library. For the grade school library, I designed a hexagonal volume surrounded by bookshelves, with clerestory lighting above and a sunken, cozy reading area in the middle. The jury concluded it was harmonious combination and a functional school. Even Ed DeCossy, one of the jurists, commented "I just love that little library,"

On the world stage in early 1962, sabers were rattling. I had pushed my student deferment to the limit; I was still eligible for the draft, and it appeared that the government was going to take military action in the Far East, possibly in Laos. One of the first things the admission chairman for the architecture graduate program, Carroll L. V. Meeks, asked me when I applied was, "After your graduation, will you be willing to stay on the Yale campus for another three years?" Despite my breezy confidence at the time that it would be no problem, I was getting tired of school, and I had this nagging issue of a military obligation. I decided, if I could arrange it, I would like to get into the six-month Army Reserve program. In the Marine Corps Dad tried his best to be of useful service to his country and felt he had failed. Based upon his own military misadventures, Dad's advice was: "Military service is a total waste of time. Get it done, with the minimum commitment possible." I could use a year's break, and the time was ripe to take his advice.

I learned that New Haven's General Hospital detachment was getting ready to send a group of recruits into basic training by June. To join them, I needed clearance from my own draft board, who reported to Fifth Army Corps headquarters in Chicago. In order for me to enroll at this particular New Haven reserve unit, they had to release me to the charge of First Army Corps headquarters at Fort Devens, Massachusetts. Most college men my age were lobbying to extend their draft deferments and stay *out of* military service. Dad and I were working the system frantically, in a tale of two cities with maximum melodrama—he from Chicago and me from New Haven—to get me *into* the Army in time to meet the deadline. A last-minute long-distance phone call from Dad, which I confirmed with another necessary phone call to Headquarters, Fort Devens, established my eligibility with hours to spare.

Sitting there at the reserve center with the recruiting officer at last, I almost blew it sky high by airing my reservations about signing a loyalty oath. The unit's commanding officer at a nearby desk overheard our interchange and said, "If this man won't sign a loyalty oath, we can't take him." The recruiter, who had already wasted a couple of days with my unusual case, wasn't ready to let me go quite yet. Accustomed to dealing with college types, he said to me, "You've stated your loyalty to your country. You just feel that your country ought to trust you without signing it, right?" I agreed with him wholeheartedly. Loud enough for his commander to hear, the recruiter then said, "Well, so do I. Then, it's solved. You can sign the loyalty oath in good conscience." Realizing all everybody had done for me to make this happen, I meekly signed the loyalty oath and the enlistment papers and entered the U.S. Army.

Echo Training Company, Ft. Dix, NJ. June 26, 1961
I'm in the fourth Row, Third from right, between Irv Gurland and Berle Engler on my right and Larry Green on my left.

11

THE ARMY: DEVELOPING THE OUTER MAN

DAD ENDURED BOOT CAMP in preparation for World War II at Camp Pendleton near San Diego. Army Reserve basic training on the East Coast was different. In the peacetime Army, we spent an inordinate amount of time shining shoes and boots and got to know each other well. Many of my fellow recruits, although not everyone in our platoon, had interrupted their college careers to get the Army out of the way. Since it was midsummer in New Jersey, we were transported to the rifle range and training sites in open trucks, made to stop activities every two hours to rest in the shade, with hydration from lemonade and iced tea, and generally treated well. I didn't catch on to this until I saw names on a couple of the uniforms at the post library. One night a tall young man with the name Sevareid spelled out the on pocket of his fatigues was reading a magazine. I engaged him in conversation and found out, he was indeed the son of CBS news commentator Eric Sevareid. A couple of other discoveries like this led me to believe that because of the well-connected New Yorkers' sons likely to be in our outfit, the training sergeants were under a standing order not to be too rough on us—with one notable exception.

We had one more obstacle to overcome before completing our eight weeks of basic training and being ranked as soldiers—a three-day bivouac. Transported into a wooded site far from any detectable civilization, we had to train, march and live in the wilderness. I'd informed my parents of the forthcoming bivouac and mentioned I wasn't looking forward to it, since I would never get rid of my cold.

While we were in the field, at our second day's mail call I received a package. I wrote back on Sunday, July 30, "now ordinarily a bundle of rags and a bottle of aspirin are nothing to attract special notice. But receiving them on bivouac was a gift from heaven. There was sand to the right of us, sand to the left of us…It was quite a struggle, but I won and passed rifle inspection. The pipe cleaners are good for cleaning the sights; the extra special good brush fits right into the chamber and cleans it out perfectly, and the toothbrushes are useful on all parts of the weapon. I was the envy of the sand-blown troops and had many requests for aspirin.

"Bivouac was not like Boy Scouts: inspection of boots and brass every morning, cleaning the rifle every night, sleeping on the cold hard ground and watching while my healthy cold flourished and settled down for a long stay. But you can't really complain about this Army. It's nothing like the Marines—no long marches, very little physical training and five or six hours sleep every night, with the added advantages of occasional weekend passes, free weekends and tea or lemonade in the middle of the morning and the afternoon. The most annoying thing is the level of instruction."

My recollection is foggy as to the specific subject matter of the lectures, but the content, reconstructed from so long ago, was equivalent to the example shown here in the amount of detail, the manner of describing procedures and the assumed level of intelligence of their target audience

Here's what I remember from a typical training class:

```
SERGEANT: Seats, men!
CLASS:Echo! (for "E" Company)
```

SERGEANT: Good morning, men!

CLASS:Good morning, Sergeant!

SERGEANT: I'm Sergeant Drawler of the Regimental
     Training Committee, here to give you your
     first hour of FM321-45, Peacetime Operational
     Maneuvers. Now you will encounter, if re-
     quested to visit the home of a civilian resi-
     dent of a municipality, certain situations.
     Among these are passing the butter. This pe-
     riod will be devoted To the Standard Opera-
     tional Procedure for passing the butter. What
     maneuver will you most likely encounter in a
     civilian home, recruit Jones?

RCT JONES:Sergeant, Recruit Jones. Passing the but-
     ter, Sergeant.

SERGEANT: Very good. Now, the
     procedure is as follows. Extend right arm di-
     rectly in front of you, palm up, fingers ex-
     tended and joined. Swing arm to the right or
     left until it is in the immediate vicinity of
     the objective. Lower arm to table, bending
     elbow slightly. By means of a slight forward
     push of the arm, engage butter plate, elevate
     four inches off the table and swing arm beyond
     original position, across the front of your
     body to the person on your right or left. You
     have just passed the butter. What have you
     just done, Recruit Green?

RCT GREEN:Which Green, Sergeant?

SERGEANT: Green, Peter H.

RCT GREEN:Sergeant, Recruit Green. Passed the but-
     ter, Sergeant.

SERGEANT:Are there any questions? Very good. That
     ends your first hour of FM321-45, Peacetime
     Operational Maneuvers.

SGT MASTROVITO: On you fee'! Stanup! When I tell
    you stanattenshun I wan' you stanattenshun.
    Now make shu' you got wada in yo' cantee'.
    Don't give you' buddy no wada. If you don't
    got no wada in yo' canteen, shame on you!

Sadly, we heard indirectly that Sergeant Mastrovito, our training company's beloved non-com, who could not have been more than thirty-five, was killed on the hand grenade range before we had completed our training cycle. That tough, pint-sized man had a heart of gold, and he had poured it into preparation that could save our lives.

Graduation day from basic training came, and we marched onto the parade ground. Our training class formed into squads, platoons and companies, and the regiment marched in review before the commanding general of the post. We were promoted to privates, E-2. Although my group had been promised transfer to Brooke Army Medical Center near San Antonio, Walson Army Hospital, our post was shorthanded. We were told we would perform the rest of our active duty working on the wards right across the drill field from our barracks.

I would also miss our platoon leader, Staff Sergeant Walker, a Black man with battle scars, most notably a chin torn up with shrapnel from the Korean War. Due to my good conduct during the first couple of weeks of basic training, he had named me leader of the first squad, and awarded me a corporal's armband to wear. He had a private bedroom with a TV set in it by the entrance to our barracks, where he spent his long evenings alone, supervising our rowdy bunch of trainees. He was there to break it up the night the city boys in our platoon yanked me out of my lower bunk from a sound sleep and doused me with a cold shower, no doubt in retaliation for for what they regarded as my "goody-goody" behavior.

RELIEVED TO HAVE "GRADUATED" from Army basic training, I returned by plane to Chicago. When I arrived at Midway airport, I waited in the baggage claim area, looking forward to my two weeks of leave and Labor Day weekend, craving my very own private room, its Simmons Beauty Rest mattress and my red faux-leather reading chair. I had not enjoyed such luxuries for well over two months, and I hoped to nurse the cold that had settled in on bivouac and enjoy a few of Mom's delicious, home-cooked meals.

When our 1954 two-tone Buick sedan pulled up to the arrival curb, the doors flew open and I was smothered in the loving arms of Linda, my sixteen-year-old sister, Mom and Dad. We had barely pulled away on Cicero Avenue when my sister, who never could keep a secret, bubbled over with the news: "We're going on a houseboat on the little Wolf River in Wisconsin—in the woods!"

Aghast, I tried to take in the new information. "Oh no, not the wilderness again! How long?"

"I've rented a houseboat for ten days," Dad announced,

My heart sank.

"Frank and Betty are going to join us for Labor Day weekend," Mom added, thrilled to be spending time with her brother and his sweet-natured wife.

"We can fish, relax and swim in the river," Dad chimed in. "They're bringing their canoe."

Not, "Oh, Pete, it's good to see you." Or "My, you look so lean and trim. The Army has been good for you. Now you can relax and enjoy being home." Instead, all I heard were plans for another bivouac, in damp, chilly Wisconsin—at the peak of the hay fever season.

What about my treasured R & R? With their carefully made plans set in stone, it looked as if I was in for some serious family time.

The first week of houseboat living went well enough. Mom whiled away her mornings, reading mystery novels in the cabin or on the deck, while Dad oiled his casting reel, restrung it with new lightweight line and organized his lures and live bait. He cast from the boat, which he maneuvered up and down the Wolf

River. Linda helped him with these tasks and threw a line in the water as well on a bamboo pole with a bobber. She alternated fishing with painting, using a tin of watercolors and her drawing pad.

I luxuriated in my freedom, at least, with no sergeants to tell me what to do. I self-isolated on the roof with a deck chair and read about a more exciting boat trip along the South American coast in Joseph Conrad's *Victory*. My hopes for a few days in our own house with filtered air and the chance to call up a couple of girlfriends dashed, I nursed my hay fever. I also tried to shake off my cold, took my doses of the old, sleep inducing Chlor-Trimiton and alternately read and snoozed the mornings away. At lunch time, Dad made sandwiches from our supply of cold cuts, stuffed in the tiny undercounter refrigerator along with a case of Hamm's beer. While we drank our beer in its native habitat, Indian drums thumped out by a beaver's tail and the tune of a tribal chant drifted through my mind:

> *From the land of sky-blue waters*
> *[Echo] (Wa-a-ters)*
> *Land of lonesome pines*
> *And lofty balsams,*
> *Comes the beer refreshing.*
> *(Ha-a-mm's Beer).*

Since Dad was in the advertising business, he had trained us to think in terms of successful television commercials.

Labor Day weekend arrived, and we made a pit stop at our home port—was it New London, Wisconsin?—for fuel, groceries, and to meet Frank and Betty. They brought more provisions, fishing tackle and a canoe atop their car. Dad and Frank launched it at the dock, tied it to the houseboat and we headed back upriver. We were now testing the full capacity of the boat, as advertised—"Ample room for six!"—in the boat renter's tri-fold brochure. Six midgets, maybe. I shook my head and shrugged: a collection of rods, reels, tackle boxes and bait cans now filled the forward deck. The tiny refrigerator bulged with Dad's beer and half of Frank's first case, while the rest sat on the counter. Their personal bags were stowed—not out of the way, but *in* the way—in a corner of the cabin.

The first night out was a trip, all right. Our crew were not into mind-altering drugs, so we would have to rely on the beer supply to help us endure it. We folded up the hinged dining table, removed the bench pad and placed it on the floor, retrieved a narrow mattress from the locker beneath and folded down a wider board from the cabin bulkhead. This was to be Linda's spot. A double bed folded down from the rear wall of the cabin, and Frank and Betty inflated their camping air mattress on the cabin floor. I stared bewildered at the jigsaw puzzle of pallets, Still, Heaven help any person who needed to use the head in the middle of the night. Because Dad, Frank and I had worked on the case of Hamm's all evening, it was a necessity. It required navigating a footpath past at least three sleeping bodies and shoehorning oneself into the tiny cubicle. Surveying the chaos, I rooted out my bedroll and climbed the ladder to the roof. Thanks to my army conditioning, even the unforgiving planks of the roof deck felt soft. I lay staring at the stars and soon drifted into a deep sleep.

In the morning, stowage and re-positioning of all sleeping surfaces was required for Mom and Betty to prepare breakfast. This required organization, and Private First-Class Ben Green assumed command—with my squad leader's corporal armband, even *I* outranked him. By the time he had taught his crew the Standard Operating Procedure for reassembling the daytime furnishings of the cabin, deflating and storing all mattresses and returning all fold-down pallets to their upright and locked positions, he had earned a new moniker. Frank said, "When I signed up for this expedition, little did I suspect we'd be trapped with Captain Bligh on his Hell ship."

Labor Day weekend proved exciting. Earlier in the week we'd motored past several boats anchored at the confluence of the Wolf and the Little Wolf rivers for an annual event they called "The Thing." They invited us back to share the fun on the holiday. When we returned for the weekend, we found at least a hundred watercraft moored gunwale to gunwale, like a downtown Chicago traffic jam. The elders laughed and scratched among the vacationers on houseboats and variety of other craft. I befriended a passably attractive girl from an adjacent boat—at this point, any available female would have looked good to me. She hopped aboard and we took off in Frank and Betty's canoe with my mother's banjo and grabbed a few hours of peace and sweet romance, apart from the chaos. Satisfying as it was for my over-bivouacked soul, we made quite a stir by our absence. A few short hours later we were distracted from our fast embrace by the water patrol, sent out by the sheriff's office, who were about ready to drag the river. When the patrol boat was gone, we sneaked back into camp and climbed aboard our respective hell ships, to be greeted with open arms by our grieving parents.

When I returned to Fort Dix a few days later, we were assigned barracks and told to await our permanent assignments. While waiting, we were put to work making repairs "in the much-neglected company area, newly occupied by the Hospital Detachment." I wrote. "A fellow architect in my barracks, Wally Wolff, a recent Cornell architecture graduate, and I were assigned the job of laying asphalt tile in a small office space. As we worked we discussed airport planning, in a Building Types Study featured in my shared copy of the current month's Architectural Record. We found a way to be creative with the two colors of tile and make the completed pattern accentuate the elongated shape of the room. We painted, cleaned and laid tile with such finesse and speed that the First Sergeant, duly impressed, granted us a pass from 5 P.M. Friday until 6 AM Monday morning as a reward." The others had to report for a work detail Sunday afternoon. Wally drove me to New York, dropped me off at Sloan House, a midtown YMCA residential hotel, and spent the weekend with his family at his home somewhere in nearby New Jersey. On September 18 I wrote:

I attended a dance there Friday night, of the International Student Council. The borrowed church house used for the function was mobbed by a crowd of stimulating people. Plenty of beautiful girls of all colors, including American Negro girls, who were quite open and danced with white boys. It was refreshing to see this simple, friendly gathering. I met an Algerian and a girl from Jamaica (she was white and, I still swear, spoke in an almost Irish accent.) I remarked that the name of the song we were dancing to was "A String of Pearls," and she replied in a broad brogue, "What do you thaink I om, some kaind of a kook?"

The only sad note in the weekend was that, arriving back at the Y, I sleepily left my watch, a high school graduation gift, in the lavatory on my floor. When I awoke, remembering it at 8 AM, naturally, it was gone. It had not been turned in by Sunday when I left. I gave them my address, and Dad made me report it to the police for insurance purposes, despite the unlikely chance it would be recovered. On September 21, I reported: "I bought a Timex watch for $10.45 at the PX. It looks as nice as the one I lost and has a factory guarantee. It will do the job. I still regret losing my good one."

We got our assignments and schedules in hospital duty for our MOS (Military Occupational Specialty) in the role of Medical Corpsmen, and our OJT (on-the-job training) began. On Wednesday, November 15, I wrote home:

"If Yale develops the inner man, the Army must train the 'outer man,' because this has been one of the most cheerful, most outgoing periods of my life. The job calls for a joke a minute, with patients, nurses and my fellow soldiers. We get seriously ill patients on my floor. Some of them die, but it is a real inspiration to nurse the others back to health and see them recover.

Needless to say, there is no shortage of real life and human drama." It went on:

> Social life has consisted of a few trips to New York, which have been exciting and fun, and a trip to Boston to see MIT …
>
> As for girlfriends, I know half of the WACs on the post but, aside from weekends with them in New York, which are expensive and difficult to arrange because of irregular work weeks, I haven't been able to think of any ways to date them. I suppose we could take a taxicab out to the hand grenade range and "neck until dead." The trouble lies mainly in the fact that I haven't met anyone I really wanted to take out.
>
> The WACs, most of whom served as nurses' aides in the hospital, were frustrated in their own way. One night when I was having "late chow" in the hospital cafeteria, which was the night shift's "lunch" period from 11:30 P.M. to midnight, I caught snatches of conversation between two young nurses at the other end of my table. "I'm depressed," said one. "I know," her companion replied. "You date some of these guys, and before you can get your hooks into them, they're transferred."

After my six months active duty in the Army Reserve, I returned to the Chicago area at the beginning of 1962. I called Stanley Tigerman, whom I had gotten to know during his whirlwind two-year stay at Yale: Already a licensed architect, he had convinced Rudolph to let him enroll for two years and graduated with both a bachelor's and a master's degree in architecture. With a referral from Stan, I got a job at Perkins &

Will, which ended in a mass layoff of personnel in April, and then obtained a drafting position at the historic firm of Holabird & Root, which I held for that summer until it was time to return to Yale.

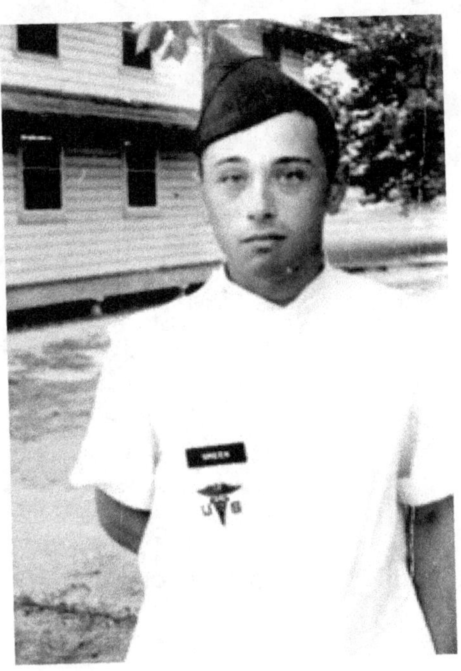

An Army Corpsman, 1965
Berle Engler Photo

Site model: Hotel project on an urban site

Vacation House on Long Island

12

PEDAGOGY IN PERIL

THE REQUIREMENTS FOR MY RETURN to Yale Architecture School were exhaustive. Claiming increased production requirements, the school required me to complete a design project to be readmitted to the school. I selected the urban design program from a recent Ruberoid competition. I prepared floor plans and elevations for a hotel sited in an urban plaza for the imaginary City of Riverton. I selected the design problem for its ability to show how the building would be sited in relation to the river, with interior room divider walls of the high-rise hotel angled toward the river for the best sun orientation and views. The main building slab was also positioned to enclose the end of a long plaza. A classical building, such as an existing city hall, fronted on the long side of the plaza. I wanted to demonstrate that I understood the importance of proper massing of new buildings in relation to existing open spaces.

The model I built to illustrate the urban design of the hotel used a skill I had acquired working with Lucio Savoia, full-time model builder at Holabird & Root, with whom I had worked for a couple of months. He and his father Attilio had first come to America to exhibit a 5' x 8' model of St. Peter's Square, including the Basilica and Bernini's arcade. They toured a chain of department stores in cities throughout America, a promotional campaign to generate shopper traffic.

A short, wiry man with large, dark eyes and unruly black curls, Lucio had an explosive personality, punctuating his expressions with broad gestures and loud exclamations, especially his passion for his native city: "If Rome were a woo-man," he exclaimed, "I would have married her!" The woman he actually did marry was Barbara, a cheerful, plump American, whom I met one Saturday when I did some contract work at their West Side apartment to help him finish a model he undertook as a freelancer. I tried to refuse payment, in appreciation of all he had taught me—Barbara had even served us a delicious lunch—but Lucio insisted.

My family enthusiastically watched the Riverton model grow in our basement. My sister Linda, who later pursued graphics and fine arts as a career, helped build and paint portions of the model. My mother even offered a tiny wristwatch to adorn the clock tower, until I discovered—as a result of Lucio's tutelage—that so much detail actually threw off the impression of scale we were trying to create in the abstract model's forms. I assured my sister in my next letter:

> Linda, the model looks great! Thank you so much for your help. Your packing was superb, family; and the model came through unscathed. I had no problems with baggage transfer.
>
> Tomorrow there will be a closed jury on the projects done over the summer. I rewrote the pro-gram to incorporate the stuff that I would have in-cluded in my talk. We aren't allowed to be present at the jury, so now I must put lots of lettering on my sheets to explain things.

Later in the week my project was accepted, and nothing impeded my re-entry into the school as part of the third-year class. Rudolph himself was to be our chief design critic. I had rented the second floor of a house near school, taken in two roommates to share our $120 per month rent and looked forward to a productive semester.

I also carried with me a note from my former employer, William Holabird, a grandson of the firm's co-founder in the 1880s. He had attended Yale and had asked me to look up the members of the Yale Corporation. When I reported back to him, he recognized couple of names and resolved to stop by Yale to visit Mr. Rudolph to see if his firm could obtain any of the college's architectural work. Mr. Holabird reported that Rudolph was very courteous to him when he stopped by.

I didn't know anything about Yale's selection process for their new buildings. But I recalled one Saturday morning in the spring of my sophomore year, when I watched from my Silliman college dormitory window as half a dozen assistants staggered into Woolsey Hall, where the Yale Corporation had its board room, bearing thick packets of 40" x 60" illustration boards. Several months later the architectural press reported that the office of Eero Saarinen had been awarded the commission to design two new residential colleges, eventually named Myers and Stiles, to be located at the northwest corner of the campus, across the road from Payne Whitney gymnasium.

Much had changed in my year's absence. While the site of the new art and architecture building designed by Paul Rudolph had been a mere excavation when I left in June 1961, the massive, brutalist structure had attained its full height, and one could make out a series of floating trays, suspended around a large interior volume. Ponderous corner towers in rusticated, finned concrete supported cantilevered floors. I could not imagine the result but was reassured by the fact that the building might not be ready before it was time for me to graduate and move on. However, the current Art Gallery was scheduled to house the Art and Architecture Schools for only one more year, so there was a chance I would finish my courses in the new building.

On my first Saturday back, I had been informed Rudolph

himself was conducting a hard-hat tour of the partially completed building. But I was on my way to a Saturday class in planning law. I looked forward to this class, because I knew architects often came up against planning and zoning boards in order to get local government approval for their projects.

As I walked toward the planning class, I passed the corner where the Art gallery faced the new Art and Architecture construction site, where I encountered a group of my classmates and the architect himself, gathering for the tour.

"You're just in time," Mr. Rudolph said. "I'm about to start the tour."

"Oh, I'm sorry," I said, "it's time for my planning law class."

The seminar was offered in the recently reborn Planning Department of the university. It was taught by Charles M. Haar, noted urban planning lawyer and author of our definitive text, *Land-Use Law*. He was joined by lawyers specializing in planning and zoning cases, Harry Wexler and David Craig. This was my initial class meeting. and it was not to be missed.

"You'd better go," Rudolph said, "you'll probably need it." But he cringed as if personally affronted, disappointment filled his eyes and he turned abruptly and began organizing the rest of the students for the tour.

Damn, foiled again. Another school year seemed to be off to a rough start, because of circumstances beyond my control.

Our first design problem of the semester was a mid-rise building with shops at ground-level and offices above, which was to include its own parking garage. Apparently we had been assigned this project because of its important location at the southwest corner of Chapel and York streets, directly across the street from the new A & A building, as it was to be known. Rudolph habitually picked his students' brains for design ideas on his own commissions. In this case, he probably wanted to explore what type of building design would best offset his signature art and architecture building. I felt this should be a modest, quiet design, what urban designers call a background building, as the most appropriate setting for the A & A building opposite.

My building fronts would hug the skewed property lines on both streets. Because two floors were devoted to auto parking and circulation, I designed their meeting as a rounded corner. The exterior appearance of the building was regular and somewhat ordinary, a plain building to form a neutral background for the sculptural tour-de-force of the A & A building. At the jury, which Rudolph chaired, he listened impatiently to my presentation and then said, "Pattern making, like the others. Next project." He stood abruptly and led the jury to the next display.

I was as concerned about architectural beauty as any architect. In this case I was designing a setting for what we supposed would be his masterpiece. My friend Mike, who knows me pretty well, observes: "your true feelings may be more ambivalent than a simple transition from 'pure' design (giver of forms) to practical buildings. As I saw when you explained the wonders of the Pantheon, you had developed a strong love of great architecture before you ran into that buzz saw, Paul Rudolph, in graduate school. I suspect that your career became a marriage of the aesthetic and the practical, rather than a transition to the latter. Second, I think I saw that part of your problem was dealing with snobbery and bullies, rather than a change of career path." Mike had found the same issue at Harvard. He even went so far as to suggest, "You began to understand that he was a bully who covered up his inadequacies by criticizing others."

Again, it came down to bullies. I hadn't let them stop me in grade school, I learned not to join them, and now I had to resist or avoid another one.

Rudolph developed a reputation for this kind of behavior. An alumnus of the Harvard Graduate School of Design, he invited many of his former classmates to serve on juries and teach: John M Johansson, Ulrich Franzen, Edward Larrabee Barnes and Henry (Harry) Cobb. He prided himself on his ability to attract diverse points of view to broaden students' concept of architecture. On juries in particular he would then challenge these colleagues openly, in front of each other and students alike. This was baffling to some, especially his students, who had not expected the chairman to take his job of exposing them to various points of view so literally and so far:

> Stanley Tigerman believes that Rudolph, as a young architect whose career had shot upward like a media arc, was inherently insecure and needed to surround himself with a wide array of rivals, whom he would seek to best at juries. Guests who didn't share Rudolph's beliefs "were often the recipients of cutting commentary. He wasn't bashful about sharing his belief systems within earshot of anyone and arguing vociferously on behalf of his position.[13]

Learning later, from Stern and Stamp's book, what other architects thought about his method and what went on behind the scenes to set the stage for the students' experience was most revealing:

> Rudolph made it a point to participate in design juries at all levels. As a result, he had a strong impact on all the students in the program, turning what had been a relatively low key, gentlemanly preserve into an intense, competitive blood sport.[14]

This treatment was evident in many of the juries I sat through, including my own. Phyllis B. Lambert, who was in my studio art classes at Yale, agreed. When I saw her more recently as a visiting architect and lecturer at Washington University's architecture school, she told me this was the reason she left Yale. She is quoted as saying that an unnamed Japanese student there, whom I also knew, interested in engineering, was not a very good designer in the sense Yale accepted and was misunderstood and treated unfairly. He had also complained bitterly to me about how he got blasted in juries, suspecting racial prejudice. Phyllis summed it up this way:

> And Paul Rudolph…I had a drawing I was very proud of. It was a perspective section through a house, and I had every story in place, all the sections through the house that you had to have. Lots of poché [diagonal line shading], lots of hours. And Rudolph just came over and said, "Where is your vapor barrier?" It seemed to me to be a school that had nothing to do with educating people, just with putting people down. Anyway, I wasn't learning what I wanted to learn. And there was all this posturing. For example: should there be a campanile at the end of a campus or not? I thought issues like this could be interesting, but I would've preferred to know how to make a campus from scratch. So I went to IIT. [15]

In the first-year architecture studio, Mr. Hansen once pointed out that my attempted design was much too complicated for my current ability level. He said, "You're on the ocean in a rowboat. You can tackle that after your skills develop a little further." What had happened to that attitude? Rudolph might have as well have knocked down children learning to walk with a full body slam. It seemed to me his purpose had gone far beyond the original intent to educate and expose students to various points of view. He seemed to need to show everyone within earshot, including the celebrity guest critics he had invited, that he was the smartest. best architect in the room.

Further, I reflected on Charlie Brewer's attitude about how I should handle my re-entry project for the civic plaza. They weren't much interested in my urban design ideas. In a letter replying to my proposal, he said "You should make sure to focus on the hotel." Where was Yale's concern with the urban issues that were impinging on us from all sides?

In my year's absence, students who had been in the first-year architecture class had finished second year, so I joined the students who remained in that class when I returned. Among them was Lucinda (Cindy) Cisler, one of several women admitted in the fall of 1960. She was from Louisville, and with her warm Midwestern ways, was a confidant to many in our class, me included. She kept me in touch with social doings and other background information. Her father, had been Dad's boss in his military assignment at WXLI – Guam. Dad had succeeded him as *de facto* radio station manager at the end of the war. Cindy was interested in planning and had read widely on the subject, including Yale's formerly prominent curriculum in urban affairs.

Other members in this class I got to know included Jonathan Barnett, whose strong interest in urban planning and design led him to a teaching post at City University of New York. Then he joined Mayor John Lindsay's newly created New York City Urban Design group. Led by Yale grad Jaquelin Robertson, it included Myles Weintraub, Lucinda Cisler, Jonathan Barnett and several other architects with urban interests who graduated from Yale's program. We used to kid another classmate, Robert A. M. Stern, who was always very talkative and socially aware, when he agonized over not receiving invitations to Rudolph's cocktail parties. It turned out social awareness was part of what it takes to engage with architectural clients. It led to his very successful career.

But my frustration with the shortcomings of Yale's program was building, along with my anger at Rudolph and his sycophants on the faculty. Perhaps my failure was manageable, and I could recover. But I felt for others, such as my Japanese fellow student and another classmate who, through no fault of their own, they didn't measure up to Rudolph's ideal.

A married student older than the rest of us, whom I'll call

Dan, had interrupted his work career to learn the craft of architecture. He had regular habits: he arrived daily in a business suit, white shirt and tie, hung his suit jacket on a chair and sat right down to work. Tall, with curly black hair, he wore rimless glasses with metal ear-pieces.

His building designs were practical, of a type that would get him though an architectural registration exam. Although Dan would never be what the master considered a "giver of form," there was no reason he couldn't learn the craft and be a provider of bread. Nonetheless, juries picked on him, and his projects seldom earned grades better than Fail. This was clearly not right, and it spurred my eagerness to escape this poisoned atmosphere for the pure air and clear skies of my own Midwest. Moreover, after a year of discouragement, Dan fell ill with a lung ailment, and even his former livelihood was in jeopardy.

Months later, when I was safely enrolled in Washington University's architecture program, I took the time to write to Kingman Brewster Jr, the new president of Yale, who had assumed the post in October 1963, several months after the death of A. Whitney Griswold. I expressed my discontent with the architecture school's treatment of Dan, who was admitted to the school and then just led on and on, and arbitrarily was failed, with very little to show for the time and money he spent on his professional advancement. From my safe distance, I also included a few choice words about what I felt was Rudolph's authoritarian regime. I received a response from one of the president's assistants, who criticized my "intemperate outburst" and confronted me with a statement from a farewell letter I had written to Rudolph, covering my reason for leaving and praising the school, "especially your teaching."

The president's aide implied hypocrisy. Because of the disparity in power between Rudolph and me, I had considered it life insurance.

But I had hit a nerve. The president's underling denied that the school had just led Dan on and on and informed me Dan had received aid from a special state fund. My student voice—

from a dissatisfied paying customer—joined a chorus of other campus protests. These were common in the early 1960s, not only from students angry with U. S. policy, but likely also from faculty, alumni and financial backers of the university. But I wasn't interested in the palace intrigue at the highest levels of University administration. I had suffered enough from it at the student level amid the strange goings-on in Rudolph's little fiefdom. When later at home, I reported my correspondence with Yale's president and the response, Mom said, "It's good to stick up for your friends."

During my year's absence from Yale, I had researched other architecture schools. While still in the Army, I had visited Boston to see Aunt Helen and Uncle Joseph's family and the MIT campus. I had an informal interview with Gyorgy Kepeş (Kep'-esh), considered one of the best architecture professors at the school. He was very open and pleasant, but it appeared that in transferring to MIT I would have to take more courses and lengthen my graduate school time. In my file I found a list of schools I had considered, including University of Pennsylvania, Illinois and others. I concluded at that time that a return to Yale would probably be the wisest choice.

In December 1962, however, after one semester back at Yale, I called on my former employer John Holabird (one of the founder William's grandsons and cousin to then company member, the younger William) and expressed my discontent with Yale's program. He sympathized and told me he had devoted considerable time and effort both as a visiting critic and to find and employ promising graduates at Washington University in St. Louis. He suggested I contact the head of the school, architect and engineer Joseph Passonneau. Just before their Christmas vacation began that year, I visited the St. Louis campus.

Arriving at Dean Passonneau's office, I was told I would find him in a computer class in a nearby building and to call him out of the class. I appeared at the door of the classroom, peeked in, and a tall, athletic man with thinning reddish-brown hair disentangled himself from a tablet-arm chair and greeted me at the door. He peeled off an old purple sweater and threw it on the floor next to the hallway door. "It's hot in here," he said. "Let's go someplace we can talk." We found an empty classroom and took adjacent student seats to hold our interview. I liked him immediately.

I explained my desire to leave Yale, mentioned my credentials, including my first Yale degree. I said John Holabird had recommended the school as open, spirited and good preparation for architects and was very positive about Passonneau's approach to architectural education.

The dean said, "You certainly can come here, but Yale is a very good school. Also, I may be leaving for the Harvard School of Design by the time you get here."

I replied that despite this I was ready to be back in the Midwest and thought the program he had built at Washington University would be better. I also felt, though I didn't express it, I deserved some time to get a feeling for student life on a coeducational campus. I made my decision to finish up the first semester of third year and transfer immediately to Washington University.

My impression of Dean Passonneau, who ultimately did not leave to head the Harvard School of Design, clinched my decision. At the time I knew little about his background, but it was impressive. Suffice it to say, after graduation from Harvard School of Design in 1949, Passonneau worked as a designer for Holabird & Root in Chicago, where his projects included work with John Holabird on a summer auditorium for the Chicago Symphony Orchestra.

I only recently learned about Passonneau's Ravinia work while researching for this book. I have a family story about that project. After a preseason winter fire destroyed the wooden concert pavilion at the CSO's historic Ravinia Festival (founded in 1904) in Highland Park, my grandfather F. J. Herlihy was called into an emergency meeting, where the president of the orchestra, Mayor Richard J. Daly, Architect William Holabird and other top city officials were waiting for him. The mayor spoke first: "Frank, we need a big favor!" They asked him to build the new concert pavilion, restore the ruined grounds and complete the work by its June opening day. Grandpa accepted the challenge, met the deadline and devoted infinite care to restoration of the 36-acre park to its former glory, including the detail of installing blooming plants by the walkways to the new pavilion in time for the first concert.

The reason we were so privileged to have this talented architect-engineer as our dean at Washington University was that he and his wife Janet's third child, a son who was hearing impaired, needed the services of St. Louis Institute for the Deaf. "I was looking for a job," he once told me, "and so here I am."

I wonder if it was fate that brought us together.

Returning to Yale to finish the semester and arrange the move, I did my final design work there, a sketch problem for a vacation house on the south shore of Long Island. Our design critic for the project was architect Paul Mitarachi. He provided the gentle kind of coaching I needed to draw out my best efforts. The final drawings rolled easily off my pencil. At the jury, aside from a comment Ed DeCossy made that the building was a bit "heavy footed," the critics, including Paul Rudolph, thought the building would make a good vacation house.

That weekend I told one of my housemates, Bob, the medical school student, that I was having second thoughts about leaving.

"I did just fine on my sketch problem. Maybe I should stay at Yale and probably be out of there in another year."

"I can't believe you changed your mind just because you've had a good week.," Bob observed. "I thought you had deeper reasons for leaving the school."

"I'm a student in good standing. It has never occurred to the faculty that I was unhappy here—of course they never asked."

"I thought you hated Rudolph—you said he's a bad teacher, with a huge ego, and the students are all after fame, not interested in helping society create better housing and cities."

"Well, Rudolph has been patient with me at times. He's sat at my drawing board and explained things to me. He's shy, but personable when you get to know him."

"You're so wishy-washy, going back on your resolve just because he said something nice to you. I feel sorry for you."

Similarly, I found a contemporaneous note in my Yale Architecture file to myself, describing my dilemma. I often wrote things down when faced with a big decision:

At Yale Architecture School, one has two choices:

1) Agree with Rudolph and have Mitarachi say, "You have no principles," or

2) Disagree, and have Rudolph say, "You know, the trouble with you is, you get a bee in your bonnet and argue in favor of it at all costs. You think it's right just because *you* did it!"

His comment stung, as intended, but to me, Rudolph was the bee. I was so sensitive to it, I feared I would go into some kind of anaphylactic shock. Would I let him sting me to death? In this contest of wills, I made up my mind to defy this man one way or another. Instead of finding it a pull, like my friend Stanley Tigerman, who became more determined than ever to redo finished work if he had to and persevere until graduation, I took his abuse as a push. It propelled me to a more congenial school—where ideas counted as much as form-making, where urban issues mattered and where polite discourse, rather than blood sport, guided the course of study.

I did what I had to do to convince Dad the change was wise. In fact, when considering breaking ties with Mother Yale, after five-and-a half years in New Haven, I pointed out to him that I had asked our trusted family friend Art Cahill whether it made sense to change schools. He replied, "You have what you need — your Yale degree. Now you can go anywhere in the world." With this assurance from one of the best business leaders the family knew, I felt confident I could move on, and it helped Dad accept my plan.

Despite Bob's and Professor Mitarachi's conclusions, my principles came back to reassert themselves. Even with these last-minute misgivings, and the feeling that I probably could succeed in finishing my degree at Yale, I concluded my instinct about Rudolph was right—and he was a bad egg, as far as my future was concerned.

I took my stand against Rudolph and his school. I sent in my resignation letter, paid my housing and tuition deposits at Washington University and packed my bags.

My instinct was soon to be proven correct—for me. Many True Believers stayed, and some became famous, leading architects. They persevered, no matter how many times the jury system and Rudolph pushed them around and knocked them down. Some, like Stanley Tigerman, were stronger for it. When Rudolph ambushed him the day before his thesis drawings were completed, he got right up and tried again. But others, including me, left and took another route to achieve their goals.

Rudolph's Art and Architecture building was dedicated and occupied in Fall, 1963. If I had stayed, I would have begun my fourth year, including my thesis project, in the new building. The gory details of the building's history are beyond the scope of my story, but they are well told in Stern and Stamp's *Pedagogy* and the press. Neither before its completion, when I missed Rudolph's personal tour, nor since, when I visited New Haven for class reunions, have I been able to visit the interior of the building, due to its being closed when I was in town.

Reactions to the building by others were mixed. Some loved its monumental presence, a sculptural tour-de-force. Others said, with multiple levels comprising its seven-story height, its faulty air conditioning system and its daily load of crumpled tracing paper covering the floors, it was nearly impossible to maintain. I report some of these comments below. I had not seen enough of it either before or after its completion to have an opinion. In retrospect, I'm glad I missed out on that period.

Rudolph announced he would leave Yale at the end of the

1965 school year, due to "competing demands" of his architectural practice. The new Yale president, Kingman Brewster, appointed Charles W. Moore, a prominent California architect and educator, to head the school. In a sarcastic mood, Moore later put it, "Kingman was not a patron of the arts or architects. …He is not the sort who tolerates artistic nonsense, so that the 'Rudolph hysteria' was anathema to him, especially when he was making these little numbers on campus that couldn't be swept or washed. It made him angry."[16]

The unkindest cut of all was the 1969 fire, in which the new A & A building was gutted. It occurred at the height of student protest and campus uprisings over the Vietnam war. Its source was of suspicious origin, and New Haven's Fire Marshal and Fire Chief never came to an agreement as to whether its cause was accidental or intentional.

Looking back, I realized, without my transfer to Washington University I might never have learned about some key basics of architecture. housing or city planning. Nor would I have met some of the finest architectural, urban design and planning educators of the day: Joseph Passonneau, Roger Montgomery, William Roberts, George Anselevicius, Shadrach Woods, and others. Nor would I have made lifelong friends Tony Layton, Cynthia Rogers Weese and Ben Weese, and other classmates. Martin Filler, a frequent contributor and architectural commentator, in an early 2015 issue of The New York Review of Books, wrote a penetrating review, "The Hard Case of Paul Rudolph," in which he discussed the architect's career in detail:

> Ironically enough, the project that halted Rudolph's rapid career ascent was the Yale Art and Architecture Building of 1958-1963, a commission he received soon after arriving in New Haven. This was the latest in university president A. Whitney Griswold's admirable program to bring the best of contemporary

architecture to the campus, which includes works by Kahn, Saarinen, Johnson and Gordon Bunshaft. As a series of Rudolph's preparatory renderings show, he gradually inflated the A & A Building (as it was known) from a relatively modest colonnaded structure in his initial version into the brutalist behemoth that was erected—a nearly cubic core surrounded by a phalanx of windowless towers as forbidding as those of a medieval castle.

The building's functional flaws soon became inescapable—thirty-seven different levels were crammed into its seven stories—and as the social upheavals of the 1960s unfolded, the heroic ethos Rudolph tried to evoke came across as authoritarian posturing. His successor as dean, scholarly postmodernist Charles Moore, held a view of architecture diametrically opposed to Mr. Rudolph's, with far greater respect for historical and vernacular traditions. As Moore slyly proclaimed, "I disapprove of the Art and Architecture Building wholeheartedly because it is such a personal manifestation for non personal use. However, I enjoy very much being in it."[17]

On the personal side, after Yale Rudolph established an office in New York and custom-designed a place to live. Filler's article continues:

Although the critic Michael Sorkin praised Rudolph's own Manhattan penthouse of 1977 as "one of the most amazing pieces of modern urban domestic architecture produced in this country," I had quite a different experience when the owner invited me and my wife to dinner there in 1986, after a gallery opening of his drawings…Throughout the multistory apartment …surface finishes and details were astonishingly shoddy. For example, railings that in photographs seemed to be made of polished chrome were actually covered in peeling Mylar. Floor levels shifted up or down every few feet for no apparent reason, and narrow Plexiglas catwalks spanned chasms open to the stories below. There was so little continuous floor space amid the cavernous volumes that guests huddled on small, carpeted platforms like Little Eva on the ice floes.

Odd sources of dim illumination — underneath stair treads and behind floating wall panels — made navigation treacherous, especially for such older luminaries as the designer Ray Eames and the architectural historian Vincent Scully. There was much stumbling and tripping as we tried to negotiate the labyrinthine circulation paths to and from the food and drinks, and even when we were seated mishaps continued. A large modular coffee table appeared to be composed of alternating cubes of reflective and matte black Lucite. But when someone set a drink down on one of the matte squares, it turned out to be a void and the glass crashed to the floor below...

As we bid good night to our host, Scully spoke for several of us when he said, "Thanks Paul, it's been a terrifying evening." [17]

Paul Rudolph died in 1997 at age 78. He was remembered by many as one of the most prominent architects of the post-World War II era. Others knew him as an irresistible force of nature. His influence remains a matter of personal opinion. Time and change will determine his place in the architectural firmament.

Paul Rudolph and his A & A Building, 1965
Publicity photo, Bing.com

Joseph R. Passonneau, Jr.
Dean, WU Architecture School

Lion House for the St. Louis Zoo—Site Model

13

BACK IN MY OWN MIDWEST

IN EARLY FEBRUARY 1963, I arrived on Washington University's St. Louis campus, checked into a single room in a suite on the first floor of a modern four-story dorm designed by architectural faculty and unpacked. As suite mates straggled in, I met Kim, a Taiwanese grad student, who received monthly packages of dried seaweed for his snacks, and Ahmet, a student from Kuwait, who had just taken delivery of his own bright red Chevy, a convertible with tailfins. My fifth-year architectural class (in a six-year program) had only a dozen students, mostly recipients of Washington University's undergraduate degree, including one woman, Cynthia Rogers. Foreign students who joined the graduate program included Julius Juracsik, who had escaped from Hungary just before the 1956 revolution, and two Chinese students from Hong Kong, Pete Chen and Jim Pai.

Our design critic, George Anselevicius, introduced the first project, a housing development of 250 units, which could be all high-rise or a combination of high- and low-rise buildings, occupying an entire block along Lindell Boulevard in St. Louis's Central West End. He took us out to the site, an urban residential setting, alerted us to "the changing face of Lindell," and stipulated that we design a solution compatible with its surroundings. In one of his early lectures, he illustrated the various types of floor plans typically used in high-rise buildings: rectangular, with apartments on both sides of a corridor; square towers, with several units grouped around a central core, and other variations. Some of us designed grouped high-rise towers, others a single high-rise slab and still others, including me, a hybrid approach, with a high-rise along Lindell combined with low-rise townhouses along West Pine, the back street facing other two- and three-story buildings. This, my first assignment at Washington University, convinced me I had made the right choice of schools. Instead of designing pavilions for the rich and monumental structures, we were solving pressing contemporary issues, such as improving the housing stock and relating to the existing context of the city.

As at Yale, we also had a fascinating parade of visiting critics. I had just missed Aldo Van Eyck, influential European architect of the Team 10 group, and Fumihiko Maki, leading architect from Japan, who had each visited the campus in the past couple of years. In addition to his St. Louis teaching duties, Maki was tapped to design a library and art gallery to connect and bridge between the architecture and art buildings.

Other faculty included William Roberts, landscape architect of the firm of Wallace, McHarg, Roberts and Todd, who taught our landscape course. His partner Ian McHarg also visited as a lecturer. Despite a thick Scottish brogue that only his countrymen could penetrate, his plentiful slides illustrating his overlay method of evaluating potential new-town sites made up for his unintelligible commentary.

Later in that semester we designed a lion house for the St. Louis zoo, assigned by guest critic Marlon Perkins, known to the public of our era from his widely viewed television series, Zoo Parade. He conducted tours of the wild animal facilities at his Forest Park zoo and coached us on the requirements for the care and feeding—very carefully, mind you—of lions and Siberian tigers. He also attended our jury and evaluated our designs.

Once again, I felt I had come to the right place, when my design solutions were rigorously examined by these knowledgeable critics. Perkins noted I had followed his recommendations for care of the animals and also liked the way it fit naturally into the carefully planned landscape of the zoo. Architect Constantine (Dinos) Michaelides, who would later succeed Passonneau as Dean, taught there as well. He filled a conference room with text and photographs of Mykonos, Greece, for his book, *The Aegean Crucible*, on vernacular architecture in the Post-Byzantine era.

As important as the improved curriculum was for me, back in the Midwest I began to enjoy life on a coeducational campus. I lived in the student dorms, ate at the undergraduate dining hall, and began to make friends in a way that seldom happened in the highly competitive graduate school atmosphere at Yale. The transfer took root, and my hopes for normal campus relationships, so strained and artificial on the East Coast, were fulfilled.

Dad used to say that friends you make in school, especially college, are the ones you keep for life. He had had a puppy-dog loyalty to them. He often declared, "My friends can do no wrong." He made it his habit to rekindle his friendships by staying in touch, planning parties and ways to see them and corresponding with them throughout his life.

Among friends I made there were Professor Bill Weismantel, whose progress I followed to employment after graduation. He offered me opportunities to prepare two riverfront plans for downtown St. Louis, one during the summer of 1963 and the second occurring a year after I had left to work in Chicago. After that stage, I stayed in touch as he became a professor at the University of New Mexico for a few more years.[18]

Seated near me in the Washington University drafting room was Cynthia Rogers, the second "Architectural Cindy" I knew in school. Tall, articulate and smart, she had attracted outside attention. One Friday afternoon, I encountered architect Ben

Weese, who had previously lectured at the school and served as visiting critic to our class, alighting from a taxicab in front of the school. I greeted him: "Hi, Professor Weese. You may be interested in seeing the new exhibit of student work in our conference room." He turned his head toward the door of the school. "Yeah, yeah, yeah—where's Cindy?" This was the first I knew of their "thing," which blossomed into romance and marriage. From this union, she launched her notable architectural career: member of the Harry Weese Chicago firm, Dean of Washington University School of Architecture and principal of their own firm, Weese, Hickey, Weese. Over the succeeding years. I visited their Chicago apartment and saw them in St. Louis several times.

Anthony Emmet "Tony" Layton had as long a memory and as strong a loyalty to his friends as Dad. I got a glimpse of his character at a presentation in our Urban Design class with Professor William Weismantel. Although we were about the same age, Tony was much further along in life than I. Already a military veteran, he was married and had family responsibilities. Soon after the semester started, his wife Tina was hospitalized with cancer.

We had each been assigned a selected city to characterize as to its unique lifestyle, culture and other factors affecting its physical design. This morning it was Tony's turn to present on Charleston, South Carolina. Tony was ten minutes late. He had told me Tina was recovering from surgery and he would have to rush off to the hospital after class. I really had not expected to see him that day.

Then Tony dashed in and took over. "Here, grab one end of this," he instructed me. I latched onto one handle of an ice chest and helped him drag it into the classroom. He brought in a box containing plastic cups, a thermos jug and paper napkins. He produced a cloth and spread it on our seminar table. He unpacked a tape player and turned it on. It played "Dixie."

Filling cups with ice, he poured us each a drink of a brown liquid and garnished it with a sprig of mint. Though surprised at a classroom redolent of bourbon at ten in the morning, my classmates and I didn't find it disagreeable. We all began to relax. A couple of the pleasure-loving wags in our class said, "All right!" and raised their glasses to Tony.

At this moment, our tall, bald planning professor, Bill Weismantel, wearing his typical inquiring and quizzical expression, ambled into the room. He took in the scene, mouthed the word, "Aha!" and nodded his approval. Unflappable, we knew he was open to just about anything—but this? He nonetheless accepted the drink Tony proffered. "Oh, that's right," he noted amiably, "if it's Tuesday, this must be Charleston." He folded his gangling limbs into a wooden desk chair and listened, content that his students were getting into the spirit of the course.

We sipped our mint juleps and awaited what promised to be good entertainment. Tony launched into a slide-and-music-illustrated description of the southern way of life that had produced the classical architecture and aristocratic charm for which Charleston is known. With the odds against him that day, by sheer force of personality and good humor, Tony had overcome his fears, raised everyone's spirits and beguiled the group, mostly Yankees, with the beauty, glamour and charm of a lifestyle they had long been conditioned to scorn.

My takeaway from that day was that Tony, despite his widely different cultural roots, was a solid citizen and a salt-of-the-earth guy, with a deep well of human compassion. Helped by his encouragement and good cheer, Tina recovered, her cancer went into remission and they enjoyed several more years of happy life together.

In his elective course in sculpture, Tony constructed an an assemblage by piercing a hole through the center of a stack of precut finished lumber at the campus boiler plant, where he heated an iron rod red hot, drove it though and then left the rod in as an axle. The final piece, seven feet tall, resembled a vertical cannon sitting on wheels with 2" x 4" spokes but no rims.

That afternoon, Tony set the finished piece on the walk

leading to our building from the street. After watching Tony apply the finishing touches, I had begun my evening's work when Tony came rushing in. "Oh my god, help. They're going to burn it up!"

We burst outside though the doors to find that the installation had attracted a crowd of sixth-year male students. Sick of Tony's braggadocio, they had plotted retaliation for his sin of pride.

"Looks like a dying swan," one said.

"Finish it off!" said another.

One of them held a can of kerosene. Egged on by the others, he sprinkled it liberally on the wooden creation. Two more students headed for the sculpture with flaming torches.

I stood between them and Tony's construction. "That's enough, you guys."

They stopped, confused.

"This is why you're here—to learn how to experiment with design," I said. "You ought to be ashamed of yourselves!"

One of my fifth-year classmates, who had more sense than the members of the older class, joined me. "Wake up, you tools. What were you thinking? You should be tackling big projects, like Tony's."

The attackers lowered their fizzling firebrands to the sidewalk. My fellow defender led the rest of the assembled mob back to their cars. Tony, who had been standing helpless to one side, joined me as we re-entered the building and climbed back to our work upstairs. Until then, my knowledge of mob psychology had been confined to grade school bullies and reading and writing about such activity. Finally, I took my stand on the right side of that issue.

In the second semester of that year, our design critic was architect and urban planner, Shadrach Woods, a member of the European and North African urbanist group, Team 10. Our ambitious semester project, he explained in a matter-of-fact, low-key manner, would be to design a new town for a site on the outskirts of the St. Louis area in the foothills of Missouri's

Ozarks. This realistic student assignment was based on the announced plans, created by Dr. Edward Ullman and developed by the U. S. Army Corps of Engineers, to build a new manmade lake at the town of Byrnes Mill by damming the Big River. The assignment assumed the National Aeronautics and Space Administration planned to create a research-oriented industry as the principal economic driver for the new town and that a contract for such an industry at the site would provide employment for 5,000 people. The new community would accommodate around 60,000 inhabitants during its first stage, expanding to 100,000 by the end of its second phase.

We piled into students' cars and Woods's rental for a trip to the site. The new town would be built at a proposed man-made lake set in the Ozark hills west of St. Louis.

Our charge was to self-divide the class of a dozen students into two teams, one to tackle a high-density town and the other to undertake planning a more spread-out community. Our team immediately undertook the daunting task of creating a contour model for some thousand acres of Ozark terrain where the lake would be created. After a week of endless discussion, argument over the techniques to be used, the assignment of tasks and the methods of fabrication to create nothing more than a three-dimensional version of the existing landscape, Tony and I quit this cumbersome group.

Confident we could make whatever model and drawings we needed ourselves, we set to work on the real problem: planning and design of the town. Instead of one large town to occupy either a hilltop site or to grow up the hillside from a shoreline of the lake, we decided to create three different districts with sub centers: one on a hilltop, one in a valley at the shoreline and others on a hillside. We proposed that this arrangement would set up a development race to see which of the three styles of living would fill up more quickly. We created a distinct anchor in each of the three districts: a commercial shopping center, a dense institutional-educational town center and a lakeside marina setting with cabarets and entertainment, water access and views.

Our revolt turned out to be providential. We were able to develop our ideas directly and clearly. We employed a method of infrastructure creation we learned from planning concepts Woods had developed for the city of Bilbao, Spain. Instead of just building streets and sidewalks to be filled in later with buildings, we adopted Woods's idea of building this infrastructure on multiple levels, separating streets and service traffic from pedestrians with grade separations, much as my grandfather had built on Wacker Drive. This called for building a three-dimensional infrastructure grid of streets and concrete sidewalks containing all the utilities, a spatial chessboard of city blocks, subdivided into lots that could be purchased and built upon, with houses, stores or public buildings. The grid could be stretched to fit the ridges and valleys of the rugged terrain, expanded vertically or horizontally in any direction at a high density and serviced from beneath with roads and streets at ground level. These would be arranged on the terrain, as shown in the accompanying photo of our site model.

By breaking away from the larger teams, Tony and I had also gained the advantage of frequent personal consultation with Woods, one of the world's most advanced architect-urbanists, who had worked with Le Corbusier on the Unité d'Habitation in Marseille. We received his blessing for our plan. Moreover, he was a warm human being and a pleasure to chat with. He didn't understand why Americans couldn't think of society as a whole, providing for the weak as well as the powerful. He'd say, "I just don't get this attitude: 'Screw you, Jack, I've got mine!'"

Since we both had crystal-clear concepts of the design, Tony and I shared the conceptual duties equally, creating both the designs and text, and quickly divided up the production tasks. He took the lead on the presentation drawings and I took charge of the project approach narrative and contour model. We shared work on the final presentation. Even after we had completed our work, presented our results to a jury of our professors for the finished project and graduated, Tony continued working through the summer. As Tony's wife Tina was fond of saying, "This man is a drafting machine. You stick a sandwich in his mouth every four hours, and he just keeps on drawing."

Because he had applied for graduate school at MIT in architecture, structural engineering and other advanced subjects, he refined the graphics. Tina re-typed the text, and they packaged it all into a handsome presentation book. The completed brochure included a photo of the site model on the cover, illustrative sketches interspersed with the narrative text and full-page sketched illustrations and foldout maps.

We kept corresponding throughout the summer and fall. The final grades came, and Tony was crestfallen to receive a B on the semester project to my A. We both wrote to Professor Woods to protest that we were equal partners in the effort. In his reply to me, he said, "The grades are comparative. If I changed anyone's B to an A, I would have to raise an A to a Super A. Tony doesn't have to worry about his future." We found out what he meant by this comment a couple of years later when Tony wrote me from MIT Graduate School of Design, "Big News: I finally got a chance to look at the letter Woods wrote to MIT & IT IS GLOWING. He called me a very talented student who uses his ability well and works hard …WONDER OF WONDERS."

In the spring of 1964, the dozen of us in our Washington University architectural class were engrossed in thesis projects and looking ahead to graduation. Despite our deeply felt loss of President Kennedy the previous fall, we learned that his Peace Corps was seeking architects to design and build housing in Tunisia. The language they spoke was French, and I was eager to travel some more before settling down to my working career. Along with half a dozen of my classmates, I applied. We filled out the forms and sent out requests for references and promptly dove into our thesis projects.

I chose a university theater, a project currently on the boards in the campus planning office, as my thesis project. Our thesis adviser was visiting critic Hans Hollein, a flamboyant

Austrian architect whose career and international reputation were on the rise. Having worked in high-school theater productions and two seasons of professional summer stock, I was quite familiar with requirements for audience circulation, seating, backstage operations, scenery handling, lighting and rehearsal space. I tackled each of these issues with great enthusiasm and generated dozens of rough sketches, some of them impressive interior drawings of the finished auditorium. Beyond that, we were expected to generate a number of details of how to support balconies, detailed floorplans of rehearsal spaces, building sections and exterior elevations.

I'm not sure how my rigid control of the schedule fell apart in that last semester. I know, after seven years of schooling, plus one in the Army and an architectural office, I was exhausted and burned out. Maybe, too, I was tired of being the perfect son, as Dad's hold on me diminished and I realized I had the power to steer my own career. But I didn't feel like starting it yet.

It was spring, and there were plenty of distractions on campus. Elections for student president were forthcoming, and one comedian in our architecture program decided to run a mythical candidate named Pum—in a campaign entitled, "Push Pum for President." His mythical name was inspired by our nickname for our instructor George Anselevicius, who was extremely knowledgeable in all aspects of architectural planning and design. But he had a curious speech tic, using the syllable "pum" to punctuate most sentences. Balding, short and chubby, he entered our drafting room each day with a new challenge. During our high-rise apartment building project, he burst into the room and exclaimed in his thick, Eastern European accent, "Vell boyss, how do you dr-r-r-ain your balconies, pum?" Although we were respectful to him in class, behind his back we called him Pum.

The election campaign generated plenty of hijinks, including a personal appearance of the fictional candidate Pum himself. Campus-wide posters reported he would arrive from out of town and mysteriously land in the middle of the campus intramural athletic fields at 2:00 p.m.

Sure enough, at about 2:15 a restless crowd of several hundred students spotted a speck in the western sky, and a helicopter hovered. The plotters of this scheme hastily cleared a circle in the center of the field of spectators so it could safely land. When it did, the door of the aircraft opened and Earl, a fifth-year student who vaguely resembled Pum in stature, waved to the crowd, mounted behind the driver of a waiting motorcycle and circled the athletic field, arriving at a stair to an accessible roof terrace of the modern library building. From there, he greeted the adoring crowd. When he raised his hands, they cheered; when he lowered them, a hush swept over the assembly. He gave a stirring speech, assuring them: if they would write in their vote for Pum, many student benefits would accrue. In the following week's election, Pum won in a landslide. The student council spent the rest of the semester trying to figure out how to install their new, but as yet unidentified, president.

Such distractions made for lots of fun and camaraderie, but they shattered my concentration, as well as that of several of my classmates, and our independent work on the thesis projects suffered. I had difficulty completing the numerous drawings required for a project so complex as a new theater. When it came time for the class banquet, a week before our presentation was due, I was so far behind, I felt I had to work that night. Despite protestations from my classmates that I ought to take the night off, I just sat there at my drafting board and stewed, trying in vain to catch up. When my name was called at the dinner to receive a book prize for the highest grades, I was not present to receive it. When the dean asked where I was, I later learned, one of my classmates said, "Oh, he's working, as usual," generating laughter at my expense.

In choosing to work the night of the banquet, I had recalled the dean's short temper about students' behavior, even in the design studio. Once, fed up with Tony's obsessively complete presentations, on this occasion almost too rich and detailed to present a simple design concept, he said, "Tony what you want to be—a renderer?" After I arrived and got into the swing of campus activity, I wrote an article about a campus event for the Student Life newspaper. When he saw me in class after it appeared, he said he said, "Peter, I thought you came here to learn more about architecture!" With my thesis project unfinished and unlikely to be, I was too embarrassed to appear in public.

Nonetheless I earned back the trust he had placed in me: In February 1964 he wrote me one of the many pep-talk letters he sent to his students: "Peter, It looks like you have had another excellent semester. Congratulations!" And on the Monday following the May banquet, he found me at my drafting board and presented me with the book prize, a copy of Henry Adams's *Mont-Saint-Michel and Chartres*, personally inscribed, "AIA Book Prize, 1964," with his signature.

At the final jury for our thesis projects, when my turn came up, I showed floor plans and most of the required drawings, in not very much detail, and I plopped down a model of the building on the master model university architects used to plan the campus.

The professors knew I had been working hard on the project all semester and were generally familiar with my progress. One asked, "Where are all your beautiful sketches of the theater interior?"

"Oh those," I said off-handedly. "They weren't complete, so I couldn't present them." Apparently the habits I developed under Rudolph's regime were still holding me back.

This professor none the less went to bat for me, and somehow convinced the others that I had thought through my design well, and if I had more time, this would have been a good, solid presentation.

The thesis project passed, and we marched in the procession. Somehow, after all my turmoil, the end seemed like an anticlimax. I had the degree, the professors were glad to see us go, and it was time to move on.

Anthony E. Layton

Shadrach Woods in Paris

Byrnes Mill New Town—Site Model
Washington Univ. Semester Project by Anthony Layton and Peter Green

14

A NEW TOWN ARCHITECT IN PARIS

SOME OF MY CLASSMATES also had the last laugh on the Peace Corps. After seven years in school, my usual determination and follow-through habits had lapsed. Something was in the air that spring. Anything but work seemed more important, and I had a couple of girlfriends to distract me. The Peace Corps had written to remind us that our letters of reference were missing, and we needed to urge those people we had listed as references to meet the deadline. Somehow, when I finally did, the date for the Tunisia assignment had passed. To my great disappointment, three of my classmates were selected to go, while my application was still pending, for assignment to another mission.

A month or so later, I was notified that I had been accepted to join the Chile project. I accepted, hopeful that it would lead to similar architectural work in Chile. I flew at government expense to San Diego, California and attended several weeks of Peace Corps training—classes in Spanish, cultural education about the people of the host country and an activity called community development. We were issued box cameras and made an attempt at a photo tour of our training site, the sterile San Diego State University campus, and were taught to develop our own black-and-white film—a skill I had already mastered. We learned food safety, public health basics and excellent Spanish classes with native speakers. They balked on defining our assignment, but we had many lectures on community development, which was vaguely defined as identifying leaders in the community, showing them how to do everyday tasks that would advance and modernize their lives and building trust with the local people. Despite many inquiries, I could not find out if any architecture would be involved until I was halfway through the course, when the answer appeared to be a definite "No."

Before joining the Peace Corps, I had sent out letters to architecture firms in France, whose names I had obtained with some personal research and the help of classmates at Washington University. Two-thirds of the way through the training course, I received a letter from one of these firms indicating they could probably use me if I would arrive promptly in September. This, and a recommendation, when in Paris, to visit the former employer of a friend-of-a-friend from my class in architecture school were enough incentive for me to plan a new trip to Europe. I promptly resigned from the Peace Corps; was regretfully driven to LAX airport for my return to Chicago by the director of the Chile program, and set out on my own.

When I arrived in Paris at the firm that had written me in late September, they informed me I was a couple of weeks too late: They had just hired someone to fill the position they had in mind. But when I called upon Jacques Binoux, former employer of Richard Rothman, my classmate Alan Appel's friend, Binoux was delighted to learn Richard was now working at Skidmore, Owings and Merrill, Chicago, and welcomed me. He explained that they were busy with a big charrette for a new town project and hired me immediately.

The project was a new housing community for the industrial town of Le Creusot, the historic coal, steel and armaments production center in east-central France, 40 miles southwest of Dijon. A new worker housing community was planned for development by CECA, the European Coal and Steel community.

I wrote home on Saturday, November 27th, informing Mom and Dad, "I've been meaning to write for a week now, but my thoughts have been long and my time short. I've been working for two weeks now. We're on charrette and I have been putting in 10- to 11-hour days…The office where I'm working is very small—only five junior architects (myself included), two partners, a spec writer and three secretaries—that's all it takes to do huge architecture and urban design projects. Both Binoux and Folliasson are robust, uninhibited and involved creative people. Binoux is a real linguist, and his French is like the best prose, with a large vocabulary and vivid expressions. He knows how to get the most out of his people, and the team spirit, mutual respect and contentment of those in the workforce is wonderful to observe. They are (cast of characters):

Rueg: thirty-five years old, Swiss, married,

Le Grou: twenty-five-year-old French boy, single—bright,

Madame CC: Marie Coucouron, thirty-two years old, married to Joseph, son born last December 25th, and

Beaudoin: twenty-six years old, French, married—witty cracks.

"The first three seem to know the most about architecture and are the ones holding down the fort.

"No English is spoken except 'O.K.' and the slang I'm teaching them. So far I've established my accuracy on detailed work, despite the inevitable fact that I have a poor sense of time and don't work notably fast. But I think I can hold the job in without any problem. And because I pick up language as a duck takes to water, there has been almost no problem with communication. We're doing presentation now, but when it comes time to design we will all be designing, myself included. The charrette was a perfect introduction to the office, for camaraderie, for a kind of work I've done often before, and for getting to know the people."

We were nearly finished with our presentation and a large model of the entire site. I was assigned to complete the main site plan, with numerous roads, buildings and walls all assembled on a sheet that must have measured four by six feet. Faced with an enormous job of tracing and inking numerous curved and straight lines on the immense drawing, I hardly noticed as people put on their coats and left for the day. Shifting to my full charrette mode, I listened to the ORTF concert on the radio and kept drawing. At about 10:00 p.m. I was hungry. I couldn't leave for food and return, because Binoux had said as he left, "Just close the door firmly as you leave and it will lock automatically." I raided a conference room cabinet on the ground floor and found a box of crackers, which I appropriated and nibbled on until the wee hours of the morning. I drew and drew. When the first light of dawn appeared in the studio windows, I finished the last corner of the drawing. At 7:30 a.m. Binoux arrived, surprised to find me still at my desk. The others trickled in. He examined the drawing. "La charrette est finis!" he declared. He asked whether I wanted to go home and sleep. I wasn't tired and had one other task to finish. At 9:30 I lost my concentration and gave up. I had done my part.

I spent the winter at Hotel California, 32, rue des Écoles, and reported that it wasn't cheap but half a block from the Sorbonne in the center of the Latin Quarter, and it took only one quarter of my salary, petit dejeuner included.

We ate lunch every day at the corner café, La Bretonne.

"Now, since you know France," I continued, "you must also know that cafés are for drinking, not for eating. And that's the first thing Mme. Yvonne told me: 'I don't run a restaurant, you know, but I feed these people that come in every day.' You get a marvelous lunch of meat, salad, wine, bread and cheese, or hard-boiled eggs, wine, bread and cheese and coffee, for three francs (sixty cents). But you never know when you'll get it. Albeit her six-year-old daughter straggles in from school and helps serve up a plate of bread or a salad now and then, Madame Yvonne usually ends up serving 14 to 16 lunch customers, plus another 8 to 10 at the bar, all by herself. And she talks a great meal… Although she assures you in flowery French that, 'All you need to do is ask and you shall have the meal you desire,' and that she's bringing your bread (without which you can't eat the cheese) or drink your wine (which you need to eat the bread) '*toute de suite*' (right away), it's usually '*toute à l'heure*' (later) when you get it.

"Owing to the common plight of the 16-odd diners, it is very easy to make friends during the lunch hour at this quaint café. It happens that this worker's suburb (Boulogne) is also a hotbed of urban design, and it is the very spot where the journals *Aujourd'hui* and *L'Architecture d'Aujourd'hui* are created. Thus I have met the people who write them—one of them a very intelligent, bubbly and cute French girl, Francoise— shows up every day on the arm of the publisher of the magazines, Mme. Renee Diamant-Berger, nicknamed by Binoux as *la môme* (the brat, or urchin) *de Boulogne* or *la môme de B—* (to make it sound mysterious, as in Balzac)—a reserved, stout matron of about 50.

"So, my lunchtime is filled not only by Madame Yvonne, who is a young looking thirty-eight and chubby, spirited and full of wisecracks—a phenomenon in herself—but also by the local color of the workers from the neighborhood (auto mechanics and construction workers as well—signs of the times in France) and two or three French mademoiselles that go there often. The mutual suffering of trying to get lunch has brought us together and gotten over the sticky problem of how to be properly introduced to a French girl. Even so, Mme. Yvonne, revealing another of her many facets, steps into the breach (when she gets a minute) and even provides introductions when she sees someone she thinks I ought to meet. A truly remarkable woman."

I worked through the holiday season in the damp, chilly Parisian winter.

One day, without previous warning, Binoux tasked Beaudoin and me to carry the large model of the new town, which featured wood blocks for houses, fourplex apartment buildings and schools, tiny lollipop forms for street trees and parks, and cutout cardboard for roads. Embarrassed because he had not worn a suit jacket or tie, Beaudoin wore his topcoat to the meeting. We loaded the model, which broke into a half-dozen pieces, into the trunk of Binoux's car. We hopped in, so we could unload it at the other end. Binoux drove, with Folliasson in the passenger seat and the two of us in back, to a grey limestone office block in the heart of Paris. We reassembled it quickly on the conference table before a board of half a dozen official-looking men. As familiar as I was with conversational French, the meeting was hard to follow, but clearly it was a group representing our corporate client and the government officials involved in approving the project.

Binoux and Folliasson made their presentation. They described the features of the community and pinned up drawings showing sanitary sewers, roads, walkways, and water supply systems—composing *la voirie,* the infrastructure of the town. I had helped prepare one of these sheets, for fire protection: fire hydrant locations, with 100-meter circles centered on each hydrant, showing the reach of a fire hose, verifying full fire suppression coverage of he new town area. The silver-haired officials, in their charcoal gray business suits and vests, walked around the model, making comments here and there, asking an occasional question and generally expressing approval. They ended by indicating to our principals that they would have word back to them within a couple of weeks.

The presentation must have been a success, resulting in moving the project ahead to the next phase. Soon we began designing the buildings for the new town of Le Creusot. I learned that architectural practice is different in Europe, requiring no structural, mechanical or electrical engineering to be provided along with the architect's design. The work consisted of designing the master town plan and conceptual design of houses, schools and infrastructure for the new community. After our work was done, the whole package would be bid by contractors, and the successful firm would provide the detailed engineering design drawings, much in the way that American architects obtain shop drawings for built-in systems, furniture and equipment from subcontractors before fabrication. This would entail the architect's review of engineering systems for design compatibility, much like the procedure Americans offices use in approving shop drawings for such items as cabinets, kitchen equipment and other built-in but separately engineered building elements.

The office routine shifted from the rush of the charrette to architectural design of buildings. While others dealt with housing units, fire stations, and the town hall, I was assigned an *préau,* (literally, water-preventive) porch to shelter students while waiting for school to start or for recess on rainy days. As I sketched various designs, Binoux advised me: "Sketch one idea after the next, never duplicating a previous design. Don't stop to critique yourself, but keep generating new ideas."

The firm of Binoux and Folliasson was to become, by 1975, one of the most important in France, designing major projects within the new Defense district of Paris.

Abbey of Cluny, Boulevard St. Michel

Rue Soufflot and Place du Pantheon, Paris

15

WELCOME TO THE HOTEL CALIFORNIA

THE OLD HOTEL CALIFORNIA. where I spent that fall and winter, was full of memories. The lobby featured a well-worn Louis XV couch and matching chairs with limed oak wood frames and a mismatched and badly distressed mahogany coffee table.

The front desk—a wood counter in front of a wall—separated the lobby from the dining room of the family's quarters. This space doubled as the room where Mme. Dutot daily served *petit dejeuner*, a continental breakfast with plump, flaky croissants, butter, jam and a large pitcher of coffee or hot chocolate. It faced a window wall opening on a barren light court. The tiny elevator, big enough for three friendly adults, featured a hand-operated interior folding gate and an out-swinging door at each level. Even that old elevator had a story.

Two American college girls from Minnesota took the room across the hall from my tiny cubicle. It faced the street and was furnished with a double bed on the corridor wall. On the side wall sat the typical washbasin. a bidet and a short wardrobe cabinet. Two dressers and an easy chair occupied the other side wall. Because they left the hall door open, I happened to meet them soon after they checked in. They were attempting to circumnavigate the room by stepping from the bed to the lavatory to the top of the short wardrobe, to a chair and so on, without touching the floor. When the shorter of the two, with close-trimmed curly hair, had completed her circuit, the other insisted upon trying it, failed and collapsed laughing on the bed. The two of them, with their silly, Midwestern sense of fun, could not have been older than eighteen. Although they seemed out of place among the mature, sultry young women of Paris, I was delighted to be reminded of their refreshing, American teen personalities.

A couple of days later, we were heading out to dinner together when we noticed some sedate older guests—two elderly ladies, an older gentleman and a middle-aged couple, obviously French from the countryside, sitting on the lobby sofa and side chairs. When we returned, they were still there, passing the time, watching the guests arrive and leave. We plotted in the elevator to give them something to look at.

The girls gagged and bound me with a a scarf around my head, tied my hands in front of me with a face towel and secured my arms with a bath towel. They put me in the elevator, pushed the button for the lobby and raced down the stairs. When the car reached the first floor, it was up to me to wedge my bound hands into the gate and slide it open. I then leaned on the out-swinging exterior door and fell through it to the floor of the lobby, just as the two pranksters casually ambled into the room from the bottom of the stairs.

"Oh my gosh," said Emily, the short curly-haired one, "a body!"

"Oh dear," the taller brunette Janie dead-panned, "There's been another murder."

The first gray-haired woman put her hands to her mouth and gasped. Her friend raised her hands and cried, «*Mon Dieu, appellez les gendarmes*! ». The oldster in a side chair looked up from his newspaper, harrumphed and resumed reading.

Observing our antics, Miguel, the Spanish night clerk, was doubled over in stitches, and his girlfriend Maria was laughing so hard tears came to her eyes. Just then another French couple arrived through the front doors, suitcases in hand, and approached Miguel at the front desk. He rented them accommodations and set them to work filling out the occupancy cards required by the police.

Meanwhile, the spectators in the lobby were still chuckling over the gag. Mischievous Maria whispered in my ear in English, "Those newcomers are also from the same town," she said, "but they missed out on the joke."

The girls gathered up the towels strewn on the floor and the three of us disappeared up the elevator. Not five minutes later, the girls ambled in from the stairway, the elevator door swung open again and my bound and gagged body collapsed in the lobby, this time to repeated outbursts of laughter, and even applause. Incredibly, they thought it even funnier the second time.

During that memorable fall and winter, as the holidays approached, my employers Binoux and Folliasson planned their annual celebration of another prosperous year. They invited the staff and guests to a holiday dinner at a favorite restaurant. Our group of eight employees, spouses and a couple of other close friends of the company ended up filling a long table occupying the entire side room of the establishment. The food was excellent, wine was plentiful and good, and I managed to join in the friendly conversation. It had not occurred to me to bring a guest, and there was no one in particular I would have invited anyway. By the third course, I had gotten into a discourse with Folliasson, the expansive, voluble and gregarious member of the partnership. With a well-padded frame, bushy dark hair, a brush mustache and a cheerful wisecrack on the tip of his tongue, he was the "outside" man of the firm, who entertained and engaged the company's clients. He was seated on the opposite side of the table with about two other guests between us.

"Hey, Green," he said, already in his cups, "how does this compare with an American restaurant?"

"Superior, with great ambiance," I replied. We began playing "Can you top this?" In French.

"And what do you think of the food?" Binoux, who was sitting right next to him, added.

"*Magnifique, par excellence*," I said, sparing no praise. Now our byplay had the attention of the whole table. I was coming right back at them in passable French.

"And what about the companionship?" Binoux demanded.

"*Étonnant!* (Astonishing!)" I exclaimed, almost running out of superlatives in my limited French vocabulary.

Not to be outdone by his partner, Folliasson supplied my next line in a stage whisper: "Tell him, *C'est la tonnere de Dieu*."

"It's the thunder of God!" I boomed in French, as he had dictated.

"Green," Mr. F. confided to me across the table, "I wondered about you, but you're all right!"

Later, after the partners had settled what must have been an enormous bill, we gathered outside in the chilly mist. "You have a ride?" Binoux asked me.

"No, I took the Metro," I said.

"Hop in." He pointed to his olive-green Renault sedan. Somehow, their spouses had gone home separately, and Folliasson took the front passenger seat.

"You know any girls?" Binoux asked before he started the engine.

For a moment I drew a blank. Then I recalled my co-conspirators in our stunts at the hotel. "If you go past my hotel I could go in and see if a couple of college girls I met are there," I offered. Moments later he pulled up in front of the Hotel California. I got out, dashed up to my room and knocked on the door across the hall. The two were sitting in the room wondering what to do next. "How would you like to see Paris by night?" I said.

The three of us crowded into the green car and Binoux, visibly amazed, said, "Very well, let's go to the Club." He drove us off somewhere on the Left Bank and led us through an old stone doorway and down a flight of steps. It dawned on me I was about to see something Americans visiting Paris only dream about. We entered a space with stout round piers topped by Gothic vaults supporting the building above. We were seated at a small round table, barely large enough for a wine bottle, a candle and our five glasses. As my eyes adjusted to the gloom, lit mainly by candles on the tables, I explained to the girls from Minnesota that this was one of the legendary Caves of Paris. On the other side of the room, a jazz combo played Brubeck, and couples clung to each other on a tiny dance floor. The atmosphere was perfect, but our situation was weird.

We had a language problem. The girls oohed and aahed, but they knew not a word of French, and even if they had, no one quite knew what to say. Binoux was proficient in English, but even he was tongue-tied. The atmosphere was perfect for seduction, or at the very least for impressing foreigners with the exclusivity of this hidden retreat. But I had long given up any romantic designs on these sweet little girls—as wide-eyed and naive as my sister's high school friends. The best Binoux could do was confide to me in French, of Emily, who was seated on an upholstered keg next to him, "She has such pretty eyes, and they sparkle so."

I couldn't help him. He had asked for girls—and here on the spur of the moment I had produced them. It actually was a nice way to end the evening. If none of the others appreciated the situation, I certainly did. I felt I had really experienced Paris as the French knew it. I had tasted the best in French gastronomy, cemented some friendships at work and made a connection. I understood a little bit more about the Frenchman's mindset and culture, and I had actually seen *Les Caves de Paris*.

Pigeons on the Piazza and the Galleria, Milan

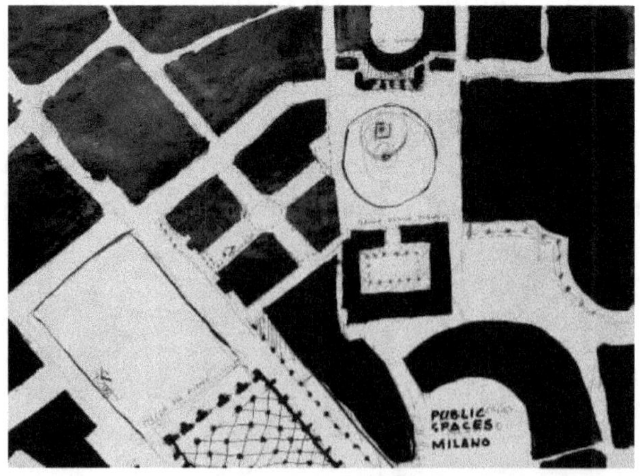

**Open Space Map of Il Duomo,
La Galleria, and La Scala**

16

WATER ON THE ORIENT EXPRESS

BY THE END OF MARCH, the charrette at Binoux and Folliasson was done, the buildings had been designed and the pace of the office slowed. We had occasional sunny days, and I was restless to move on. I had met a student in Paris, Elias, whose father worked for an American construction company in Istanbul. They needed some drafting help and might be able to put me to work when I got there. I had learned about the fascination of the country by staying in touch with a Turkish girl from the art school at Washington University, who had described the fascinating architecture and culture of her native Istanbul. I wrote her and told her I planned to travel to Istanbul to work for a while and would like to visit her family there. She alerted her parents to my visit, and later wrote that they would welcome me and invite me to their home and, both being art curators, would help to arrange some gallery visits. She also put her younger sister in charge as my hostess and guide to the city. Coincidentally, at the Hotel California I met a Turkish girl named Painas, who coached me in some of the basic travel words and phrases of the unusual Turkish language.

I resigned from my Paris job and planned an itinerary that would take me to Istanbul and allow me to work my way slowly back to Paris in the summer. I informed the Army Reserve that

I was planning to move again, and again the machinery went into motion to reassign me to another control group, which usually involved a couple of months' delay and a consequent extension of my unassigned and off-duty status. I checked the train schedule and learned that the only way I could make it all the way to Istanbul was either to wait until Thursday for the through train or proceed on Monday's train to Milan, its endpoint, and wait there for Thursday's train to arrive on Friday and take me to my final destination. Impatient to get going, I packed my essentials: my "European student costume"—a suit jacket and contrasting color slacks, sketchbook and ink pens, planned a few days' stay in Milan and set off on my new journey.

Although Arthur Frommer's *Europe on Five Dollars a Day*—a 1957 travel guide that showed Americans how to travel cheaply—had inflated to about ten dollars by 1965, I was still a budget traveler. After two weeks of planning, I checked out of Hotel California and bought a third-class ticket on the Monday Paris-Simplon (Orient) Express.

Arriving in Milan on Tuesday, I found a hotel with a French-speaking concierge, who warned me to be careful: "*Il y a des voleurs* (There are thieves) *en Milan*." Taking advantage of the three-day wait for the Istanbul train, I explored the great Italian industrial city. I began with an investigation of what people back home had told me: Pizza is a favorite in America, but it's not really an Italian dish. Regardless of its patrimony, I found it in northern Italy—a Four Seasons variety with a different topping on each quadrant—sausage, sardines, ham and cheeses—and it was very good.

Next I explored the original Galleria of shops and offices, the legitimate ancestor of America's enclosed pedestrian malls, which any real estate developer will tell you must be located along the path connecting at least two major anchors. Even a century earlier, architect Giuseppe Mengoni followed this rule when he designed and built Milan's Galleria, a four-story double arcade spanning two blocks between the major anchors of the Piazza del Duomo, in front of the late medieval cathedral, and

La Scala opera house. Named after Vittorio Emmanuel II, the first King of Italy, the gallery's interior enclosing walls are finished Renaissance stone facades, with gabled and pilaster-framed window openings above a second story of arched, glazed openings, with stores and shops on the ground level. The entire length of the two-block arcade is roofed above these four-story facades by a continuous glass vault, with an elegant glass dome at the crossing.

While I entered the imposing cathedral and toured its complex interior, I did not venture to sketch its multi-spired façade, the interior with its myriad statues nor investigate the crypts, which hold remains of the good St. Charles Borromeo, Bishop of Milan. Figuring that "a picture is worth a thousand words," I opted for a few of the words—of Mark Twain, that is. In 1869 he said he and his companions, in his account, *The Innocents Abroad*, were duly impressed:

> The central one of its five great doors is bordered with a bas-relief of birds and fruits and beasts and insects, which have been so ingeniously carved out of the marble that they seem like living creatures—and the figures are so numerous and the design so complex that one might study it a week without exhausting its interest.

In the cathedral's vast interior, the master writer had additional observations of the marvel he and his companions had experienced:

> Within the church, long rows of fluted columns, like huge monuments, divided the building into broad aisles, and on the figured pavement fell many a soft blush from the painted windows above. I knew the church was very large, but I could not fully appreciate its great size until I

noticed that the men standing far down by the
altar looked like boys, and seemed to glide,
rather than walk. [19]

Mark Twain devoted many pages to describing this wonder,
all worthwhile and amusing to read. Rather than sketch this
masterpiece of exquisite detail. I chose to study the dynamics of
shopping mall development as originally practiced in Milan. In
a fraction of the time it would have taken for such drawings, I
found the wide plaza before the Galleria and its pigeons more
approachable subjects, and much more easily depicted.

After sketching the mall and visiting the Cathedral, I
attended *The Barber of Seville* at La Scala. I found the
performance so enchanting I didn't even mind that I had to
accept standing room behind the last row of orchestra seats. By
the time the Istanbul train arrived on Friday, I had a vivid sense
of Italy's cultural splendor and her prosperous northern
industrial city.

I climbed aboard the Orient Express for the second leg of
the journey. Killing time, I learned from a fellow passenger how
to count to five in a Yugoslavian dialect—*bir, iki, uç, dort, besç* —
which turned out to be the same in Turkish. I struck up a
conversation with three young South African girls on their trip
of a lifetime throughout Europe and the Middle East. After
Turkey, they intended to visit Petra—the City of Rock, with
temples, tombs and classical-style facades carved into red desert
cliffs, about 100 miles from Amman, Jordan—and other Middle
Eastern sites. We then became acquainted with two boys from
Australia, who were hiking and backpacking toward
Afghanistan. Company was congenial, and sleeping
accommodations were nonexistent, so we chatted into the night.
We had each brought along food but were thirsty, and the water
available at the end of each car was labeled Non-Potable. I knew
from my Peace Corps training that water can be made potable
by boiling it for fifteen minutes. As one of the Australian boys
had Sterno canisters in his backpack, we spent the next five

hours from midnight to about 5 AM boiling water over Sterno in one of their canteen cups, so each of the six of us could have a drink. Although the minimal amount of clean water produced left us still thirsty, through this activity—in addition to consuming time—we all became friends. Near dawn we pulled into Edirne, the first station in Turkey, and vendors climbed aboard swinging trays of *chai*, sweetened Turkish tea. We each paid gladly whatever they asked, slaked our thirst and had our first Turkish treat.

While we boys had busied ourselves overnight with water supply on the platform connecting cars, back in the passenger seats the girls had adopted a bedraggled Turkish fellow with several days' growth of beard and a very sweet personality. They called him Smush and, despite ignorance of Turkish, somehow learned he had been visiting his sister in Bulgaria. They promised to find him at his stall in a certain Istanbul market the next day.

We all agreed to stay at the same hotel and, after several hours of makeup sleep, set out to find this fellow. They had only been able to identify his location through their sign language and his scribbled note in Turkish. Asking directions and showing the note as we proceeded, we found him at the designated market, sitting on the ground between some constructed stalls, with a few trinkets set before him to sell. The girls greeted him joyfully, bought the combs and compacts he had to offer and wished him well. After a couple of days and a meal or two together, our little band broke up. Both the boys and the three South African girls continued on their tours and I stayed to see Istanbul.

Santa Sophia, as it looked in 1965

17

ISTANBUL: MY WORK CAREER RESUMES

I CONTACTED ELIAS'S PARENTS and was promptly invited to dinner at their apartment in a fashionable neighborhood on the outskirts of the city. Both of apparent Spanish origin, Madame B., tall and matronly in a black dress, had jet-black hair coiffed in a bun. Her husband José, his head balding and his figure spreading comfortably in middle age, stood almost as tall as she, but had a less formal, modest manner. In excellent French they showered me with questions about their son's doings in Paris. I knew very little about his activities, but he seemed to have no gainful employment, except to sketch and listen to samba music. I reported that he was in good health, seemed content and passed along what I had learned in our conversation.

Elias had invited me to his apartment to get his parents' contact information. I went to his tiny room on the fourth floor of a walk-up building with a hall light on a thirty-second timer. By the time I had climbed to the second floor, the hall lights went out and I had to find and press the nearest button to restore them. Repeating this process twice, I found his door and knocked. He admitted me to his tiny pad, which had just enough room for a desk, a chair and bed. He was a sensitive, artistic type, tall, with a pretty face and gentle gestures. He played records of an orchestral arrangement of Manuel de Falla's "Nights in the Gardens of Spain" and the Miles Davis jazz version, noted the similarities, and I agreed. That seemed to end the conversation, and we listened. It dawned on me that he might be gay. I got the promised contact information and left. I repaired to the nearby café where he had introduced me to his attractive French friend, Catherine, in hopes of finding her again. He had left us together to finish our wine. In our continuing conversation, she had asked, « Tu as le feu dedans? » (Do you have fire in the belly?) Slow to react, I failed to pick up her signals and respond in time. Knowing what I now knew about Elias, I understood why he had left us together. But I had missed my chance. She wasn't there.

With little to report about their son, I told them about his interesting music history lesson. I didn't know what they knew about their son's sexual interests, and I couldn't say for sure, so I didn't bring it up. After dinner, the conversation turned to work, and José, the father, said he was in charge of engineering at Morrison-Knudsen's Istanbul field office. The company was building a chain of U. S. missile bases strategically placed along the southern coast of the Black Sea to deter Russia, at Samsun, Ordu and Trabzon. They needed drafting help to produce reinforcing steel shop drawings for missile silo complexes. They would pay me hourly. I was all in.

The following Monday, in a pouring rain, I stopped at one of the many pastry shops near my hotel in Taksim Square and ordered a sweet roll and a glass of fresh-squeezed orange juice. A stainless-steel rack displaying oranges filled the entire wall behind the counter. It was a Rube Goldberg-style contraption: oranges rolled down the stacked, sloping rows of the rack by gravity, like a giant vending machine, to dispense them one at a time. The proprietor taught me the names of each of the Turkish delights displayed in his glass case. Each morning when I stopped for my breakfast, he introduced me to a different sweet pastry, such as *mendil*, so named because of its triangular shape, like a folded handkerchief. Then I hopped on a bus labeled Yeni Levent, Turkish for the suburb New Levant, the geographical name for countries bordering the Mediterranean Sea's eastern end.

On the ground floor of a modern, steel-and-glass suburban building, I entered the small office of M-K's Istanbul headquarters and met its four occupants. Elias's father José, chief engineer, introduced the others: Art Campbell, office manager, who constantly complained in a Texas drawl that every other day was an official *bayram* (holiday) and he never knew whether his staff were going to show up or not—Irini, a frenetic multilingual secretary, and Çalyan (Charlie), the laid-back chief draftsman, who spoke enough French to communicate to me what was needed to do the work. I was to draw details, called shop drawings, specifying how to cut and install reinforcing bars in the forms for poured concrete. This was to be my job for the foreseeable future. I stayed while the rains continued and awaited suitable weather for touring archaeological and architectural sites around the city.

They also needed a field engineer, I learned, who would soon be arriving from the States. Weekly, we heard news that he would be delayed. Finally, a few weeks later, Stan arrived, a slender, fiftyish Oklahoman, with a graying mustache and a friendly, shy manner. As I drew my reinforcing bars with ink on vellum, he sauntered over to my desk and told me his life story.

"I think they hired me because of my refrigeration skills," he confided. "I'm good at all kinds of welding, refrigeration piping and electric motors. Only trouble was, one day when I was welding, I forgot to put on my mask. I don't know if you know it, but welding of refrigeration piping can sometimes produce phosgene gas, which is poisonous."

"So, did you get hurt?" I asked.

"Oh yeah, I was in the hospital for a long time." He chuckled in his offhand, apologetic manner. "So, it left me with only one lung."

This had to be chilling information about the company's new hire, imported all the way from the United States at great expense. I wondered if Art knew, or if it was my place to rat on this guy. In his shy, forthright manner, maybe he had already told Art about it. But the money was spent, the man was here, and he obviously needed the work. I let it slide.

Art found out soon enough. The chilly drizzle continued, and Stan stopped by the office two weeks later, after visiting several sites. He said jokingly that the climate didn't seem to be agreeing with him: He had a bit of a cough. A week after that, word reached the office that he was in the hospital, where he remained for another couple of weeks and died, ending his career, poor soul, and leaving the firm without their anticipated, highly skilled field engineer.

Charlie kept feeding me drafting work. Fascinated with the electric calculator beside my drafting board and eager for something to occupy my mind, I made more of my job than necessary. Where a concrete beam was designed to taper, the longitudinal reinforcing bars converged and were held in place by tying the lengthwise rods together with rectangular rings of steel rebar, spaced one foot apart. While Charlie pointed out all I needed to do was dimension the first and the last ring, I took the time to calculate the dimensions of each one. Charlie shook his head and sighed. But my drawings were neat, complete and met the approval of management.

Charlie's cool manner contrasted with the rest of the office. Art was a hands-on manager located hundreds of kilometers from his job sites. He had half a dozen job superintendents to keep in touch with by telephone, that is, when he could. This did not always include rainy days. Nonetheless, he kept pressure to connect on his trilingual Turkish secretary—when she was not on one of her many holidays. The phone lines were full of static and unreliable. Irini, who also served as telephone operator, filled the air at most hours of the day, with her yelling into the phone, "Effendi, effendi! (Sir, sir!)," diligently and loudly attempting to establish and maintain contact with their remote outposts.

I soon contacted my college friend's well-placed parents, both art curators, who welcomed me to Istanbul with open arms and familiarized me with their art history and culture. They invited me for lunch on the following Sunday. It was quite an experience, with about a dozen of their friends and relatives plastered in chairs against the four walls of their modest living room, all talking excitedly. I didn't understand a word of Turkish, but I smiled and tried to be friendly. Of course, my hosts. who were multilingual, translated for me anything they thought I should know.

The nation shed her Muslim ways abruptly in the 1920s. On 24 July 1923, the Treaty of Lausanne was signed by the Allied Powers with the Grand National Assembly of Turkey, thus recognizing this provisional body as the government of Turkey. Then on October 29, the Republic of Turkey was proclaimed and Mustafa Kemal Ataturk, the military leader who helped the Allies win World War I, notably through the victory in the Battle of Gallipoli (1915), was made the first president of the new republic. He subsequently proceeded to abolish the decrepit Ottoman Empire. On 4 October 1926, under the new code, women gained equality with men in such matters as inheritance and divorce, since Atatürk did not consider gender a factor in social organization.[20]

Turks love to retell the story that on the very next day, women of Turkey put away their burkas and hijabs and appeared on the streets of the cities in modern dress. Ataturk's liberation, legal reform and civil transformation of the Republic of Turkey still stand out as monumental achievements in modern times.

On weekends during my employment, I sketched on the seven hills of Istanbul. It's curious how many cities claim to be built on seven hills—Rome, Istanbul, Torquay, Cincinnati—who knows what other places claim such unique topographical origins? I drew the Blue Mosque, commissioned by Sultan Ahmet, and the ancient Hagia Sophia, which faces it across a large public square, rebuilt for a third time by Emperor Justinian after an earthquake.

Suleyman Mosque, in the historic district of the city, was named by his son in honor of his father, called Suleyman the

Magnificent, and also the Lawgiver. The tenth and longest-reigning Sultan of the Ottoman Empire, he ruled from 1520 until his death in 1566. He initiated many of the city's modern features—fountains from a central water supply, an organized city plan, and its infrastructure. Implementing his ruler's plan was Sinan, an architect, the great master builder of Turkey in the Renaissance era. I admired and sketched his Suleyman Mosque, its domes climbing in rhythmic sequence to their summit.

I bought a Turkish-English dictionary and a Teach Yourself Turkish manual and learned enough Turkish phrases for a rudimentary traveler's vocabulary. An extremely useful word not in that dictionary, *dolmush*, described a fleet of privately owned, communal jitney cabs, which made the rounds of the city's public squares, picking up and dropping passengers and charging each a lira or more, based on the number of stops traversed. While such public ride-sharing was efficient and had in the past been common on U. S. cities, including the South Side of Chicago, this method would be likely be considered too risky in America today. It has emerged recently in another, similarly risky mode, with Uber and Lyft, which lack the ride-sharing feature.

One day, off a main boulevard of Istanbul, I was exploring crooked streets no more than fifteen feet wide in the old city, crowded by buildings of three to six stories, with shops below. Throngs of people, some in modern dress, others in robes and turbans, crowded these byways, hurrying to work, shopping, meeting or taking in the scene at sidewalk cafes.

A laborer trudged slowly into the passage, bearing a sheet of plate glass twice his height on a leather harness covering his shoulders, from which leather straps projected to corners of his burden, securing it in place. Just then a truck burst into the alley, horn blaring. People scattered to the safety of the two-foot sidewalk that lined the street, and the laborer did his best to crowd to one side of the narrow passage. The truck sped wildly down the street, missing the bearer but nicking an edge of the plate glass pane, effectively ruining it for its purpose as a shop window. I've often thought of that unfortunate delivery man. His employer's investment in that pane was wiped out in a few seconds of bad luck on the chaotic streets of this city. I wondered if the laborer could return and resume work at the same job.

My friend's younger sister acted as my guide, helped me learn a few more Turkish words, and persuaded a male friend of hers to drive us around Istanbul to see the principal sights and landmarks. She recommended I take a boat ride on the Bosporus to the quaint Buyuk Ada, literally translated, "little island." I bought a ticket and set out on a rainy day. The boat ride revealed an historic island town frozen in time, free of neon or stainless steel, where transportation was on foot, horse or donkey cart.

She also took me to the house of one of her friends, who served us tea in an elegant setting. Our young and beautiful hostess conversed in excellent English, discussing the art of making tea, and just when to stop boiling the water and mix in the tea leaves. I got a glimpse of what fine, young Turkish women were like, and felt a bit grubby. I was merely a tourist, who had been living out of a suitcase for months. I felt I should have cleaned up first and worn my jacket and tie, to fit in properly and associate with Istanbul's finest citizens in this very polite and formal setting.

I was to be rescued from my scruffy state and my unfamiliarity with Turkey by another young man my hosts introduced me to, named Bulent. He was fluent in English and eager to show me real Turkish life. He proposed that we go to a *hamam*, a Turkish bathhouse. Delighted to take part in such a traditional custom, I followed my guide inside a blank-walled building, surmounted by multiple roof shapes and domes, occupying the better part of a city block. We signed up at a desk, paid a modest fee and were assigned a partitioned cubicle at least six feet square, fitted with hooks for our clothing and lined with wood benches. We disrobed and donned large bath towels and swimming trunks: Turkish men seemed more modest in locker rooms than Americans. We entered a large pool area where men sat on benches or the edge of a very large pool and swam or lounged in cool water. Off these main spaces were stone-walled, semi-cylindrical alcoves, with statuary in ornate wall niches and a series of intersecting pools at various levels. We passed through a doorway in one of these alcoves and entered a steam bath, where we sat for about 15 minutes and chatted while the cleansing warmth soaked into our pores. We emerged and took a dip in very hot water in a small pool. Adjacent to this, we stepped into a larger pool where we soaked in pleasantly warm water.

My first shock of the day was an attack by my guide. Bulent climbed out of the warm pool and joined me on a bench. Nearby he found a strigil, an instrument with a curved blade, this one made of plastic or bone, an instrument directly traceable to ancient Greeks and Romans for scraping the skin at the bath and in the gymnasium. He applied it vigorously to my back, shoulders and arms and scraped off a remarkable quality of dead skin. It stung and I let him know about it. "But look how much I got off," he protested. Having traveled for weeks with only infrequent shower facilities, I realized this was the first time I had felt really clean in months. I performed the same task for him. We rinsed off in a fountain and dipped in another pool of warm water on the other side of the alcove.

My second shock came when, expecting refreshment, I dove into the main swimming pool. For the next few seconds, the icy water paralyzed me and left me breathless. After a minute, I recovered and swam a couple of laps along its immense length, which competed more than favorably with an Olympic-sized competition pool. I think the Romans called this large, high-vaulted room the *caldarium*, but to me it was more like a *frigidarium*.

My third shock arrived when we reassembled in our cubicle, relaxed and refreshed. Bulent started talking. He complained about Turkey's current government and mentioned problems of corruption and inattention to the people's needs.

My guide continued his critical commentary at length, which surprised me. I looked beyond the divider partition at the high-vaulted ceiling above and wondered how he could get away with such talk where there was so little acoustic privacy. I wondered if Ataturk's miracle had been so pervasive that free speech in modern Turkey had been fully secured. Perhaps he felt protected, although inside an open enclosure, by speaking in a foreign tongue, I concluded there must be an unwritten rule that what one says in the hamam, stays in the hamam.

Next he introduced me to the covered market, *Kapalıçarşi*. Occupying an expanse of several city blocks and roofed over with Gothic vaults springing from a forest of columns, the Grand Bazaar contains every commodity imaginable. While Milan's Galleria was an example of modern development principles, it cannot claim the honor belonging to Istanbul's bazaar, considered one of the first and largest shopping malls in the world. Today, with 61 covered streets and over 4,000 shops it covers 30,700 square meters, or over 300,000 square feet, almost seven acres. In 2014, it was listed first among the world's most-visited tourist attractions, with over ninety-one million annual visitors.[21]

Bulent took me through a portion of the vast roofed emporium, divided by covered pedestrian streets and avenues into districts, each displaying a different type of retail goods or commodity in their stalls. We joined throngs of shoppers, in all varieties of dress, from black robes to brightly colored modern costumes, crowding through passages so narrow they forced our attention on the adjacent stalls. A babble of languages greeted our ears, and smells ranging from pleasant to putrid, from exotic perfumes to rotting produce, met our noses as we passed diverse displays. We entered a neighborhood of carpet dealers with an aroma of coffee. I paused to examine an intricate figure on a deep red-and-blue patterned oriental carpet.

"Isn't it exquisite?" said a man in casual dress with a black mustache and friendly smile. "It's only four thousand dollars."

"Oh, I'm just admiring it," I hastily replied. "I couldn't

possibly buy such a fine carpet. I would have no place no put it."

"Ah, I understand," he said, "perhaps this smaller one in the same pattern would interest you?" He pointed to an adjacent display. "Look, why don't you and your friend sit here with me and tell me about yourself/"

I looked inquiringly at Bulent.

"Why not? It's the custom in this market." He gestured for me to follow the carpet dealer.

We moved inside the stall to a small conversation area walled in by carpets and sat on low, padded stools.

"Would you like some coffee?"

I looked to my companion for direction. He spread his hands, shrugged and smiled. It was up to me. I accepted.

He introduced himself as Omar and asked about me and where I was from. Bulent introduced himself in Turkish, indicating he was just showing his visitor around the city. I detected an edge in his voice as if to warn the merchant, "Don't mess with him."

I ventured some conversation about myself and how I had been visiting the city in recent weeks to work in an office.

Omar brought the coffee, served it to us and launched a narrative about how he had settled upon this style and brand of the brew.

Both Bulent and I complimented him on its flavor.

He told about his family and small children and abruptly said, "You know that little rug is only two hundred dollars."

"Oh, I'm sorry," I said. I had no intention of buying anything.

He asked what I did. I said I was learning how to be an architect.

"Mimar!" he said and began discussing the architectural wonders of Istanbul. "One hundred dollars."

I looked at Bulent, who addressed the merchant in Turkish, thanked him for the coffee and rose from his stool. I did the same. We shook hands with the man and left.

Afterwards, I asked, "What did you tell him?"

"I explained that you were a student and not interested in furnishings at this point in your career. I said if he treats you right, someday you'll come back and be a very big customer."

"Thank you," I said, sincerely grateful for his help. I was beginning to understand how things worked in the Grand Bazaar.

Street Stairway, Istanbul
*Curved, to "gagner sur la pente," or
gain on the slope, as José commented.*

Sultanahmet Mosque, Istanbul

The Citadel: Ancient fortress at Ankara
*Welliver would approve of my depiction of these
vast spaces and volumes with economy of line*

Honat Hattum Medrese, Kayseri
Imams taught astronomy, sitting around the reflecting pool

18

ADVENTURES IN ANATOLIA

THE WEATHER WAS GETTING SUNNIER by the day, and my shop drawings were almost finished. This was my opportunity to part happily with my friends at the construction company. After I completed work at Morrison Knudsen's Turkish office, I bade farewell to my office mates, Art, José, Irini and Charlie. I took my earnings to a bank, bought some more traveler's checks and spent another week completing my sketches of monuments throughout Istanbul.

On one occasion, as I sat sketching outside Hagia Sophia, an engineer from the complex, who was conducting a tour of the monument for two visitors in French, stopped to look at my drawing. He told them the building was originally a church devoted to the Virgin under early Christian rulers Theodora and Justinian. When I addressed him, he pointed to my sketch and explained that the pairs of heavy buttresses on two opposite sides were added by architect Sinan in the sixteenth century, in response to cracking of the main dome. The roof surface, he added, was made of small sheets of lead, a malleable metal, easy to shape and crimp, still used for roofing today, Due to its chemical stability, he said, it had resisted environmental conditions over many centuries. Entering the interior, I made another sketch. I noted how glare through the small arched windows encircling the base of the dome made its supports disappear, inspiring a poet to say, "it looks as if suspended by a golden chain from heaven."

Whenever I sat down to sketch, on a bench, on a low wall or even on the ground, I attracted a crowd of admiring sidewalk superintendents. One day, a shopkeeper saw I was uncomfortably situated. He went into his shop and returned with a chair, so I could balance my sketchbook on my knee and improve my view of the historic multi-domed mosque I was sketching. My admirers called me *ressam* (artist). One knowledgeable spectator pointed to the mosque and said, "Sinan mimar," explaining that Sinan was architect for the mosque. Another day, I was sketching the Blue Mosque, with its many minarets, just at prayer time. The air filled with the cries, "Allah... ." Mullahs from all over the city were calling the faithful to prayer, followed by a chant in Turkish. A helpful observer of my handiwork pointed to a little bump I had just drawn at one of the circular balconies on a minaret and said something that sounded like, "Oparler," which I noted on the sketch. It later occurred to me that it was French, "haut parleur," for loudspeaker.

My friend's father was curator of the Topkapi Museum, His wife, also an art curator, led me on a private tour of the museum. She showed me the jewel the Pink Panther had stolen in the Peter Sellers film. We then entered the harem, at that time closed to the public during archaeological restoration. She showed me the sumptuous living areas where eunuchs once guarded the Sultan's wives, and a pool where the Sultan threw gold coins and watched nude slave girls retrieve them for his amusement.

They also suggested I tour Anatolian Turkey—it was inexpensive and easy, they explained, on a fleet of modern Mercedes-Benz buses that served the interior of the country. They mapped out a wide-ranging bus route across Anatolia. My hosts provided their own business cards, the names of art gallery directors and a list of sites to visit along the way. The route took me through such historic towns as Pergamon, Bursa, Ankara, Kayseri, Konya and Antalya. This fortuitous guidance enabled me to immerse myself even more deeply in the Seljuk architecture, great food and hospitable charm of Turkey.

Now it was time to leave my friend's family in Istanbul with great thanks. I set out on my Turkish odyssey. At the downtown bus terminal, I climbed aboard a modern Mercedes-Benz bus, along with rural men and women in robes, some with masks, in *chaderi*, wearing a hijab to cover the face and hair, bearing bundles, carpet satchels and old suitcases tied with rope. The bus driver piled some of the bundles between guardrails on the roof of the vehicle. We took a ferry across the Bosporus to Anatolia, drove off the boat and set out southward on a two-lane open highway. We climbed into the Anatolian hills. The driver announced we were coming to the town of Gemlik, and my seatmate, clad in a robe and turban, pointed out olive groves on either side of the road.. "*Gemlik zeytin*," he said," *çok guzel* (Gemlik olives, very good)."

We made a tourist stop at Pergamon to see the amphitheater and were told we had an hour to visit the site and return. A young man in lederhosen and a Tyrolean hat followed the sign to the amphitheater and I joined him. Like most German students, he spoke English well, and we chatted while we hiked to the top along a narrow road that spiraled around the conical hill whose summit held the ancient Greek amphitheater. During our long climb, he gave me a German lesson, and we made a joke out of it. By the time we had reached the summit, with his corrections, I was able to say, "*Wir haben nach Pergamon gegangen. (We have gone to Pergamon)*."

We stood at the top of well-preserved stone semicircular seating, facing south across the valley toward more distant hills and the seacoast. The acoustic qualities of this natural theater were apparent, carrying the hushed murmur of daily activity in the town of Pergamon beneath us all the way to the last row. We learned that the amphitheater was still in use for summer concerts and plays on the broad stage in front of the seats. The enduring achievement of the ancients silenced us and held us in its thrall.

Our descent was much quicker, and soon we were on our way again. As the road flattened out, the speakers on the bus played jarring, atonal music of tinhorns and primitive stringed instruments in a repetitive rhythm, as our driver blazed through pastureland at seventy miles an hour. When we neared a town, a peasant was crossing the road leading a group of ducks. The driver employed his horn instead of his brakes. Ducks and peasants scattered for their lives in all directions. When we came upon a shepherd herding sheep across the narrow road, however, the speeding bus screeched to a halt: The animals had the right-of-way. The minutes ticked by until the very last sheep and shepherd had cleared the roadway, and we resumed our speeding flight across the landscape.

My route next took me to Bursa, in the southwestern corner of Anatolia, one of the industrial centers of the country, where most of its automobile production takes place, the first major capital of the Ottoman State between 1335 and 1363. Often called Green Bursa for its many parks, gardens and surrounding forest, it also has the mausoleums of early Ottoman sultans. I sketched the Green Mausoleum, known for its green and blue interior tiles, tomb of Mehmet I, sultan before the Ottoman conquest of Istanbul in 1453.

The route my art curator guides had recommended took me through the country's new capital, Ankara. Beginning with his reform and modernization of Turkey in the 1920s, Kemal Ataturk set out to establish a new capital. He detested the cosmopolitan and vulnerable city of Istanbul, whose history and ancient culture of deposed sultans would never be expunged. He also wanted to establish a government presence in the heartland of Anatolia, thus solidifying and defending his nation's borders from a central point. Outside of town, on its own open manmade mesa sat Ataturk's austere, classical style mausoleum, stripped of ornament. On a hilltop above the old town, an ancient fortress loomed above the modern four-story structures of the city's main street, Ataturk Boulevard.

Beyond these places, the city offered few attractions to the visitor. As my Petite Planete French-language travel guide put it, "A city to see, certainly. Between two trains."

The bus rolled on.

In Kayseri, the principal city of Cappadocia and one of the former capitals of Seljuk culture, I visited a medrese (sometimes pronounced ma-dra'-sa in English), a small residential college, with a central courtyard and a pool reflecting the sky, where imams taught Islam, mathematics and astronomy. I made sketches of the medieval Seljuk architecture.

Penetrating this deeply into the heart of Anatolia, I found it harder to find hotels for a night's lodging. One night in Kayseri I stayed at a hostel with dormitory-style sleeping hall, improvised in a large, high-ceilinged gathering space. Its only privacy separation consisted of makeshift wooden dividers extending vertically to the height of a standing man and what appeared to be bedsheets suspended on crisscrossed clotheslines.

At the check-in desk, I met Hagen and Hiltrud, a young German couple who were hitchhiking through the country to reach Afghanistan. They said they had hired a car the next day to take them out to the hills of Göreme, over an hour's drive east of the city, and invited me to come along. They promised archaeological and natural wonders of a kind I had never seen..

When it got late, they entered their sleeping cubicle and I entered mine, along with several other guests who had already retired. I wondered what kind of acoustical privacy could possibly exist in such a setup, what intimate sounds I might hear and whether I could get any sleep. Apart from a few snores, a hush prevailed in the vast hall. The other occupants were no doubt more seasoned travelers than I. They must have learned that an absolute silence was essential to privacy within such an irregular hostel.

As we approached Göreme the next morning, we drove into a lunar landscape, a valley of conical hills. Our driver explained they were carved into the porous volcanic rock by the action of wind and water over the centuries. Raids of Arabs, Mongols and Turks through the eras had forced monastic communities, originally Greek, first to retreat to these desolate hills and then, in the Christian era, to burrow into them, accessing them only though narrow, hidden tunnels. To hollow out homes, churches and cathedrals into the stones, they used templates to guide their carving. They created colonnades, vaults, domes and interior features, such as tables, benches, niches for oil lamps and cisterns formed from the rock for pressing wines. Once secure, they decorated their refined interior surfaces with sacred images, at first with paint, and later with Byzantine mosaics of the finest quality.

Konya, an oasis in a denuded, desolate plain, has a history dating back five thousand years. Originally the Greek town of Iconion, and next the Roman town of Iconium, where Perseus is said to have cut off the head of Medusa, Konya was the first capital of the Seljuk people, whence emerged the first power of the Ottoman sultans. It was the home of the famous whirling dervishes, those dancers so ecstatic with their faith that they could not stop spinning, one arm raised toward the heavens and one lowered toward earth. Until the 1920s the dervishes were also a political force, until Ataturk demoted them with his governmental and civil reforms. He converted their former local headquarters, the *mevlanas*, which heretofore had served a function like American political precinct offices and meeting houses, to museums of charming but mainly historical interest. I visited the Mevlana Museum in Konya, which formerly had been comparable to the Washington, D.C. headquarters of a major political party. Now it contained an exhibit that charged admission to their bejeweled treasures—artifacts, jewel-and mirror-encrusted fezzes and colorful, richly embroidered robes.

After establishing myself at last in a hotel, I happened to meet a bank president, who spoke excellent French and invited me out to dinner. While he introduced me to some very fine Turkish dishes, he plied me with questions about America. I could sense his hunger for news of the outside world. I realized he was one of the most privileged men in this small historic town, but he was tethered to it and starved for experience in the modern world. He impressed upon me, barely concealing his envy, my very great privilege to be able to travel widely at such a young age and see so much of the world.

A final stop on my itinerary was the seaside resort town of Antalya, its Mediterranean harbor overlooking mountains on the opposite shore. As I sat and sketched those hills. a bystander told me there lay the birthplace of St. Nicholas, forerunner of the modern Santa Claus, a real person who spent his life giving his worldly goods to the poor.

I found the modern world a bit stingier. In the front courtyard of the town's art museum, I met a bright local boy, who was admiring the garden sculptures and asking questions in pidgin English. While we waited for the museum to open, he told me he liked to draw. When the gallery opened. I presented the Topkapi museum director's card and was cordially greeted a few moments later by the museum director. He gestured for me to enter but held up a warning finger, "but not the boy." Although out of courtesy he had refused to accept my admission fee, I offered to pay the boy's fee. "No, it's not that," he said. "Among these priceless artifacts, these urchins are too risky."

I explained that in my country, we provide special museum tours for school children. "I have been talking with this boy, and he wants to be an artist, *ressam*. I'll make sure he stays with me and doesn't touch anything." He threw up his hands, refused to take any money and allowed me to take the boy into the museum with me. We spent the next hour touring the exhibits. among them a Hittite necklace. Another artifact, a carved reindeer, was very moving to me, since it transported me into the past: The artist made it with his own hands: a tiny image of the animal in semi-precious stone over 2000 years ago. The boy's eyes were wide with wonder at these marvels to be found right here in his own town.

Throughout Anatolian towns in Turkey, sidewalk cafés were occupied exclusively by men. I had seen rural women on buses, herding sheep alongside the road and elsewhere, but never at their leisure. I imagined the women were far too busy for this kind of inactivity, sweeping their homes with straw brooms, washing clothes, minding children, shopping and preparing meals. The men idly drank coffee, argued politics, and discussed how to run the country. Impressive ambitions, true, but hard to achieve from a seat in a café. They sat in the dusty, crumbling streets before buildings needing basic maintenance. Even a coat of paint would help, in towns that seemed not to have changed in centuries. What if someone organized them, I mused, and made them do some of these tasks?

As I boarded the bus back to Istanbul most seats were full, except for two at the front window next to the driver, with a full view of the road ahead. An attractive young woman took the one alongside the driver, and I claimed the one next to her. As we began the long haul I tried to make conversation with her, using a combination of Turkish, French words and sign language. She had been home to visit her family and now she was returning to her job in Istanbul. I asked her what job she did. "*Pavyonda*," she replied. I had been in Istanbul long enough to know that dance halls where men were entertained in Istanbul were called *pavyons*, for the French *pavillon*. I assumed she was a waitress and was even pretty enough for a showgirl. After that I couldn't think of much to talk about, much less express it in any words she would understand. We rode along, pointing out interesting sights and exchanging smiles along the way.

After two hours, the driver entered a town and stopped at a dusty, unpaved parking lot next to a café, where passengers could take a break. Men piled off the bus, some entering the café, but the rest stood around. I remained next to the girl, trying to keep her company. She indicated she was going to take a walk and headed toward a steep-sided drainage canal at the far side of the parking lot. I accompanied her. Some of the men grunted, and many began to follow us. I realized they were not happy, either with the girl or me. It dawned on me I was the only one not in on the story. With her good looks and modern, slim-fitting clothes, which I was used to among urban girls, here in a rural area she stood out. Her compatriots tagged her as a "loose woman," and me, with my goatee and my western clothes, as her pimp. I was alarmed at the appearance of the situation and glanced at the canal, with its rock side walls, wondering if the sullen villagers were going to push us both in. I realized the best thing for me to do was to leave and let her fend for herself. I went into the café and later climbed back on the bus, where another seat was now available. I had offended the moral sense of a medieval culture. What a different world from modern America I had encountered in Anatolia!

Back in Istanbul, I met a group of young men who had just graduated from the university, and they invited me along on their celebration. First, they took me to a *pavyon*, basically a night club. Despite Istanbul's comparative sophistication, in conservative Turkey, these places were considered risky and scandalous, yet patronized by prosperous men in Turkey. A *pavyonda*, it turned out, was an entertainer at a night club—at best a singer, at worst, a stripper, featured in the show. Afterward, we went to an open-air café in a public park. They spoke enough French and English so we could converse. We ordered tea, and then the waiter brought around the main attraction, a silver plate laden with pillow-shaped nuggets. We each chipped in a few lira and with his tongs the waiter placed one on top of the coals already glowing on the hookah, a shapely jug of water as tall as the table. One of the young men grasped the rubber tube attached to the smoke chamber above the water, took a puff and passed the mouthpiece to the man on his right. Conversation turned to memories of our college days, as we continued passing the pipe in this manner until each of us had had several tokes. The voices at our table, as well as our spirits, rose. One of my companions broke into song. I responded with a favorite song from summer camp. They sang a chorus of school songs, and I sang college favorites. We left the café in the park and paraded through the streets of the city, arms across shoulders. We went to different schools and didn't even get each others' jokes, but we had a wonderful time. It dawned on me that what had raised our spirits so high was some very good hashish. But thank Allah, we didn't have a drop of alcohol to drink.

Present diplomatic relations with Turkey notwithstanding, the timing of my 1965 visit was fortuitous. I benefited from the Turks' good relations with us during World War II. They remembered Americans as their friends and defenders. When one older lady I met learned I was American, her eyes misted up and she cried, "Kennedy! How we miss him here."

My adventure had allowed me to immerse myself all over again in architecture, good food and the hospitable charm of Turkey. Bordering on the Mediterranean Sea to the south, Bulgaria and Greece to the west, the Black Sea and Russia to the north and Syria, Iran and Iraq to the East, my hosts had said, this westernmost Middle Eastern country plays a strategic role as a land bridge which connects Europe and Asia.

Antalya, Turkey, Birthplace of St. Nicholas

The Parthenon, Sixth Century BC, Praxiteles, Architect

From my vantage,   I was overwhelmed by the immense scale of this monument, Compare the size of the two tourists clambering up the base to the temple floor.

The Acropolis with Mt. Hymettus beyond

Vincent Scully liked this view, with the man-made temple boldly asserting man's place on Mother Earth in the Athens landscape, perched between its twin peaks and the sea.

19

GREECE: THE COLUMN IN THE LIGHT

Our form of government does not enter into rivalry with the institutions of others. Our government does not copy our neighbors' but is an example to them. It is true that we are called a democracy, for the administration is in the hands of the many and not of the few. But while there exists equal justice to all and alike in their private disputes, the claim of excellence is also recognized; and when a citizen is in any way distinguished, he is preferred to the public service, not as a matter of privilege, but as the reward of merit…While we are thus unconstrained in our private business, a spirit of reverence pervades our public acts; we are prevented from doing wrong by respect for the authorities and for the laws, having a particular regard to those which are ordained for the protection of the injured as well as those unwritten laws which bring upon the transgressor of them the reprobation of the general sentiment.

— from the Funeral Oration of Pericles, honoring the dead of the Peloponnesian War, c. 430 B.C. (Thucydides transcription)[22]

I PAID A LAST VISIT to my friend's Istanbul family, thanked them for their hospitality and planned a leisurely tour back to Paris to see if employment opportunities had improved. I told them about my plans. They advised: "If you're not in a big hurry, the best and cheapest way to travel to Greece is to take a speedboat ride from Çeşme to Chios, a Greek island only an hour off the Turkish coast." Once in Greece, I could take the overnight Greek tourist ferry to Athens via the port of Piraeus.

I made the arrangements and set off late one afternoon on my journey. After a one-hour speedboat ride, I boarded a multi-decked ferry, with staterooms and snack facilities. In an economizing mode, I had passed up a reservation for a stateroom, which would have cost a days' pay at my drafting job, assuming I could sleep on a couch. After scoping out the ship I immediately realized I had made a serious mistake: the furnishings of all the public rooms consisted of chairs at tables, vinyl and chrome side chairs and narrow benches. As we pulled away from shore, I had some dinner, toured the ship and watched us sail into the sunset. Since few passengers were making the trip on this particular night, I made myself as comfortable as possible in an armchair in one of the vacant public lounges and tried to fall asleep.

A couple of hours later a steward came through the lounge to clean tables and noticed my uncomfortable position. I could speak only a few words of Greek and he spoke nothing else, but he motioned to me to follow him. He raised a large ring of keys, opened the door to a stateroom and bid me enter. The enclosure and the bunk looked like heaven to me. My Turkish was sufficient to offer him my heartfelt thanks. I tried "*çok teşekkür ederim*" in case he understood Turkish, and "*efcharisto*," assuming he was probably Greek. He accepted all of my remaining lira, amounting to a few dollars' tip, bowed and withdrew, closing the door behind him. I stowed my suitcase, collapsed on the bunk and was immediately dead to the world.

When I awoke, I ventured out on deck. The rising sun glinted off deep indigo waters. I was reminded of Homer's words: *Dawn climbed from her rosy bed and flecked the wine dark sea with her glow*. I sighted a rocky coast projecting out toward us from the right. A Greek temple appeared atop the cape, glowing in the rust-red rays of sunrise. My map of the Turkish isles revealed it was the Temple of Sounion. Ignoring my perch on a modern vessel, I imagined how the Greeks must have rejoiced at this sight when they returned from a sea voyage to their beloved home. Within two hours we reached the port of Piraeus and the chaos of stevedores, passengers, cranes hoisting freight aboard seagoing vessels and the mew of seagulls, blaring taxi horns and blasts from steamships embarking on ocean voyages.

I found a taxi to take me to Athens, landed in Omonia Place and consulted my guidebook to recheck the address of the reasonably priced hotel I had selected nearby. With only two blocks to go, the handle on my folding suit bag gave out. A helpful street urchin noticed I was having trouble carrying it. I made hand gestures of winding, and he caught on that I wanted some wire to repair the handle. He grabbed one side of my bag and I took the other, and he led me through winding streets and alleys to a little shop, whose proprietor understood, produced some wire and fixed my suitcase handle, When I offered to pay, he held his palms toward me and refused. The boy then guided me to my hotel and more than earned his tip.

The Greek *taverna*, I learned, was a late-night affair best experienced in a group of friends. Instead, I ate well at a sidewalk café and turned in early, to make up for my restless journey the previous night. I started early the next morning to explore the Acropolis, entered through the Propyleaia, climbed to the manmade mesa, sat on a parapet wall and sketched a close-up view of the Parthenon. I had worked about an hour when an official guard came up and said I couldn't sit on the wall. I tried to explain that, as a Greek, he ought to know enough about architecture that I could not change my point of view or it would ruin the perspective of the drawing. He understood enough English to tell me he didn't care about that—I was not allowed to sit on the wall, period. I quit and was forced to finish up the drawing that night at my hotel.

What fascinated me about the ancient temple was its immense size. Art Campbell had mentioned back in Istanbul that, as a builder, he would have loved to have the marble supply contract for that job. Similarly, the stone maidens supporting the entablature of the Erectheum looked to me more like colossal Amazons than dainty females. A couple of days later, from a hilltop vantage I managed to capture a view of the acropolis in its landscape setting, as Vincent Scully had described to us: a man-made temple aggressively posited between the sea and the double-peaked, mother-earth symbol of Mount Hymettus.

I recalled Scully's lectures about Greek architecture and democracy, his reading of the funeral oration of Pericles, and his fascination with the sculptural qualities of the column in the light. The Parthenon offered an army of columns supporting the roof of the temple. There were so many columns, and their mass and strength were so great, a good portion of the building survived its misuse as an arsenal—strength in numbers. A new interpretation of Scully's words occurred to me. A democracy survives on the strength and dedication of its individual citizens. Athena, the goddess inhabiting the temple, symbolized the eternal light of wisdom. The column is the individual. The combined support of enlightened individuals—as symbolized the column in the light—protects the republic's collective defense and endurance into the future.

Back in Paris at the hotel I had met a talkative Greek businessman, Marios Trevizas, a travel agent. He gave me his card and promised, if I ever visited Athens, he would give me a free tour. I'm sure it was one of those things he said a dozen times a day. When I showed up at his door, he was taken aback, but he recovered quickly. He had to leave for an appointment but told me to come back in an hour and he would keep his promise. When I returned, he put me on a bus bound on a day trip to Corinth. After crossing Corinth Canal, a narrow man-made gorge excavated from solid rock for a shipping channel, we entered the ancient city's site..

Strategically situated between two harbors on a four-mile-wide isthmus between Athens and the Peloponnesus, Corinth has been occupied since Neolithic times in the seventh millennium B.C. During the Trojan War the leader of the Corinthians was Agamemnon, brother of King Menelaus of

Sparta. Seven columns remain here of the Temple of Apollo, one of the most authentic and ancient examples of the archaic Doric style. For a period of 800 years, the sick journeyed to the nearby sanctuary of Asklepion to be healed—a site dedicated to Asklepios, the god of healing, and his daughter, Hygeia.

After seeing these highlights of Greece, I took a daytime boat to Naples. We negotiated the narrow passage separating Scylla and Charybdis—the wandering rocks, probably explained, according to my high school Latin teacher, as the change in perspective as the ship moved through the narrow strait between Messina (in Sicily) and Calabria, the toe of the Italian boot.

The Naples Museum provided an excellent collection of antiquities, from Greek and Roman statuary to an impressive bowl some six feet across made entirely from a single rock of porphyry. Factory tours, shops and stands located everywhere around the city offered rings and portraiture in cameo, an art form carved from a mollusk shell. The white calcium deposits of the main shell are sculpted away from the convex surface, revealing its pink lining. The artist creates a portrait or an oval image in relief on the shell surface, surrounded by the classic pink background from the inner shell, to be mounted in a ring setting, a picture frame or an oval brooch.

The most memorable side trip I took was to Pompeii, where by 1965 significant ruins had been excavated to reveal an instantaneous snapshot of an ordinary day in 79 A.D., when the life of the town was cut short by an eruption of Mt. Vesuvius and its thick deposit of ash and lava. It occurred so suddenly that people and animals were captured in their poses for eternity—a man crouching, trying to protect his face; a dog arrested in mid stride, running to warn his master, and a table set for a meal with food ready to be eaten. An exhibit at the St. Louis Science Center in 2019 recaptured that poignant moment for me with casts of these remains and the results of even more complete excavations made in the intervening 55 years.

Santa Martina with the Roman Forum beyond
A fortuitous sketch, depicting mass and volume with economy

Nave, St. Peter's Basilica, Rome

20
ROME'S DOMES AND HOME

For in this place Christ stood when he said to Peter: "Thou art Peter; and upon this rock will I build my church…and I will give unto thee the keys to the Kingdom of Heaven." (Matthew 16:18-19)

—Latin inscription in letters five feet high at the base of Michelangelo's dome, St. Peter's Basilica, Rome

ON MY FIRST VISIT TO THE IMPERIAL CITY, Mike and I had visited the Pantheon, a temple to the Romans' many gods. In fact, one visiting Rome soon begins comparing domes. While the dome of St. Paul's in London by architect Sir Christopher Wren is impressive, Rome's domes, so to speak, top them all.

We had visited in the Pantheon 1959 on a sunny day with a clear blue sky. We passed through the tall classical columned and gabled porch and left the realm of the rectangular to enter a literally spherical world. It astonished me that the flawless tiled floor was not, in fact, protected against the weather. On that bright morning, sunlight pierced the perfectly round oculus, open to the sky at the apex of the coffered interior surface, the progressive tapering of the recessed squares proceeding in radial symmetry to the circular opening, without any glass or other membrane to keep out the rain. Sunlight poured through the aperture and carelessly cast an oval bright spot across the columns, entablature and gable of one of several side chapels that line the cylindrical side walls. Just as sunlight came in, I reckoned, so must the rain, sleet and snow on the immaculate tessellated tile, all the more impressive for enduring the weathers throughout the past one-and-a-half millennia.

Another day I left the car horns, buses, pedestrians and pigeons on St. Peter's Square and entered the Basilica, quiet with a calm murmur, far different from Rome's bustle outside—perhaps a celestial hum from the Other Side. A coffered vault loomed over Bernini's nave, bordered by arches so vast in scale I could not assimilate their size. But each side arch was supported by smaller arches parallel to the nave's length and each resolved into four rectangular piers forming a vaulted side chapel. A group of visitors, clustered at the right side of the main nave around a wall niche enfolding a small marble statue brought the immensity of the interior volume into focus. Logical stair steps from the height of the humans to the arches gave me a measure of the cathedral's immense interior volume. Fellow architect Laurent Torno calls this feat the hierarchical orchestration of human scale.

The crowd in the side aisle had moved on. I approached the object of their fascination and faced Michelangelo's Pieta. Although one could reach out and touch the statue, I merely beheld the creamy white marble surfaces, marveling at their delicate rendering in stone. Mary caressed the body of Jesus, feeling his skin still warm, smooth, the unforgiving stone glowing, yet with the pallor of recent death. The tenderness of her sorrow was so moving as to put a lump in my throat and tears in my eyes. When I heard the news a few years later, that a vandal had attacked the unguarded treasure with a sledgehammer, I wept. It was later restored, to the extent possible, alarmed and railed off from public approach. I felt undeservedly lucky to have seen the masterpiece in its pristine condition at close range.

At the crossing, I stared upward at the dome and the inscription encircling its base, which I could readily translate from my high school Latin scholar days — "Thou art Peter; and upon this rock will I build my church... And I will give unto thee the keys to the Kingdom of Heaven." The guidebook said the basilica was built on the rock that supported the original church.

What's in a name? I mused. According to Thornton Wilder, who taught creative writing to my mother at the University of Chicago, Gertrude Stein had a theory that one's given name, such as Ulysses or Romeo, presupposes some prescience on the part of the parents, or else guides one toward his lifetime mission. In discussing her essay, "Four in America," Wilder says,

> The section on Ulysses S. Grant begins with a lively discussion of the relations between people and the Christian names they bear. Miss Stein relates it to superstition and religion...

> Miss Stein is talking about religion throughout this section, and she is furnishing analogies to the kind of "knowing" that goes to make up religious belief. One of them is the haunting sense that your name is the right name for you[23]

If Stein's theory is correct, St. Peter's name, the Latin word for rock, was appropriate to its bearer.

My parents claimed they picked my name out of the phone book—one that sounded good with my family name. But when they came up with Paris Green—coincidentally the name of a common rat poison of the day—the obstetrician roared and shook his head as he left the delivery room. Daunted, they kept going down the listings until they came to Peter, a safe choice my mother felt would fit in well with her Irish surname which, as our tradition required, would be my middle name. It also had a familiar ring to it, the name of one of her mother Mary Howard's twin brothers. So much for that theory of destiny.

But when her father died, Mom held me tightly to her and said, "Peter, my rock." Even today, I can't help but wonder whether there might not be some substance to Gertrude Stein's theory.

A white-robed altar boy lit candles. Roman ladies garbed in black knelt, a businessman genuflected in the aisle and hastily took a seat. Tourists in shorts and brightly colored shirts, toting cameras and purses, occupied seats or stood further back. Beneath Bernini's serpentine-columned Baldachin, a bishop appeared in a white miter and cassock, faced the crucified Jesus and began the Mass. His censer swung on a chain and the sickening sweet smell of incense wafted forth. Since I had only attended mass at family weddings and funerals, I hesitated, wondering what my lapsed Catholic mother would do right here and now. My heart, full of the strong impressions of the setting, the Pieta and my maternal family's Irish history, was overcome with emotion, and I knelt in the pew.

Spring rains moved in and reflected my sorrowful mood. I'd had my fill of visits to the Campidoglio (Capitol), the Roman Forum and the many museums full of ancient and modern art treasures. I was jaded and could take in no more. It was time to end my wandering, get a steady job and apply what I had learned.

And yet when I got back to Paris I found lodging again at Hotel California, looked for a few friends and re-contacted some of the firms I had interviewed. I let my parents and friends know of my arrival back in Paris. I called Monsieur Lasry and left a message that I was still interested in the job I had applied for.

A few days later, I received a telegram from home. It was from Dad: "ARMY CALLS. CALL HOME." I called late in the evening, which was dinner time at home. Mom answered and said that Dad was in the hospital. I could hardly believe that this man, who had never missed work for a sick day in his life, was ill. Apparently he had some kind of intestinal inflammation, which resembled a bleeding ulcer, and was in for tests. She read me the information the Army had sent. They wanted me to report to a base north of Paris, so I could draw uniforms and be ready in the event of deployment.

I awoke from my traveler's dream. It was time to attend to important matters at home. I booked a return flight for the following week. I called Monsieur Lasry's architectural office and told him, contrary to my message, I had decided to leave Paris. "Are you sure?" Lasry asked, "Because we have just begun a new project and we could use some help." I wondered where all this demand had been when I was first searching for jobs in Paris. But I replied, "Yes, I am sure. But thank you for your interest."

I received a festive card from Aline, the attractive younger sister of Françoise, Madame Diamant-Berger's assistant at *l'Architecture d'Aujourd'hui*. I had taken her on a dinner and dancing date. This was an invitation to a party she was planning in two weeks. I had to call and refuse her kind invitation. Now that I was leaving, I realized that working one's way into the life of a foreign city is possible—it just takes a while to be included.

When I informed Monsieur Dutôt of my plans to leave, he expressed regret and thanks for all my patronage. He then recalled that, when I left my room before, they had found a foam-lined overcoat in the wardrobe. I couldn't fit it in my suitcase to tote around with me for months. I had simply left it there. "Is it yours? he asked.

"No," I said.

"It is necessary to be sure," he said.

"I am sure." I hoped he would excuse the convenient lie. I could not carry the ragged thing on the plane and hoped he could find someone who needed it more than I.

By now I had received the paperwork with the official orders from the Army. Back home I would follow my normal procedure when relocating and file the necessary change of address form with the reserve unit. It would take another two or three months to sort this out and reassign me either to a reserve unit near my new Chicago location or a "control group." This would mean I wasn't obligated to show up anywhere and no effort was required on my part. I sold the typewriter I had bought from my fellow hotel guest Mark when he left for home.

I revisited the Café de l'Odeon on the corner for a final *sandwich à sauçisson sec et vin rouge*. I thought of the friends I had joined there. The young man from Algiers who was an hour late for our lunch appointment, so I ordered and ate lunch. I was just about to leave when he arrived, brimming with apologies, and insisted I join him at his apartment. Before I could object, he took out a steak and began cooking it on his stove. He watched me consume every bite until my plate was empty. Desolated by my rudeness in not waiting long enough for him, somehow I managed to stuff in another meal to show my gratitude for his generous hospitality.

I could never forget my lunches and dinners with sweet little Sophie from Nîmes, who wore her heart on her sleeve. She stole mine when she kissed the cartoon of a wolf on a subway poster. "Such a cute little wolf!" We toured the Ile de la Cité together, admiring Notre Dame's flying buttresses, in their pre-2019-conflagration glory, peering upward into the vast darkness of its Gothic ribbed vaults and deep into its interior. She genuflected as we crossed this main aisle, and a distant priest conducted Mass at the altar. We discovered the underground Holocaust Museum, with its grim reminders of six million perished Jews. Tucked away in the courtyard of the Palace, residence of kings until the 14th century, which serves in modern times as the central police headquarters of Paris, we explored the unique architectural gem, La Sainte Chapelle. This dazzling chapel, with the slimmest possible limestone supports and the maximum expanse of brilliantly colored stained glass, was commissioned by King Louis IX of France to house his collection of Passion relics, including Christ's crown of thorns, which he collected in the First Crusade.

We had spent several weeks together and pleased each other well, until I quit my job and decided to leave for Istanbul. When I returned to Paris, I could not find her. Miguel, the night clerk and unfaithful boyfriend of his funny and delightful compatriot Maria, gave me an address across town for her, which I chased down. Only this time, I was the victim of his deceit. But it was fair play, after all. I did find a friend of hers on my return. Sophie told her she had met an American boy: she was going to marry him and have a big family. Did she mean me? She was warm, willing and delightful, but we had never discussed the future. Yikes! A perfect example of our disparate outlooks. I was on a fantasy tour of the imagination; she was rooted in reality.

My thoughts returned to a Moroccan who said he wanted to get to know me and introduce me to couscous. He took me to his favorite native restaurant. Comfortable there, he ordered a big lunch for us and taught me all about the different varieties of couscous. Then he ranted for an hour about how France oppressed his country. Over my offer to split the cost, he told me I should pay: I was a rich American, he claimed, and owed it to his country. Because it was only way to leave the place quietly and get away from him, I paid.

One night I brought two American girls who had never eaten French food to my corner café. They were still not inclined to try it. After wine, burgers, French fries and ice cream for dessert at à la carte prices, they cleaned me out. They had no French currency to help pay the bill. The waiter was furious and pointed out he would have to pay the difference or lose his job. I skulked back there the next night with the rest of what I owed him, plus a very generous tip.

I recalled Mrs. Campion, one of the regulars at a nearby haunt in rue de la Harpe, where she and a group of students, artists and retirees on limited income dined on the *prix fixe* menu of 6.5 Francs, which included an appetizer of *salade Nicoise*, *salade de crudités* (raw seafood and vegetables) or *rollmops* (rolled sardines), and a table de hôte selection, such as pot roast or chicken, with potato, vegetable and coffee or tea. Madame Campion managed to keep conversation flowing among the lone occupants of adjacent tables, both English and French speakers. After seeing me there over a couple of months, she invited me along with the others to her salon to have a drink and discuss the arts and topics of current interest to the intellectuals of the quarter. She wasn't exactly a Gertrude Stein, nor were her guests—the *prix-fixe*-dinner denizens of the district—the great writers and artists of the day. In fact, I learned I had little in common with this motley crew. While I admired this lady's noble intentions, I felt uncomfortable in the group and didn't bother to return.

Rain was falling on the Boulevard St. Michel, as it had so often that fall, winter and now spring. The drops fell equally on the speeding Citroëns, rattling *deux-chevaux* and lumbering buses; on slicker-clad walkers, benches, pissoirs and awnings, cleansing them of the detritus of the day. The aroma of roasted chestnuts drifted past my table under the peeling, white-barked plane trees, on the rain soaked sidewalks dutifully cleaned daily by *pensionnaires.* These retirees manned the Metro stations, swept the streets and conducted hourly patrols past the folding chairs of the of Jardins du Luxembourg, to collect a few centimes for the privilege of sitting amid the faded Beaux-Arts glory of the former palace grounds. It was hard to leave all this behind in France, especially my friends, perhaps never to see them again.

I had squeezed every last ounce out of my cultural and architectural adventure. It was time to give up my drive to keep moving and discovering. My travel urge was gone, my sensibilities jaded and my longing for home, family and friends insistent. Besides, I had strayed too far and stayed too long: they needed me at home It would be some time before the thrill, irritations and weariness of travel faded and were converted to memories. Mark Twain expressed my feelings best:

> We are at home again. We are exhausted. The sun has roasted us, almost. We have full comfort in one reflection, however. Our experiences in Europe have taught us that in time this fatigue will be forgotten; the heat will be forgotten; the thirst, the tiresome volubility of the guide, the persecutions of the beggars— and then, all that will be left will be pleasant memories of Jerusalem, memories we shall call up with always increasing interest as the years go by, memories which some day will become all beautiful when the last annoyance that incumbers them shall have faded out of our minds never again to return. …
>
> Travel is fatal to prejudice, bigotry and narrow-mindedness, and many of our people need it sorely on these accounts. Broad, wholesome, charitable views of men and things cannot be acquired by vegetating in one little corner of the earth all one's lifetime.[24]

I would have to hand it to Binoux, however, when a couple of years later, he called on Richard Rothman, my original connection to him. We were both working then at Skidmore, Owings & Merrill in Chicago. Richard, who was very busy finishing a project that week, passed him off on me to give him a tour of the University of Illinois, Chicago Circle campus, and a chance to reciprocate a bit of his warm reception and kind hospitality. Back in France, the talented and industrious Binoux and Folliasson continued to succeed in impressing clients and government officials alike, adding their signature designs to a high-rise tower and other structures gracing the newest Paris business district—la Defense.

Paris became part of me, and I was to be lucky enough to return twice, once in 1997 to show it to my wife Connie and two daughters Lisa and Lori—and again in 2002 with Connie, as part of a pre-retirement tour of Central Europe. We enjoyed bargain prices due to the disruption of tourism caused by the 9-11 attacks. I held out hope for another visit, to celebrate our fiftieth wedding anniversary, but it would have to wait until after the pandemic and a return to normal life.

Boulevard St. Michel

Part III: An Architect At Last

> When spring came, even the false spring, there
> were no problems except where to be happier.
> The only thing that could spoil a day was people,
> and if you could keep from making engagements,
> each day had no limits. People were always the
> limiters of happiness, except for the very few that
> were as good as spring itself.
> —Ernest Hemingway. *A Movable Feast, 1957*

IN MY SCHOOLING AND PREPARATION for architecture, I was able to develop my potential for visualization, drawing and writing, In the postwar era of growth, professional design firms and the construction industry expanded to an extent never before seen. My role, however, had yet to be written. Skill, time and chance would determine the next phase of my development. All the while, my father and then my professors groomed me for perfection in word and deed, with expectations (theirs) that my achievement would be unlimited.

But these gains came at a cost.

In architecture, as in my early life, I was always pressed for time. Starting with my suburban high school, we ate dinner whenever Dad got home and off the phone, running his out-of-town businesses. Some nights we ate as late as 8 p.m., and I was expected to help with the dishes. Then I tackled my homework, staying up past midnight. The next morning without fail, Dad would wake me from the dead at 6:00 a.m. to catch the commuter train to high school and start the whole brutal cycle all over again.

Technical theater and set design were labor- and time-intensive, building flats, painting backdrops and fashioning props. At Music Theater, running the shows, with complex scene changes, required split-second accuracy. And strike night involved 36 hours of continuous hard and work with little or no sleep.

Undergraduate Yale was no picnic, with weekly themes due, monumental reading loads and budgeting scarce time. Added to this were social pressures to get a date for the football weekend, participate in extracurricular activities, and fitting into a new group as a Yale man, whatever that meant. Somehow I powered through and got my degree,

Graduate school was even worse: the tension of creating just the right thing, executing the design well and then preparing the presentation. This required creating eye-popping final drawings in India ink and entailed arduous labor and time, always time, during the sleepless charrette, with the risk of a misstep—spilled ink, a misdrawn wall, or a forgotten detail always in play. It all ended abruptly at the deadline.

Out in the world of architecture, we played for keeps. Competition was brutal, stakes were high; the workload was a roller coaster, too busy or not busy enough, and time was money. Dad, who sold his time and advice, often said, "Don't get stuck in a service business. You're better off if you make something that people have to have. This will always sell and make money for you, whether you're at work or not." But he offered no advice on how to get into that kind of business.

By the 1960s, when I entered the working world, all America was fast becoming a service business. Like Dad, I was out of luck.

The toll this pace took on me made time my treasure. I adopted the attitude Hemingway expressed in *A Movable Feast:* "The only thing that could spoil a day was people, and if you could keep from making engagements, each day had no limits." People stopped to talk, told you jokes, filled your mind with irrelevant concerns and wasted your precious time.

The frantic pace gave justification and made excuses for the bad, bred-in habits I had to overcome from my childhood—especially the personality quirks, such as shyness, resentment of authority and failure to trust others. I was trying to break into a profession my family knew little about, which my grandfather had only viewed negatively, and which had a high bar to new members.

Dad played his part in that. He had clawed his way up from poverty to success in the business world. One of his techniques for countering anyone who disagreed with him was to belittle him with sarcasm and ridicule. He could put me in a corner and shut me up in a hurry.

I recall one incident during a vacation at home, when I was just starting architecture school. I explained at the dinner table how Sullivan had evolved his method of architectural expression, "form follows function," with an example: "The columns in a building are burdened with more weight of each added floor, so in some of his taller buildings, they are thicker at the based than at the top."

"That's preposterous!" he boomed. "In my experience in downtown Chicago, the columns are the same from top to bottom."

"But, it's such a simple idea, you add weight—" I sputtered.

"Ridiculous," he said.

"Oh look, there's that pretty bird again," Mom said, pointing out the window. Her defense against family conflict was changing the subject. I was flustered, unable to spell out a simple concept for my father. He insisted on being heard, but felt no obligation, when challenged, to listen to me. The topic was closed, and I remained silent for the rest of the meal

My positive qualities, innate or learned, were hard work, a promotional sense and a stubborn "stick-to-it-iveness," as my mother called it, which served me well. I used my opportunity to travel widely. I followed theatrical director David Tihmar's advice: "Feed on the arts as grist for your mill." I honed skills in planning, architectural design and visualization, including a facility in freehand sketching I improved throughout my lifetime. I developed my verbal skills as well, which enabled me to translate visual concepts into words for the business world. I used both visual and verbal tools to influence and win clients. But were they enough?

To win the confidence of clients, one needed people skills. When, I wondered, had I ever had time to learn them?

21

PUTTING MY HOUSE IN ORDER

FOR MY FIRST JOB after I returned to Chicago from Europe, a friend of a Glencoe neighbor offered me an opportunity to join his firm, which specialized in commercial and industrial building design. He was a mature architect seeking younger people to take over his design, production and, ultimately, management responsibility. He was honest about the lack of prominence of their projects, helping industries expand their factories and warehouses, designing stores and other workspaces for business clients.

Although it was a good offer, I passed it up in favor of joining Skidmore, Owings and Merrill, a glamorous, high profile design firm—a leader of the profession. But glamor had its drawbacks. At the prominent firm I had to stand in line behind scores of graduates with master's degrees who performed menial drafting jobs in hopes of attracting the notice of the star design leaders. After a year of this, I finally left this famous firm for a position where my skills were rarer and much more in demand, a course-correction after what I realized might have been an error in judgment.

Former May Company president David C. Farrell credited his success to a strategy of following the path of least resistance to the top. In retailing, everyone wanted to be a buyer, and competition was stiff to rise within and beyond that group. Instead, he pinned his hopes on learning the business side of the company—marketing, administration and money management. While his peers were still selecting merchandise and trying to get ahead, he began running things.

Ultimately it served me well to have SOM on my resume. Advising my young self from my 2020 point of view, however, I would say: "Take the path of least resistance to the top. Jump on the industrial architecture opportunity. They need you and will teach you everything they know. They will allow you to progress and run their operations for them. Then you will be free to pursue bigger and higher-profile projects, once you have acquired the skills to accomplish them."

From Skidmore, Owings and Merrill, the new position I was offered took me back to Fruco & Associates, St. Louis, an architectural and engineering branch of Fruin-Colnon, a long-established construction company dating back to th leather and lumber interests of St. Louis history.

Recruited by my former professor Bill Weismantel, I returned to St. Louis to resume employment on another riverfront project with this firm, where I had worked that summer of 1963. By now I had caught on to the principle of taking the path of least resistance, but I always wondered what my career might have been like if I had started doing it from the outset—I could have been a firm principal much sooner, with an even stronger base of experience and good will, more easily acquiring new work.

After a year of work experience, I took the four-day exam for my architectural license in Jefferson City, the state capital. As part of the approval process, a few weeks later I was called to a downtown office, where the three architectural members of the State Board of Professional Registration conducted the required personal interview. It began in a collegial, chatty manner. But then, without any prompting, I turned defensive, concerned about failure. I damaged my image by calling attention to my employer firm's design-build operation and defended them.

This awkward discussion must have given the registration board members pause. I had passed all my objective exams, except they found fault with the design portion of the test, the only subjective judgment available to them. They held me over to retake the design test the following year. By then I had changed employers to a growing, "pure" architecture firm—without any taint of construction ownership. I made small talk in the interview and two weeks later received my architectural license.

In the 1960s when I was starting my career, architects were known for marrying beautiful women. It made sense to me since they recognized beauty in all things. But I didn't understand why they also had a high divorce rate from these beauties. I eventually concluded that their relationships were based on external, physical appeal, rather than friendship, love and understanding. What I didn't recognize, however, was my own tendency to judge women in the same superficial way.

I have often wondered why I seldom asked more questions of these lovely young women, learned more about their history, their families, their hopes and dreams. It took me a dozen more years to change my attitudes, however imperfectly, and to ask, to listen and to learn more about the other people in my life.

And then in St. Louis during the summer of 1970, a work colleague suggested I join him, his wife and her college friend on a blind date for a day float trip on the Current River in the Ozarks. He said her name was Connie Sulkowski and gave me her address. I picked her up at her house in a north suburb. I almost got a ticket for parking my car, with its Peace symbol on the bumper, in a No Parking Zone at her front curb. She explained to the cop I was leaving soon and had just stopped to pick her up. I should have known then that I was in trouble. But to use Congressman John Lewis's phrase, it was "good trouble."

That long, perfect day in August, we swam by a sandbar, frolicked in the river, paddled our canoe and couldn't wait to say goodnight to our friends so we could spend time alone together. We found a café and spent another two hours discussing everything under the sun, including beliefs, hobbies, likes and dislikes. I finally dropped her off at 10 PM, after a marathon fifteen-hour day.

One the next weekend, out of habit I attended yet another singles event. I wasn't much interested in mingling, but I met one picture-perfect blonde, who told me she had been married and divorced. She said, "I married for looks alone and ignored things about his personality which I later came to dislike." Here I was, attracted by her looks alone. I was so stale on this scene, I stood aside from the crowd—their chatter had risen to a dull roar—commiserating with a guy who stood beside me, whose mood seemed to match mine. "You know," he said, "I'm ready to settle down. There's a limit to the number of cans of beer you can drink by the pool."

The following week I picked Connie up for a company picnic. I parked legally across the street this time, and we sat on the stone bench in front of her house. I proposed with a diamond solitaire I had bought the day before, and she accepted. I made that drive to North County every day until our wedding, which I wanted as soon as possible. We settled on the day after Christmas. Her mother, a professional seamstress of wedding dresses, had a rush order for the job of her life. Moreover, she had to plan the event. Connie said her mother achieved sainthood in the process. While I avoided more parking tickets, I stayed in good trouble for the next fifty years. Two married children and three grandchildren later, we had grown into a happy family.

Connie, whose common sense, independence and thinking process were totally different from mine, was to be my best mentor. She helped me overcome many of my hesitations and fears. To the extent I paid attention, her realism and doubts kept me from pitfalls. When I became impatient with uncomfortable, dead-end work situations, she was quick to point out errors in the course of my career. And yet, like my father, I was still a dreamer.

I made other mistakes before Connie could point out the

error in my impulsive ways, I put her through a lot of worry and stress. I quit a paying job which, in my opinion, had turned sour and started my own firm. I had some success with clients I had worked with at previous firms, but earnings were slow to materialize. At Connie's prompting, I took a Dale Carnegie course to overcome my shyness. It was an era of expansion, and marketing professional Stuart Rose discovered that our entire industry thirsted for training seminars on how to find and win new business. I signed up for his seminars, took them seriously and heeded advice from colleagues on potential good clients. My "mistake" forced me to learn the marketing side of the business. At end of ten difficult years, I found my niche and began learning how my dad's promotional and advertising outlook applied to marketing professional services.

I had no shortage of big ideas. I thought about and sketched concepts for enclosing trees, gardens and rooms within geodesic domes before John Portman had ever built a Hyatt Regency Hotel. I was hired to create plans for the downtown St. Louis riverfront. My Washington U. professor, urban planner Bill Weismantel and I imagined and illustrated a theme park and a visitor recreation plan for the land surrounding Eero Saarinen's Gateway Arch. Over my career I proposed three different reuse plans for the St. Louis and Illinois riverfront near the Gateway Arch—among over 200 such plans SIU Professor Robert Mendelson enumerated in a 1970s survey of modern planning studies for the St. Louis region.

With all these unbuilt concepts, I worried I'd be like Claude N. Ledoux, Russell Sturgis or Eric Mendelsohn, more famous for their unbuilt visionary concepts than for constructed projects. I was fortunate, however, to have clients adopt some of those ideas and to see them grow into major projects. Moreover, a lot of this was paying work, which employed me for years and led to our firm's success. When clients found themselves stalled, waiting for zoning approvals, lower interest rates and markets to catch up with their ambitions, they hired our services to flesh out and visualize their bold plans. As a result, planning work helped to recession-proof our workflow.

In my interpersonal relations, especially in regard to forming friendships, allies and business contacts, I felt I could have done much better. Through developing better interpersonal skills, I might have learned more, found good mentors sooner and trusted in others to help me advance.

But every wrong turn teaches something—fortunately I learned from those errors. Yale Architecture School confirmed my ability to design and my choice of a career. Changing schools broadened my definition of architecture. Traveling increased my visualization skills, broadened my knowledge of people and deepened my understanding of architecture in its social setting. Switching firms showed me various ways to practice. Starting my own business required me to learn marketing. Finally, joining with the engineering profession to seek new work showed me the universality of marketing techniques in different types of business. I was lucky to have great mentors at each step along the way. Marrying the right woman and building a family helped correct for these mistakes and stay on a steady course.

In my relations with peers, I would encourage my younger self not to compete so hard with my rivals. If I helped them advance, they would have reciprocated later. In my early career I wasn't very good at employing the common-sense wisdom then current in business, "What goes around, comes around," and "I'll scratch your back and you scratch mine." My company allowed me plenty of time to get to know our clients on a personal basis, and these relationships grew into the trust necessary for easy communication and a good understanding between them and our staff. The result was successful projects and continuing business with them in the future.

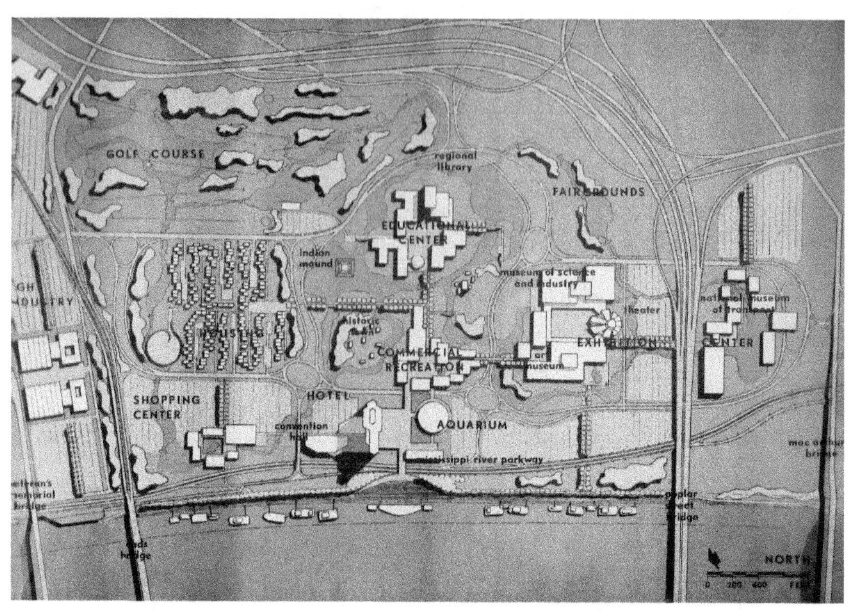

Illinoistown Master Plan. showing Industrial, Housing, Education and Recreation Uses
Fruco & Associates, Architects-Engineers, 1963

Central Riverfront Study: Old St. Louis District
Even the new buildings respect the historic scale.
Fruco & Associates, Architects-Engineers, 1966

22

RESTORING OLD SPACES

FOR THE SUMMER BETWEEN THE FIFTH AND SIXTH YEARS at Washington University architecture school, my planning professor Bill Weismantel, as a consultant to Fruco & Associates, Architects-Engineers, hired me and David A. Roth as urban designers for the 524-acre site on the Illinois side of the Mississippi River facing the Gateway Arch. The client was the Port Authority of Southwestern Illinois. Professor Weismantel researched potential land uses and available markets for the vast acreage, then occupied by railroad yards, a grain elevator and scattered housing neighborhoods. He analyzed the needs of Illinois, the national potential of the site and the area's history, dating back 10,000 years to Modoc man. The Illinois tribes also roamed the region, including the Mound Builders (about 1200 AD).

By 1814 a small settlement had grown where Wiggins Ferry crossed the Mississippi to St. Louis, called Illinoistown. Weismantel concluded in 1963, that this should be the name for our site master plan, with land uses as follows:

> A careful, realistic study revealed a concept which promises to focus national attention on the east side of the Mississippi as well as on the Jefferson

National Expansion Memorial, national trends indicate major influences in America:

1). An almost insatiable demand for recreation of all types,

2) An increasing desire for education at all levels.

The master plan for this site, now referred to as Illinoistown, has as its basic theme education and recreation of national interest. Illinoistown has been designed for the following activities: National Museum of Transport, aquarium, golf course, art museum, residential townhouses, river museum, educational complex, museum of science and industry, riverfront activities, industrial display area, and recreational development of theaters, restaurants, bars and active physical sports. It is designed to be a place where people come to be refreshed and renewed.

To do this, it must have a character all its own.

While working two years later at my first job in Chicago at Skidmore, Owings & Merrill, I got a call from my former planning professor, Bill Weismantel. He told me of a second planning project he was working on with Fruco: a Central Riverfront Study. the client this time, the City of St Louis, Board of Public Service. The purpose was to study potential land uses surrounding the Gateway Arch. He offered me a job as urban designer, with the further option of continuing as a junior architect at Fruco & Associates. Bill, acting as project planner also hired an economist and planned to use the architectural firm to present the study.

Because our analysis identified the shifting function of downtowns from office and retail uses to tourism, recreation and sports facilities, we proposed visitor attractions; education and recreation uses north and south of the Arch grounds, and a transportation loop to connect downtown and a ring of surrounding parking lots with the riverfront. These included sports parks, a historically focused theme park and re-use of the nine-block district of three to five-story historic warehouses for offices, apartments and ground floor tourist drinking, dining and entertainment venues.

During our study period, two rival real estate developers each proposed plans for the valuable nine blocks immediately north of the Arch grounds. The first plan envisioned re-use of some of the historic buildings but included clearance for new construction of three apartment towers; the second proposed total clearance for eleven towers of high-rise housing, most of them to be financed with federal grants and loans. A vigorous internal debate ensued among city staff and elected officials, who traded charges and counter-charges of impropriety.

Shortly thereafter, in November, 1966, our study was published. Included was our recommendation that there be no towers:

> Applying the principle of conservation of resources, we can conclude only that, next to a consciously historical monument such as the Jefferson National Expansion Memorial, demolition of this ready-made museum of architectural, social and economic history could be an irreplaceable loss. There should be no large-scale clearance for redevelopment here. Nor should there be any high-rise buildings east of the Third Street Expressway…for the comfortable scale of the low buildings would be threatened.

An internal recommendation by the Planning Commission to follow our historic preservation guidelines—which clearly stated there should be no new towers—was suppressed. The cover-up was then revealed. Eventually a plan similar to ours was adopted, and a sluggish redevelopment market (as abetted by the decline of HUD under a new administration) killed both opposing plans and ensured that our limited-growth recommendation prevailed.

Other features of the study were also implemented,

confirming that the plan had a positive influence on development. Transit loops and a pedestrian bridge over a sunken highway, connecting downtown and parking lots with the riverfront, are now permanent features of our system. A mix of office, residential and visitor commercial restaurants, bars and entertainment spots now occupies the nine-block historic area, rechristened Laclede's Landing. The downtown continues to attract additional sports facilities, such as the newer convention-football complex, an ice hockey arena for the St. Louis Blues and, most recently, a new stadium for a St. Louis-based soccer team. Moreover, conventions and tourism have become a significant factor in the regional economy.

Our study received good publicity in the local newspapers and caused some excitement about downtown revitalization. I was getting traction, along with a sense that what we were doing mattered.

After I had started working for the firm now called PGAV, I began laying out industrial plans for their best developer client, who was in search of new industrial and office park sites. I introduced the developer to the need for planning with a discovery I'd made. I had sold them on the idea of doing a survey of available land throughout the region for new business and industrial parks. While I was prospecting sites at the Corps of Engineers for this study, one project manager there pointed out: "See this highway embankment over here, and then on the other side of this large floodplain, that rail embankment?"

I saw.

"All you would need to do is connect the two with a levee and you could enclose over 1000 acres of land and protect them from flooding."

It looked easy to me. If I had known how complicated it would become, I would have said "you're crazy" and brushed him off. I showed the parcel on one of the presentation boards for the land survey. When I presented the results, the real estate developer was astounded. He hired a helicopter to check out the sites I had shown on my regional maps, liked and proceeded to acquire all the property I had shown between the two bridges—contingent, of course upon his obtaining rezoning for the whole package. An early adopter of computers, he made Return-on-Investment calculations comparing land and development cost with potential sales price and profits. The results based on present worth were off the charts. The 1200 acres involved was in St. Louis County, about one-sixth of it in the adjacent city of Bridgeton, a separate political jurisdiction, guaranteeing us double the fun and excitement.

What we had never heard of in 1970 and hadn't bargained for was the environmental movement. Environmental preservation groups came out of the woodwork, pointing out how levee systems always fail, how they raise river levels and how development adds internal runoff from the land and adds to flooding downstream. While we couldn't see how our little 1200-acre parcel made much difference one way or the other on what happened to the global environment, one would have thought we were starting World War III.

The small but proud community of Bridgeton was the first to hear our rezoning arguments, and it became the tail that wagged the dog. All the newspaper publicity the project generated just to add 200 acres poisoned the well and threatened our proposed rezoning action for the larger acreage within the boundaries of unincorporated St. Louis County.

When, a few years later, the exaggerated and overheated heated arguments cooled, I realized that several of their contentions were true. In retrospect it would have been easier all around to leave the river floodplain alone and look harder for open parcels on higher ground.

After two years of elaborate planning, and expensive zoning lawyers, our project got the zoning, all right. The county was too motivated to increase its tax base to be distracted by such a minor concern.

Nonetheless, the developer hired a respected civil engineering firm to design the levee. Their experienced experts did it well—it was one of only two levees on the Missouri River that survived the 1993 Flood—and the site became an important development client for Horner & Shifrin over the next forty years. Eventually I joined that firm, broadened their interests to include planning and helped increase their workload in both architecture and engineering,

Center for Independent Living, East St. Louis, Illinois

Shorewood Place, Michigan City, Indiana

23 CLAIMING MY TURF IN ST. LOUIS

FTER SOME DISILLUSIONMENT and lack of control over my career working for others, I left stable employment in 1973 to form my own firm. I had relationships with a few existing clients I believed would engage my services: an office-park developer, the St. Louis District–Corps of Engineers, a small denominational college and a parochial elementary and high school. Among these, a developer I had met working for a former employer preferred to work one-on-one with me. Over several years he became a steady client and commissioned the design of several new, small office buildings and a chain hotel. Through a former Horner & Shifrin civil engineer, a member of the congregation, I was employed to design a church school and a master plan for a denominational college. Through Connie's contacts, I was hired to design code compliance upgrades for a parochial school and a new classroom building for the campus.

While I saw great advantages to establishing my own architectural practice, staking a claim for individual recognition and developing my own clients, in some respects it was a self-inflicted wound. After serving these clients, I learned their work was not enough: I needed a system for generating repeated work and a higher volume of activity. I would have to develop new business more effectively to maintain a steady stream of work.

In my own smaller operation, while in complete control of my activities, I learned I was out of the running for the big commissions. I lacked the designers, detail technicians, specification writers and office support staff to compete with established firms with more capabilities. In a small, new firm, I may have been in control but did not have the established track record of experience in some of the building types, such as the office buildings, libraries, housing complexes and hotels that were currently being built. Nor did I have the financial staying power to wait, nor knowledge to become instantly successful in the marketing of architectural services. I also envied those who had saved for years or inherited the magical ingredient necessary to start a new business, investment capital. While only one of several ingredients for success, ready investment capital would have helped jump-start those activities.

I would be limited to competing for smaller jobs: owner-occupied office buildings, store design or single small businesses, and increasingly rare commissions to design houses, usually custom homes for the wealthy. Even in these building types typically performed by smaller firms, competition was fierce. I would have to beat out firms with more completed projects in their portfolios, yet I offered less expertise and experience than some of those smaller firms could demonstrate.

One positive benefit growing out of this dilemma included the need to venture out and seek new work. With the encouragement of a fellow architect in another small firm, I called Missouri's Division of Design and Construction, the state agency that managed new building and expansion and maintenance of the state's physical plant. I received my first assignment and, over ten years, progressed to larger jobs on numerous state-owned buildings and campuses.

One of the larger projects I designed for the State of Missouri was conversion of a National Guard Armory to an Armed Forces Reserve Center, a joint-use project between the U.S. Army Reserve and the State of Missouri, located in Rolla. The project added a common lobby for the existing National Guard offices and new offices for the U. S. Army Reserve unit based there, an Army kitchen and other improvements for parking and vehicle maintenance. The project required extensive cooperation among state National Guard headquarters and federal Army Reserve offices, especially in review and approval of plans. The result was efficient joint use of the armory for expanded use by an Army Reserve Bridge Truck company and National Guard meetings, as well as making the upgraded facilities available for community use.

Following this model, I eventually cultivated ties with federal, state and local design agencies in adjacent states and developed longstanding relationships. I tried joint marketing with healthcare and housing consultant John Coggeshall, who knew how to access federal funds set aside for this purpose, and designed small group homes for the mentally ill, essentially assisted communal living facilities with a home-like atmosphere. I learned how to make cold calls on government offices throughout the Midwest and procured contracts from several district offices of the U. S, Army Corps of Engineers.

The small group home projects had a complex history. A product of Rosalynn Carter's vision for deinstitutionalization of the mentally ill, they were designed as places where these, mentally ill individuals could live, learn or relearn the activities of daily living, some holding outside jobs, while they had visits from health and service professionals to improve their lives. Most had 12 to 14 beds, divided equally between men's and women's individual bedrooms, communal dining, kitchen and TV rooms and common areas for social functions. They were funded by the U.S. Department of Housing and Urban Development which provided forgivable direct loans for construction to Community Mental Health Centers under Section 202 and rent subsidies from Section 8 Rental Assistance programs of the Housing Act. From 1978 through 1982, John and I designed and saw completed five such buildings funded under this program in Illinois, Indiana and Missouri.

Armed Forces Reserve Center, Rolla, Missouri

While still in my own smaller firm, I discovered that the Illinois Department of Transportation also required labor-intensive submissions similar in complexity to the federal process. Since I was seeking smaller assignments such as the design of wayside rest stations, I asked a senior IDOT official whether there was any way around this cumbersome procedure. He laughed and said, "You're not the first to ask this question. One firm principal recently said, 'We know each other. Couldn't you just call me up and let me know when you have some work and then allow me submit all this paperwork to get the job?' I had to tell him it doesn't work that way—we use this paperwork to decide who is qualified in the first place."

I had been doing many of the right things to compete in the newer, more sophisticated project marketing world. I wrote good proposals, learned the tricky art of completing state and federal qualification paperwork, making our firm known to the many people in state and federal agencies and cultivating relationships with their staff. At the Corps of Engineers I learned any professional on the government's staff might be called in at random to serve on a selection committee, and the more of these dedicated public servants I knew, the more likely was my firm's selection. For several years I scrambled for sufficient work to support a living wage, while developing long-term relationships with good clients.

Then in mid-career, an interesting opportunity opened up.

My former clients at a midsize civil engineering firm needed help, both in the occasional architectural assignment they acquired and, as it turned out, in marketing and new project acquisition. They were accustomed to mining a "good-old-boy" network, calling on their friends in various military and other public agencies. Now they were up against the new, merit-based system, under which expertise had to be catalogued, described in great detail and submitted in written form, in order for a selection committee of an agency to consider hiring a design firm. While I had been chasing such work for my smaller operation—with never more than four staffers as support—in this firm I could represent an accomplished team of over 50 established professionals and support staff.

At first I was hesitant, having to give up all the goodwill I had built up over the previous ten years for my own firm. But when my wife pointed out the advantages of the offer—a good salary, benefits, support staff— she convinced me I could greatly increase the stability of our life. It was also a chance to apply my hard-won knowledge of the profession on a much larger scale.

Like many architectural and combined engineer-architect firms, this one had a fifty-year record of achievement, but the old guard of clients they had dealt with were the only ones who knew about it. They lacked the promotional habits to inform the next generation of decision-makers about their wide-ranging capabilities and fine reputation. In this regard, the senior principals of this grand old firm had had lost the thread and no longer held a key to developing new government business. When they made me an offer of a salaried job at a handsome, steady wage, I found it too good to refuse.

This would also be a comedown for me from the glamour of a pure architecture-only firm. But the multi-disciplinary operation opened up my reach to engineering, as well as architectural services. This was a golden opportunity to follow the path of least resistance to the top.

In my new role, representing a larger, 50-years-established firm, I at once had the much greater capabilities and credibility of an accomplished team behind me. Soon my efforts gained traction: we began winning the larger state and federal contracts for which my small firm had previously been ineligible. Furthermore, I learned that these marketing skills applied not only to my own architectural field, but also to the much larger market for civil, structural and environmental engineering services as well. In the federal market, the architects were still considered essential: the jobs we pursued, after all, were called Architect-Engineer contracts.

Seamlessly, I broadened my goals. From my chosen field of architecture, I moved into the arena of design firm marketing, which I would study and master for the rest of my career. I learned how to build larger teams by partnering with other engineering and architectural firms that had the skills our firm lacked, but which were required for a specific contract. This technique, and the skill of continuing to market, reminding the client of what else we could do for them when we already has the contract, led to relationships with public agencies lasting over many years.

In advising my young self, I would counsel him to compete less and care more about others—they may hold the key to my future. Ask others for advice and listen to them, I would say— they will tell you whatever you really want to know. Pose your problems out loud to them. Even if they don't have the answer, just stating the issues may help you to see them more clearly. Get to know others, with easy questions: "How did you get here?", "What do you like to do?" and "What are your hopes, dreams and goals?" You'll find they are dying to tell you.

In joining a larger firm, I had stumbled upon a much expanded career. On the way to this point, I had committed missteps, taken wrong turns and made false starts. Nevertheless, I did some things right. I deserted Yale as a sinking ship when I sensed there was something very wrong with the architecture school. The program also ignored the urban context, architectural history and the larger meaning and purpose soon to be demanded of the built environment. The arbitrariness, sycophancy and hero worship that prevailed in Rudolph's art and architecture building after I left in 1963, was soon to be consumed in an almost symbolic inferno and reincarnated in a better program by others, like a phoenix from its ashes. The important lesson from this experience was, at least it was experience: The human mind has a remarkable capability to distill it into inspiration, vision and new directions.

I would achieve my goal of designing and completing numerous useful and attractive buildings, planning several campuses, urban downtown revitalization projects and business parks. I would support myself in an architectural career and attain a position of leadership in my firm and my profession. I would be able to support a family and show them some of the world I had had traveled. I can say, at least, I took a stand and saw it through.

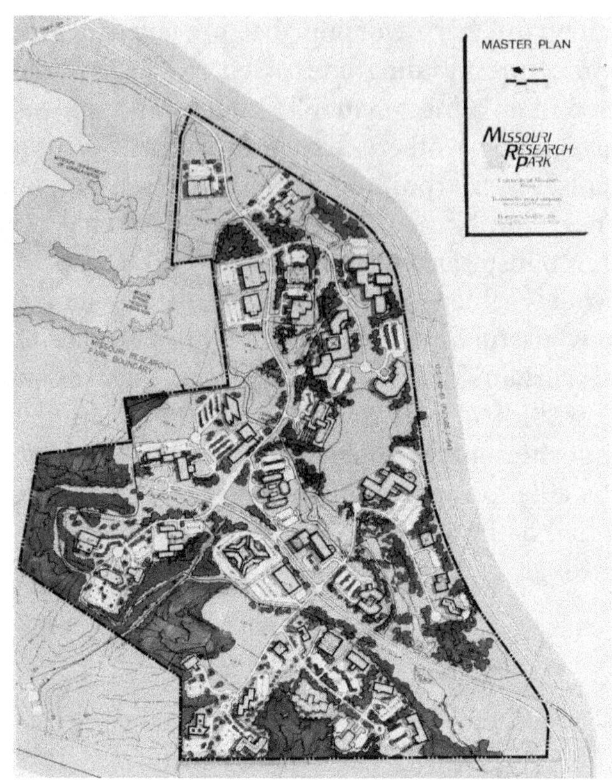

Missouri Research Park Master Plan
University of Missouri, Owner

Sixth and Cherry Parking Structure
City of Columbia, Missouri, Owner

24

DESIGNING NEW PLACES

I N THE 1990s, while the architectural profession was wringing its collective hands about the growth of Design-Build contracting, the federal government began hiring such teams anyway—usually a consortium composed of a General Contractor, an Architect-Engineer and a Construction Manager—in order to obtain the best designed, most cost effective and most efficiently constructed new buildings for public use. They were determined to have the benefits of these three worlds, obtaining close coordination with contractors, architect-engineer teams and construction operators during the design and all subsequent phases of the construction process.

Federal agencies, and even some private corporations, sought courthouses, office buildings and headquarters buildings by requesting two-stage proposals, the first for finalist selection of qualified teams and then for competing design, cost and value proposals from the chosen finalist teams, sometimes offering a stipend to finalist teams for the second phase, an expensive process of preparing and bidding such detailed designs and proposals. As far as federal and corporate integrators were concerned, the simon-pure architects could either continue to fight the consolidators of all these construction services or join them: the world had moved on.

We rarely joined such teams, mainly used for large scale, high-profile projects, such as Illinois Center in Chicago, the new Lincoln Museum and Library in Springfield, Illinois, and big city, high-rise courthouses, none of which were in our target marketing plans. They attracted the very large architecture and engineering firms, to which we had little to offer, since they duplicated most of our services with their in-house personnel.

Meanwhile, we were expanding architectural and engineering practice by another means: working on a larger scale to influence urban design. We were planning and designing projects with in-house or closely-allied consulting realtors, planners, architects, economists, landscape architects and engineers—civil, structural, mechanical and electrical. Viewed another way, we were providing concept-to-completion services for industrial and business parks, research campuses and educational institutions: a different route to expanding our design practice to meet modern needs. We, too, were redefining and expanding the scope of architectural practice.

When I joined Horner & Shifrin in early 1983, Ron Dyess, the company's sole architect, and the marketing staff had developed an industrial portfolio including several clients: Gusdorf Corporation, maker of knocked-down office furniture kits; Harris Corporation, a manufacturer of radio transmitting and receiving equipment; a local dairy, and the design of accessory buildings, on-site laboratories and public works buildings for the firm's engineering clients. With the help of David Lee, a British-born industrial engineer and marketer, project engineers familiar with local governments, my own contacts with local, state and federal government agencies and our marketing staff, we were able to add several new types of work. For DeSoto, Missouri, we converted a former U.S. Post Office to a City Hall and government center. With the enlarged staff I now represented, we obtained an Indefinite-delivery Architect-Engineer contract with the Kansas City District Corps of Engineers for numerous building conversions, renovation projects and new training buildings at Fort Leonard Wood, Missouri. Soon we got a new assignment for the State of Missouri to replace security windows and upgrade the water supply at Algoa Correctional Center near Jefferson City. After figuring out their system, we also received assignments from the Illinois Capital Development Board for buildings in our region of Southwestern Illinois.

Under its former owners the firm, with a distinguished 50-year history behind it, was coasting along with an older master-apprentice system commonly found in many older firms. Productivity was low, and best employees were leaving on a regular basis to seek more opportunity and better pay. Some in the industry were even considering the formation of unions, first among draftsmen and then even among professional engineers and architects, to remedy the problem, a solution distasteful even to many of the workers themselves. The reason I had joined the firm was also related to limitations on what I could earn in a single-ownership small firm and the ability of a larger firm to invest in and adapt to the coming computer revolution. What was to be done?

Leonard Kirberg, an aspiring engineer trained at the University of Missouri – Rolla had some ideas. He had worked briefly at McDonald Douglas Corporation and had spent the balance of his career at Horner & Shifrin observing, while earning the confidence of, the firm's management

In 1986 the firm's president and officers agreed to retire, let a new generation take over and appointed engineer Leonard Kirberg as the new president. The first task he tackled was transition of the firm's ownership from its former principals to all of its employees. His path was not to be easy. While he had been appointed by the outgoing president, who had agreed to the formation of an Employee Stock Ownership Plan (ESOP) in mid-1987, he encountered a serious obstacle.

The critical step in the process was establishing a sale price for the company's stock, to be acquired by the ESOP, which would be responsible for the repaying a loan to compensate former principals. The original valuation consultant hired by the outgoing principals set a price, which Kirberg, representing the incoming management, considered artificially high. The matter went to court, and transfer of stock to the ESOP was delayed for many months. Nonetheless, Len held his ground, and demanded a fair acquisition price, which would not saddle the new ownership with an unwarranted and unreasonable debt. At last, the judge rendered his decision, agreed to the new management's sale terms and settled the case, while he admonished the previous ownership for their unreasonable demands and unnecessary delay.

As a result of Kirberg's victory, our newly enfranchised employees worked with increased drive and determination. One example was the firm's role in a multi-company consortium that won the contract to design MetroLink, a new light rail transportation system for St. Louis. Spurred on by pride of ownership, the firm's employees worked evenings and weekends to meet strict deadlines and match the quality and speed of the other much larger firms on the team. This new spirit characterized the firm from that point forward and led to its continued expansion. The seed Len Kirberg planted gave the firm's employee-owners a stake in success, and their motivation, pride and achievement has resulted in the firm's exponential growth to the present day.

At that key moment, Len Kirberg appointed me Vice President - Marketing Services, and I applied everything I had learned from my family and in conducting my own business to meet the challenge. In my own firm I had already begun marketing my architectural services to military and governmental clients with limited results. Due to Horner & Shifrin's larger staff and longer history, however, I soon established traction in these efforts and began to succeed.

Although I had previously illustrated projects for the St. Louis District, U.S. Army Corps of Engineers, I was now able, with a larger firm and my familiarity with the federal paperwork necessary, to update the firm's relationship with this local federal office and obtain an Indefinite Delivery, Indefinite Quantity (IDIQ) contract for civil works. Numerous structural and civil engineering feasibility studies followed, including design of roads in southeastern Missouri, floodgates along the Meramec River at Valley Park, levee repair evaluations and scope-of-work determinations for rapid local bidding after the 1995 flood.

Under this contract we had the opportunity to make some new science on one assignment with the St. Louis District. We assisted in the setup and execution of a Bubble Screen Mitigation Study to reduce the impact of underwater blasting on fish, with Dr. Greg Hempen, PhD. We helped him prove that surrounding an underwater demolition blast with a screen of air bubbles significantly reduced the impact on the river's fish population. By demonstrating a method of saving the lives of fish during necessary demolition operations to construct the new Lock and Dam 27, we made the task of removing old bridge piers and former lock and dam structures more friendly to the river environment. As a result, this experiment earned an American Society of Civil Engineers Honor Award. for Horner & Shifrin and the St. Louis District, U. S. Army Corps of Engineers.

Another high point in planning occurred with an assignment under this open-ended contract with the St. Louis District, U.S. Army Corps of Engineers, a Rail Relocation Study to support negotiations with the Burlington Northern, successor to the same rail company that my grandfather had helped build, for the acquisition of a Mississippi River bridge to make way for the Lock and Dam 27 replacement project. Brad Susman, an economist with Team Four Research, the consultant we hired, established the facts and provided the basis for the Corps of Engineers' own estimate of the railroad's cost caused by the bridge's removal. The railroad claimed this change would require rerouting coal trains around the bridge to cross the Mississippi elsewhere for the transport of hard, long-burning coal from the northwestern states.

Susman drew out enough information from the railroad company on rail traffic to establish that the company no longer used these sources of coal, but instead others that did not require trains to cross the Mississippi. Based on our report, the Corps negotiations with the railroad resulted in six million dollars in savings to the federal government. These negotiations reduced the railroad's estimate of over $44 million of economic costs to $37 million. Brad joked that I should have taken this job on commission, based on a percentage of the savings achieved. I observed that the government did not offer such a basis, but instead granted our highly respectable hourly rates for principals and his own ample consulting fee.

Brad, a strapping six-foot-tall, deep-voiced bachelor, with a suntan and buzz-cut black hair, customarily appeared at my office in his charcoal gray suit about lunchtime. After a quick update on our project, over lunch, he regaled me with tales of his sail fishing in Baja California, travels to other exotic locales and project trivia, These included a phone conversation with John Walker Barriger IV, President and Owner of a surviving Illinois branch of the Chicago, Milwaukee and Western Railroad, which served one route to the bridge. He had very little to do except watch over the traffic of three trains a week, but he was happy to consume two hours of Brad's expensive time: He related his family's history in detail—apparently his father J. W. Barriger III, had been a prominent figure in American railroading.

On another of our projects with Brad, engaged by the Corps to analyze the feasibility of a new marina at Mark Twain Lake near Florida, Missouri, birthplace of that renowned author, we stopped for the night at a small junction motel where our route met the main lake road.

Over drinks before dinner, Brad shivered. "My God!"

"What is it?" From his alarmed tone and his pinched facial expression, I wondered if he'd had a heart attack.

In a tone worthy of a British Lord horrified to discover a fly in his soup, he uttered, "In this key lake location, a potential tourist mecca, I can't believe it—they've *watered* the gin!"

He quickly remedied this fault with the waitress and warned the management, continuing this policy, would amount to commercial suicide.

In order to break into a new market for our firm's services on the Ohio River, I formed a working relationship with a firm already established as a long-time client of the Louisville District Corps of Engineers. I met and made friends with Mickey Jones, a cheerful, confident and accomplished engineer and marketing principal with Mason & Hanger Engineering, of Lexington, Kentucky. Mickey had built great relationships with the Louisville District and established a continuous good performance record on contracts with Corps project managers over several years on federal architectural work at military bases and related architectural assignments. For this one, he knew he needed to ally his firm with an accomplished civil engineering firm with a track record on federal river work.

In preparation for our submittal on forthcoming civil works at McAlpine Lock and Dam, I made an appointment with Dr. Snow, the storied dean of lock and dam engineering at the civil works branch of Louisville District. I had never met Dr. Snow. When I arrived I met a stocky senior engineer with a kindly face, snowy white sideburns framing a bald crown and wire-rimmed glasses. We chatted for a few moments, and he escorted me to a conference table in the civil engineering area, around which were assembled a dozen younger and senior men and women—all project engineers in the civil works division. Aghast at this golden opportunity. I hoped the talk I had prepared would measure up to the task.

I introduced myself and the firm, presented our experience in large civil works projects and mentioned the team we had formed with the established Louisville firm. I pointed out that the Corps during the past 20 years had very little funding for lock and dam work up and down the river systems. I observed that, due to Congress's inability to pass a new water bill during those years, neither did other, very large firms have recent work to show within the federal funding area of the continental United States. I pointed out, however, that we had kept alive our qualifications with private levees, such as the 500-year flood protection system we had designed for Earth City, and other recent levee maintenance contracts for St. Louis District Corps of Engineers.

The meeting was cordial, questions from the group were relevant and I spotted among them a couple of familiar faces, including that of Larry Dalton, a slow-talking a laid-back gentleman with a Lou-a-vull drawl, a man of few but carefully selected words. He was one several of project managers I had called on before. I hoped I had said enough to convince the group of our sincere interest in working with them on this important project and our excellent qualifications for the work. I thanked Dr. Snow for his welcome reception. I called on the contracting officer before I left to inform him of my meeting, climbed into my car and practically sailed home through the lovely hills of southern Indiana on the wings of hope.

Apparently these marketing efforts were on target. A month or so later, after we had incorporated all these ideas, thoughts and qualifications into an inch-thick submission booklet, we got the magic phone call from the contracting officer and the head of the selection committee. In response to their routine questions, we told them, yes, we still wanted the contract; yes, we still had the team we proposed in our submission, answered a few detailed questions, and asked a few questions of our own about the project schedule and scope. They promised to let us know their decision. A couple of weeks later, we received another phone call notifying us of our selection, followed by a huge packet of paperwork in the mail with the contract offer.

We began work on numerous assignments for the Louisville District on an architect-engineer contract for the design of a replacement lock at McAlpine Lock and Dam on the Ohio River at Louisville. I managed the individual project negotiations but, thanks to skillful engineering leadership, our contract was renewed repeatedly over the next dozen years.

Specific tasks, called delivery orders, were managed under these contracts by structural engineer Duane Siegfried, who later became company president. Assignments included:

- Instrumentation and monitoring plan for Olmsted Lock: Developed with Shannon & Wilson, Inc., to measure and track movement and structural shifts, creep, expansion, seismic effects and other performance data for the new lock structure.

- Studies and design of working mock-ups of alternative navigable pass structures for Olmsted Dam on the Ohio River, including contracting for on-site monitoring and reporting services of construction progress. (A navigable pass dam slows water flow by lifting gates from the river bottom to reduce flow but still permits barge navigation, maintaining a navigable depth of water above.)
- Design studies for a new 1,200-foot lock structure at McAlpine Dam, including, excavation protection, sheet piling shoring and temporary dewatering systems.
- Feasibility study for safe removal and temporary replacement of a steel bridge accessing McAlpine Lock. This assignment was handled primarily by Mason & Hanger Engineering, with our structural engineering support.
- Construction monitoring and reporting contracts during building of McAlpine Lock.

In addition to these projects, which represented steady revenue for the company, we won other design commissions from public agencies. For one contract with the State of Illinois, Ron Dyess and I received special training from the state, so we would be qualified to design improvements for handicapped accessibility under the Americans With Disabilities Act. We designed accessibility of improvements—ramps, accessible toilet room improvements, and power-assisted doors for 22 buildings, at the amenable campus of Southern Illinois University–Edwardsville (SIU–E). With the addition of Stephen G. Knarr, architect, we designed fire stations and more city halls, adding to our portfolio of architectural projects.

For communities that had known our firm primarily for design engineering of streets, bridges, water supply and sewer collection and treatment facilities, in addition to city buildings, we also had the opportunity to design parks, bike trail systems and pedestrian bridges. For the City of Columbia, Missouri, we designed a 200-car parking structure. Because of the city's concern to blend public buildings with the collegiate atmosphere of the town, we paid special attention to blend our design with the nearby "red campus," or Georgian brick, buildings of the University of Missouri.

Also interested in working directly with the university, we submitted our qualifications to design a pedestrian bridge for the University of Missouri–Columbia campus. The bridge would connect the Dan Devine practice pavilion and adjacent parking lots across a major artery, Providence Road, to the football stadium, Faurot Field. The challenge of the assignment was to ensure safe passage of players and large crowds of spectators to and from parking lots and practice fields across the busy north-south artery to the stadium.

Their facilities office called us in for an interview. In the conference room, Glenn Smith, a Missou alumnus and structural engineer with our firm, and I met the project manager from the university facilities office, an architect from that office and two representatives of the athletic department. As an architect and marketing officer of the company, I took the lead. My first challenge was setting up the slide projector. When I turned it on, the bulb burned out with a flash. Panicked, I recalled we kept a spare bulb in the projector case. Using minutes of our precious time before the fidgeting selection committee, with seconds to spare before their patience ran out, I managed to get it installed.

I introduced Glenn as the project leader, the structural engineer who would be in charge of the project, and gave him the floor, while I stood aside and recovered from my last-minute, near-disaster.

Glenn offered a relaxed introduction, recalling his happy

days at the university and describing the bridge design qualifications of his capable staff. As an architect, I had a special role in the project: to integrate such an ungainly structure as a wide span bridge with the human scale and architecture of the Dan Devine pavilion and the football stadium, with its new press box recently added above the near side of the structure. My personal contribution to our slideshow was a conceptual sketch of the pedestrian bridge, which Glenn and I had imagined might best be a Warren truss, the type in which the steel diagonals meet in an M-shaped configuration at the center. In a whimsical moment I added the bright yellow M logo of Missouri University at the center of the bridge. I believe to this day, all other factors in qualifications of the competing teams being equal, that this afterthought won us the job.

This curious detail aside, the outcome of the story tops even that. The bridge was to be built with 90 percent federal funding, the remainder supplied by the state. When the project was designed and a state financial administrator reviewed the plans, he objected: "Federal regulations prohibit advertising on a federally sponsored bridge."

"But this is not advertising," rebutted Mike Alden, the tall, plainspoken and legendary athletic director from 1998 to 2015, who ranked as royalty on the campus. "It identifies the university and is a symbol of our pride."

It took a summit meeting between the Vice Chancellor of the University and the Director of the Missouri Highway Department to settle the meaning of the term "advertising," but the University's will would not be denied, and the logo remained.

These were but a few of the dozens of combined planning, urban design, architectural and engineering projects the firm completed during my 21 years with the company. Len Kirberg, our president, and I promoted the advantages to our clients of integrating planning and architecture with engineering.

Pedestrian Bridge, University of Missouri—Columbia
Horner & Shfrin, Inc., Engineers-Architects-Planners

Our architects collaborated on a City of St. Louis bridges to ensure that streetlights had a warm color temperature and human scale, far different from the high-pole, cobra-headed lights casting harsh, cold mercury vapor illumination typically favored by civil engineers. We completed several projects where roads, parking and landscape features—such as stands of trees, hills, pedestrian-bike trails and lakes of Earth City and Missouri Research Park—were gracefully integrated with the landscape. We convinced our clients that engaging our professionals to do this extra work added long term value to their projects.

We kept building on our success with Earth City. When I became a Vice President of Horner & Shifrin, the University of Missouri selected our firm to plan and design a site of 600 acres for a university research park on land it had acquired in St. Charles County from the federal government—part of 22,000 acres the federal government had purchased for a munitions plant and as an emergency seat of government, if necessary, during World War II. The university, as represented by Jim Edson for the university and Scott Jenkins, of Trammell Crow, their development manager, and later Dr. Rick Finholt, as Director of University Research Parks, presented our planning and design challenge.

The initial phase of the project, was to develop a Master

Plan to accommodate research facilities in a park-like setting, with all the amenities needed to attract research companies, who could train personnel from around the world and provide facilities to attract and retain high-value researchers. Facilities envisioned were state-of-the art research buildings, parks, trails natural beauty, a conference hotel and a championship golf course.

To ensure Missouri Research Park's high quality with a detailed implementation strategy, the university commissioned us to prepare a Master Development Plan. A component of this document was a project manual, "to provide a structure whereby Missouri Research Park can develop to its maximum potential."

We hired a landscape firm, Landscape Architecture Resources, to join us in enhancing and ensuring high-quality development, attractive surroundings and increasing property value long after we had finished our work. Elements of our Land Use Plan was based upon the following planning standards:

- Establish Height zones: L (low), to preserve the existing skyline of tree cover adjacent to neighboring residential properties; M (medium), height in a mixed-use area, with a critical mass of site interaction, visual enclosure and pedestrian accessibility in a campus-like setting, and H (high), at key locations, where vertical landmarks will be visible at focal points for site orientation, to provide open views to and from these buildings.

- Maintain self-sufficiency of the site by providing a mixture of uses: administrative, office, commercial and conference activities, within walking distance of each other in a "university core" and other added activities, to ensure the continued self-contained functioning of the park.

- Preserve natural site features, such as contours of the land, woods, and wildlife habitat and enhance them with lakes, walks and trails within an open space network, easily accessible to building complexes.

- Promote phased development for roads, landscape features, site utilities and buildings. to ensure a completed look to each phased development withing a reasonable time period.
- Re-establish and maintain a low-maintenance, natural landscape in areas reserved for future development, through the use of indigenous trees, shrubs, grasses and wildflowers.
- Coordinate the necessary entry features, landscape elements, sculpture, signage utility structures, light standards and other man made site features to create a high-quality visual environment.
- Provide convenient, quick and safe access and circulation for police, fire, ambulance, delivery and user vehicles; separate pedestrian and vehicular traffic, and provided rights-of-way for expansion of local and arterial roads to accommodate anticipated traffic at the time of the park's completion.

To implement the Master Development Plan's objectives, we created the following documents, in addition to the Master Plan: Land Use Plan, Preliminary Subdivision Plat, Conceptual Guideline Sketches, Conceptual Landscape Plan, Open Space Plan and Protective Covenants, which building owners in the park must agree to follow at the time of contract execution. This approach went far beyond the normal range of services architects and site planners had provided for developers in the past, and has resulted In creation of a high quality successful research park: This 1988 plan predicted:

> Implementation of these principles over the years to come should produce a development attracting the highest quality tenants and investment which solidly increases in value. A Missouri Research Park success will create new employment, products, ideas, technology; it will

strengthen and diversity the regional economy and become a cornerstone for high technology in the Midwest.

This project's bold predictions have been largely fulfilled. Over thirty-five years later, the project is fully occupied by scientific and research companies, with the features envisioned. Moreover, along with aggressive efforts by regional development officials, it has helped spur creation of other research campuses by Monsanto Company, (now a Div..of Bayer), Washington University and the Danforth Plant Science Center and helped make St. Louis a nexus of plant science and world food research.

Moreover, it has been one of many programs which rewarded architects' efforts to expand our influence beyond building design to exert a wider impact on urban land use, environmental preservation and land planning. It has tapped vast opportunities for growth into environmental planning, through collaboration with other professionals. Further, it has demonstrated how architecture can be broadened to include planning and urban design. This innovation represents progress toward the urgent goals of slowing global climate change, design with nature and preservation of our planet,

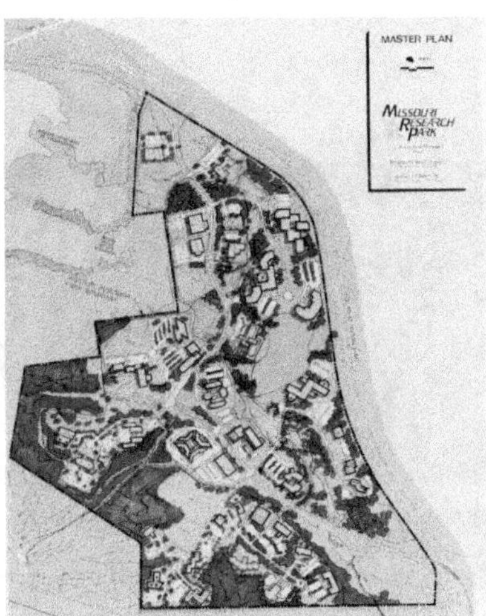

Missouri Research Park
Open Space Plan

Concept Sketch: Buildings around a man-made lake

Missouri Research Park: Lake and Research building

Missouri Research Park – Bike-Pedestrian Trail

**Missouri Research Park
National Weather Service Building—and friends**

Leonard C. Kirberg 1943-2019
Colleague, mentor and friend
Horner & Shifrin photo

25

MISSION CREEP

THE BOOK WAS FINISHED, but the pandemic was not. We could see light ahead, but we still needed everyone's cooperation to re-establish public health in America, not to speak of the challenge of defeating the virus and its variants worldwide. One thing this slowdown accomplished was to allow me time to reflect on my life.

Telling my family's story caused me to launch a second career and resulted in two biographical memoirs. Encountering the adventures, unusual characters and near disasters in my career had also spurred my creation of three architectural mysteries. My own life story, with my voyage of discovery into architecture, has rounded out the picture. The results of all this activity amounted to a range of activities far beyond my original intent.

Mission creep is the unintentional broadening of a venture's or project's original scope. This is a condition we monitored in business, in case it caused us to spend more time and effort on a job than we were being paid for. When it occurred, we pointed it out to our clients and negotiated changes to our contracts to ensure fair compensation for the extra work. In evaluating my life's goals and achievements, I found that mission creep, as in business, had a most beneficial outcome.

I wrote this story for my grandchildren, other young people—avatars for my young self—and anyone else who might find it useful in planning their career. And not just those who want to be architects. For all, I can offer the benefit of my experience.

How I wish I had paid more attention to the family stories my parents, grandparents and other mentors who had time for me.. What attention I gave to what they knew and how they reacted to problems, opportunities and events was invaluable. In some cases I was the only one who knew their experience, in a unique position to report about these treasures to the world. My mother saved all of my father's World War II letters, his written stories, and her own writings, as well as my college and travel letters. All these enabled me to remember those past scenes and my interactions with family. When I was not directly quoting them, I was often paraphrasing. Also, when I start to write freely about a past event, other details came back to mind.

It is also vital to evaluate inherited opportunities carefully. I had a chance to join my grandfather's construction company, and perhaps take it in a new direction. But I wanted to step back from building projects and help clients decide what to build in the first place and how it should be designed. Construction projects require different skills.

I did inherit my grandfather's megalomania, both Mom and Dad's writing skill, a bit of art talent from all sides and also my father's ability to dream. Architects are the first to conceive of a project, before the builder, and I wanted a key role in the whole process.

I was lucky, in that I could visualize something that didn't exist yet and describe it in both words and pictures—talents that enabled me to develop an architectural and urban design career. My dad used these talents in the advertising business and to sell his client's products to the mass market. At first I didn't know how to apply his knowledge of promotion and persuasion to selling architectural services, especially when competing with other architects.

Then I heard the story of an architecture professor who was speaking to a large class of incoming students at a major university. The speaker asked, "How many of you are interested in finding new business for your firms?' A few hands shot into the air. 'Will you please stand?' Half a dozen individuals in the large group rose. Then the professor said, "Now, I want the rest of you to note who these people are, since many of you will be working for them someday."

Whether or not one intends to work as an architect, in another field, or eventually become a firm principal, it pays to understand where the work comes from, in other words, how to market professional services.

At the very least, to get started you need to go to the library and force yourself to read a couple of books on sales and marketing, so you get a feel for the subject matter. It's very different from the design process or producing anything else you want to sell, and it involves quite separate activities. For generations, architects have looked down on any form of advertising or promotion, as if it were beneath them, claiming it puts the competition for services on price alone. A wise buyer if any product or service knows better than that: Sometimes you have to pay more to get the best. For heaven's sake, acquiring new work is our lifeblood! The public must understand what we do.

And marketing is a broader concept than sales.

In the post-World War II era the term "marketing" became a buzzword for a newer approach to bringing goods or services to consumers. Salesmen are limited to filling orders for various quantities of predesigned and prepackaged goods the customer wants. Even in mass marketing to the general public, customer feedback and market research resulted in the creation of many new products and gave consumers many more choices on store shelves.

That's a different problem than producing a new building or place for a single client or even where you're making a place for a specific industrial process, designing a building for a specialized purpose, or even planning a new community or neighborhood for larger group. It's essential to acquire in-depth knowledge of what your clients need. This is a two-way communication between the customer, or client, and the architect.

To win a new client you have to hold in-depth interviews with the owner and the users of the new building. If you're not good at everything the client wants your firm to do, you have to find out what part of it you do best and stick to it—never oversell, that is, promise special expertise you, with the help of others, can't deliver. Often you can add to your own firm's capabilities to provide what the client needs. That's why you have a team.

Based on what you find out from the client, you can add experts to the team to handle specialized project requirements—such as an acoustical expert for an auditorium, a laboratory specialist or a refrigeration engineer. Then you'll be equipped to customize the proposed building to respond directly to the owner's particular needs. The team that does this best often wins the commission to design the project.

Also, you need to specialize in the things you do best. I like preliminary design best—it sets the direction for the project and convinces the client of the firm's skill in solving their problem. I was impatient and results driven. This suited me better for the challenge of marketing and planning work, where the results could be produced within days or weeks, rather than than taking months or years. At the front end of projects. I also found the work process in planning and urban design is fast paced, a lot like marketing. Plus, ten years in my own firm forced me to overcome my shyness, take more risks and learn how to succeed in winning new commissions. This experience prepared me to hit the ground running when I moved to a larger firm with more capabilities.

I learned the most important thing to remember about marketing our services from Len Kirberg, the best firm leader I ever worked with. He was unflappable, a steady hand at the helm. He cared about our own people's growth and our clients' interests, their hobbies and their families. As well as giving clients your expert personal attention, you need to get to know people and build their trust.

In a high-pressure field like architecture, it's vital to keep your life in order. You wouldn't trust a forgetful or disorganized surgeon, an alcoholic roofing contractor or a womanizer as a school principal. Architects had the reputation, especially in the 1960s when I was starting my career, for marrying beautiful women and then going through messy divorces. During that period, architects, advertising executives and business owners known to ne and my family were committing professional suicide, because their chaotic personal lives sapped their energy. It's important to concentrate seriously on family life, save money for the future and build a career.

Now at the end of one career and in the middle of another, it surprises me how my original goals have been transformed and my achievements broadened from my earliest expectations. My classmates in architecture school admired my simple intention to "return to Chicago and design beautiful buildings." Eventually I left Chicago for a job opportunity and broadened my goal of building design to include urban design and planning. As a result, I not only influenced the development of the City of St. Louis, I found ways to steer development in the future and thus continue influencing my projects' physical form after my work was finished.

I had always wanted to have my own firm. I tried that and found it had limitations—competition from more accomplished small firms, the need for a much broader understanding of marketing and finding new business, and enough capital to buy computers and wait patiently while early projects were being completed and a continuous system for acquiring new work had been established. When I had the opportunity to work with a larger firm, I influenced its growth and helped ensure its continuation from its fiftieth to its seventy-fifth anniversary and into the future.

Starting out, I believed architecture was a solitary act and wanted to create masterpieces. I learned that architecture and urban design require an army of skilled professionals to finish a large project or to promote, adopt and implement a town plan. This effort would not be complete until long after our work was done. I learned how to set guidelines for future design to be finished by others and how to regulate, influence and guide the future beauty of place without further need of my presence.

In order to earn a living, I made a choice between two careers for which I was qualified: architecture and writing. I nonetheless found that in architecture I would need to use my writing skills for obtaining new work, envisioning my designs and describing plans for new communities. This skill opened up a second career during my retirement. I became a writer after all, without having to sacrifice an alternate career I had originally considered.

When I retired from active architectural practice, I found that my writing skills, while useful in my job, could increase far beyond what I imagined. In addition, I had discovered people whose mischief and exploits made interesting topics for fiction. I realized that readers found my parents' stories interesting, funny and heroic, and that my own story had more of these qualities than I previously thought. I realized I had accomplished a lot more in life than I gave myself credit for, and I began setting down my personal history.

There have been plenty of challenges, for sure. But architecture took me places I never thought I'd go and led me to meet some fascinating people. It challenged me to do more than I ever thought I could. I made friends all over the country and shared many good times with them. Len Kirberg expressed it best: "What it always comes down to," he'd say,—and I believe this applies to friendships and romance as well as business— "is building relationships."

The unintended expansion of my mission also opened up a purpose for the rest of my life. I proved for myself the converse of Socrates' maxim—that the examined life is indeed worth living. Moreover, it continues to provide a new mission for my retirement years.

There is no doubt that I had to fight for every achievement. I struggled to let my true nature out, seeking understanding more than money. Le Corbusier's maxim, "Creation is a patient search," was correct. In my choice of schools, career path and design decisions, my search for meaning in architecture was long and difficult. I sought to fulfill the needs of my clients, to provide users and community dwellers with functional, sturdy and pleasing designs. When all these things happened, my colleagues and I were fairly compensated, took pride in our work and treasured our lasting relationships.

ENDNOTES

1. *The New Yok Times,* July 28, 1945.

2. Wednesday, May 17, 1944.

3..Aeginetian (or Eginetan) marbles: A collection of sculptures originally decorating the pediment of the temple of the goddess Aphaea in Aegina, now held by the Glyptothek museum in Munich. (www.lexico.com/definition. Quoted in: Adams, Henry *Mont-Saint-Michel and Chartres,* Houghton Mifflin Company, The Riverside Press ed.(Cambridge), 1905, P. 74.

4. *Ibid.,* Adams, P. 73.

5. *Ibid,* Adams quoting Viollet-le-Duc, P.64

6, Wikipedia https://whc.unesco.org/en/list/1025/

7. Wolfe, Tom, *From Bauhaus to Our House,* Pp. 59-61.

8. Gill, Brendan, *Many Masks: A Life of Frank Lloyd Wright,* G. P. Putnam's Sons (New York), 1987, P. 430.

9. *Ibid,* P. 1

10.*Ibid.,* P. 73

11 Stern, Robert A. M. and Stamp, Jimmy, *Pedagogy and Place,* Yale University Press (New Haven), 2016. P. 215

12 *Ibid.,* P.184

13 *Ibid.,* P.201

14 *Ibid.,* P.185

15 *Ibid.,* P.195

16 *Ibid.,* P. 241.
17. Filler, Martin, New York Review, 2015, "The Hard Case of Paul Rudolph."

18 Weismantel, William L., Attorney, St. Louis, Missouri; B.S., Missouri School of Mines and Metallurgy,1949; LL.B., Harvard University, 1953 His specialty was urban land use law, but his knowledge of urban planning issues was encyclopedic.

19 Clemens, Samuel, *The Innocents Abroad.* (Kindle Locations 2088-2093).

20. Wikipedia, https://en.wikipedia.org/wiki/Mustafa_Kemal_Ataturk, Tab, Modernization Efforts

21. Wikipedia, https://en.wikipedia.org/wiki/Grand_Bazaar,_Istanbul

22. https://www.thoughtco.com/pericles-funeral-oration-thucydides-version-111998

23. Wilder, Thornton, *American Characteristics and Other Essays,,* Donald Gallup, Ed., Harper & Row, Publishers, (New York), 1979. Essay: "Gertrude Stein's *Four in America*", P.207

24. Clemens, Samuel, *The Innocents Abroad.* (Kindle Locations 2088-2093).

ACKNOWLEDGMENTS

This book owes a lot to my parents and family, who gave me the chance to accomplish what I describe here. Moreover, fellow writers in my second career have played a major role. I met most of them through St. Louis Writers Guild, guide to acquiring much current information about the writing and publishing industry.

Specific help came from my beta readers: David Margolis, author of well-crafted and humorous fiction; T. W. Fendley, friend and fellow writer of imaginative fiction; Bob Little, architect, former Chicago resident and avid reader, and Mike Lederer, scientist, fellow traveler and lifelong friend. I can't say enough good things about the interest they all took in my early efforts and later drafts of this work and the sure guidance they provided about issues I could not have recognized without their aid. Also, author Cherie Postill coached me on finding beta readers, Moreover, almost a dozen of my fellow architects and graphic designers provided expert advice on the book's design and content. I'm especially grateful to Jerry Pratter, attorney and architecture fan, for providing the Martin Filler article on Paul Rudolph. Thanks to you all.

Special thanks is due Catherine Rankovic of BookEval.com, who reviewed and edited this book. Not only did she introduce the concept of Creative Nonfiction to me in her course at Washington University's Summer Writers Institute as I launched my second career, she has also critiqued and edited most of my nonfiction work. With this background, she was able to identify quickly what belonged in this volume and what did not, suggesting many significant improvements. Thanks again, Catherine, for all your invaluable contributions.

While I credit these individuals for their positive contributions, any remaining errors are my own.

—Peter H. Green , St. Louis, September, 2021

ABOUT THE AUTHOR

Peter H. Green, AIA
Architect and Author

Peter H. Green spent a 40-year career as an architect, urban designer and city planner before launching a second career as a writer. His design organizations include the American Institute of Architects, American Planning Association, American Institute of Certified Planners and the Society of American Military Engineers, where he is a past St. Louis Post President and Fellow.

Peter earned a Certificate in Creative Writing and a Bachelor of Architecture degree from Washington University, St. Louis, and a B.A. from Yale University. He served as Vice President, Programs, for St. Louis Writers Guild from 2009-2014. He is a member of Sisters in Crime, St. Louis Publishers Association and Missouri Writers Guild.

He lives in St. Louis with his wife, Connie, and has two married daughters and three grandchildren. An illustrated. Thurberesque story, "The Night We Ruined the Dog," on the life and times of the last pet they owned, can be found on his author website: www.authorpetergreen.com

CONNECT WITH PETER

His website is: https://www.authorpetergreen.com

Facebook page: http://www.facebook.com/
AuthorPeterGreen
Twitter handle: https://twitter.com/writerpeter
LinkedIn ID: Peter H. Green

Before you go...

Authors depend on the approval and
reactions of readers. Please leave a brief review,
even just a few lines, at this book's detail page,
available at:

Amazon Author Page:
https://www.amazon.com/Peter-H-Green/
e/B008749FPC

Goodreads Author Page:
www.goodreads.com/author/show/
5864519.Peter_H_Green519